RELIGIOUS

VEGETARIANISM

RELIGIOUS
VEGETARIANISM

From Hesiod to the Dalai Lama

Edited by

KERRY S. WALTERS
LISA PORTMESS

STATE UNIVERSITY OF NEW YORK PRESS

Excerpts from *The Presocratic Philosophers* edited by G. S. Kirk, J. E. Raven, and M. Schofield, pp. 314–319, copyright 1983, printed by permission of Cambridge University Press. Excerpts from *The Laws of Manu*, translated by G. Buehler, copyright 1986, printed by permission of Oxford University Press. Excerpts from *Vivekananda: The Yogas and Other Works* edited by Swami Nikhilananda, Trustee of the Estate of Swami Vivekananda, copyright 1953, printed by permission of Ramakrishna-Vivekananda Center of New York. Excerpts from *The Science of Self Realization* by A.C. Bhaktivedanta Swami Prabupada, copyright 1981, printed by permission of The Bhaktivedanta Book Trust International. Excerpts from *Sources of Indian Tradition, Vol. 1* edited by Ainslee T. Embree, copyright 1988, and *The Renewal of Buddhism in China* by Chun-Fang Yu, copyright 1981, printed by permission of Columbia University Press. Excerpts from *To Cherish Life* by Philip Roshi Kapleau, copyright 1981, printed by permission of the Rochester Zen Center. Excerpts from *Worlds in Harmony: Dialogues on Compassionate Action* by His Holiness The Dalai Lama, copyright 1992, printed by permission of Parallax Press. Excerpts from *Vegetarian Judaism* by Roberta Kalechofsky, copyright 1998, printed by permission of Micah Publications and the author. Excerpts from *Tree of Life* edited by Philip L. Pick, copyright 1977, printed by permission of The International Jewish Vegetarian Society, London. Excerpts from *The Lights of Penitence, Lights of Holiness, The Moral Principles, Essays, Letters and Poems* by Abraham Isaac Kook, translation and introduction by Ben Zion Bokser, copyright 1978 by Ben Zion Bokser, printed by permission of Paulist Press. Excerpts from *Animal Theology*, by Andrew Linzey, copyright 1995, printed by permission of University of Illinois Press. Excerpts from *Liberating Life* edited by Charles Birch, copyright 1991, and *Good News for Animals* edited by Charles Pinches and Jay B. McDaniel, copyright 1993, printed by permission of Orbis. Excerpts from "Vegetarianism and Religion" by Francis X. Clooney, copyright 1979, printed by permission of the author and America Press. All rights reserved. Excerpts from *Tales of the Masnavi* translated by Arthur J. Arberry, copyright 1993, printed by permission of Curzon Press Ltd. Excerpts from *Al-Asma'ul-Husna, The 99 Beautiful Names of Allah*, "Explanation of Qurban," copyright 1993, and from *Come to the Secret Garden: Sufi Tales of Wisdom*, "The Hunter Learns Compassion from the Fawn," copyright 1985, by M. R. Bawa Muhaiyaddeen, printed by permission of Fellowship Press. The excerpt entitled "Animal Psyches and Communities" by Al-Hafiz B. A. Masri, from *Animal Sacrifices: Religious Perspectives on the Use of Animals in Science*, "Animal Experimentation: The Muslim Viewpoint," edited by Tom Regan, copyright 1986, printed by permission of Temple University Press. The painting *Slumbering Ox* by Martha Ekyo Maezumi is printed by permission of the artist.

Published by

STATE UNIVERSITY OF NEW YORK PRESS

ALBANY

For information, address
State University of New York Press,
90 State Street, Suite 700, Albany, NY 12207

Production and book design, Laurie Searl
Marketing, Fran Keneston

Library of Congress Cataloging-in-Publication Data
Religious vetgetarianism: from Hesiod to the Dalai Lama / edited by Kerry S. Walters, Lisa Portmess.
    p. cm.
Includes bibliographical references and index.
ISBN 0-7914-4971-8 (alk. paper)—ISBN 0-7914-4972-6 (pb : alk. paper)
    1. Vegetarianism—Religious aspects. 2. Spiritual life. I. Walter, Kerry S. II. Portmess, Lisa.

BL65.V44 R45 2001
291.5'693--dc21

                                                                00-054795

10   9   8   7   6   5   4   3   2   1

For our children

Jonah

K. S. W.

Andrew, Corinne, Colin

L. P.

Contents

Preface

This book gathers writings on religious vegetarianism from several different faith traditions. Collected here are excerpts from ancient Orphic and Pythagorean authors, writings spanning centuries of Indian and Buddhist thought, and a variety of readings from Judaism, Christianity, and Islam. The focus is on spiritual questions raised by the slaughter of animals for food: whether such practice can be defended by fundamental religious teachings, whether human violence toward animals is ordained or the result of human sin, whether an authentic relationship to God requires vegetarianism, and so on. The answers, so manifold, unpredictable, and provocative, illuminate both the entangled destinies of human beings and animals as well as the path to a more profound compassion for all life.

A few words need to be said about how source material was selected.

Meditations on the relationship between human beings and animals exist in all spiritual traditions, many of which are obviously not represented in this volume. To keep the text to a manageable size, we included only those writings that consider vegetarianism from the standpoint of the world's great living faiths, in addition to one other, the Orphic-Pythagorean, which has had an enormous impact on Western thought. The literature of religious vegetarianism collected here is not narrowly focused on dietary practice, but reflects the deepest intuitions, hopes, and insights of the religious life.

As was the case with our previous volume, *Ethical Vegetarianism from Pythagoras to Peter Singer* (State University of New York Press, 1999), one of the most difficult tasks in preparing this anthology was determining what sources to omit. The literature of religious vegetarianism is even more vast and richly diverse than that of ethical vegetarianism, and space limitations demanded a drastic culling of faith traditions as well as spokespersons, ancient or contemporary, from each of them. Readers interested in wider exploration of the pertinent literature are invited to consult both this volume's concluding biblio-graphical essay and the references mentioned in the notes that follow a good number of the selections.

The problem of source selection for this volume was compounded by an additional one. Whereas Indian and Buddhist sacred texts are replete with explicit discussions of vegetarianism, the scriptures of the "three religions of the Book"—Judaism, Christianity, and Islam—are not. Advocates of vegetarianism who are members of these three faith traditions argue that their sacred texts eas-ily accommodate (and indeed point to) a nonviolent diet. But they also con-cede that vegetarianism as a spiritual goal is implicit rather than overtly pre-scribed in the Bible and the *Qur'ān*. The consequence is that the Indian and Buddhist sections in this volume are more heavily weighted with primary scrip-tural texts than are the sections devoted to Judaism, Christianity, and Islam. But in choosing writings by Jewish, Christian, and Muslim exegetes, we were espe-cially careful to include ones that made their case with generous quotations from the Bible and the *Qur'ān*. On balance, then, there is proportionate scrip-tural representation throughout the entire book.

In *Ethical Vegetarianism*, we included selections from some authors who were inconsistent vegetarians (for example, Bernard de Mandeville, Oliver Goldsmith, and Albert Schweitzer) and rigorously excluded authors who advo-cated vegetarianism from a primarily hygienic viewpoint (such as Upton Sinclair, John Harvey Kellog, and George Bernard Shaw) as well as those whom the vegetarian community too hastily claims on thin textual evidence (for instance, Plato, Henry David Thoreau, and Leonardo da Vinci). Our thinking was (and is) that a person can offer perfectly cogent ethical arguments for veg-etarianism without being a thoroughgoing vegetarian in practice; that even though ethical and hygienic motives for a meatless diet are not mutually exclu-sive, many vegetarians who operate from the latter are relatively indifferent to the former; and that the case for ethical vegetarianism is weakened rather than strengthened by uncritically claiming famous-named "proponents" who at best penned an ambiguous line or two about diet.

In this volume, on the other hand, we've included—with one under-standable exception[1]—only those authors who unambiguously preach *and* practice vegetarianism as a spiritual discipline. Whereas it's possible (albeit awk-ward) to intellectually endorse an ethical argument without consistently acting upon it, an analogous compartmentalization in the spiritual life is especially problematic. Spirituality aims to integrate religious ideals, beliefs, and principles with concrete, everyday behavior. Its goal is a holistic transformation of the person rather than mere philosophical analysis or conceptual clarification. This transformation is neither quick nor easy, and charity rather than judgment is the appropriate standard when examining the progress of others. But a good faith effort to live rather than just think about one's religious ideals is a *sine qua non* for spirituality in general and religious vegetarianism in particular.

NOTE

1. That exception is the Dalai Lama. Although an eloquent and insightful spiritual champion of compassion for all living beings, he confesses that a life-threatening bout with jaundice led him to follow medical advice and reluctantly adopt a minimally carnivorous diet. For more on his decision, see the editorial Introduction to his selection in this volume.

Introduction

AMBIGUOUS PERMISSION,
JOURNEYING SOULS,
RESPLENDENT LIFE

Toward animals we manifest ancient ambivalence: awe, love, fear, cruelty. In their flight we envision the spirit's flight, against their strength and grace we gauge our own, with their bodies we sustain human life, and our infliction of suffering on them prompts the deepest religious perplexities. Whatever the sacred and the holy are thought to be, the human slaughter of animals questions it, renders it paradoxical, demands reflection.

Such questioning inescapably originates in religious traditions that first shape how the human relation to animals and to the sacred is thought and lived. Whatever the fundamental religious or metaphysical insights of a tradition, vegetarianism emerges illuminated by them, and in turn interprets and elaborates on them. Whether from the Orphic-Pythagorean belief in soul transmigration, Indian belief in the oneness of all things, the Buddhist recognition of impermanence and pervasive suffering, the Judaic-Christian sense of God's love for all creation, or the Sufi mystical sense of the unity of life, religious vegetarianism trails its origins in its very formulation.

The world's religious traditions do not speak with a single voice. No truth about how we should understand redemption, enlightenment, the nature of the holy, or our relation to animals is uttered independent of its own complex tradition. Similarly, religious arguments for vegetarianism draw on particular theologies, stories, or metaphors derived from specific material cultures and faith traditions and historically conditioned visions of necessity and possibility. Even rebellion against prevailing practice remains entangled with religious legacy. What truths there are to be known—of life's sanctity, of divine will, of the kinship of all creatures—are embedded in particular historical periods, particular

1

geographical settings, and particular cultural matrices. Even within individual spiritual traditions, defenders of vegetarianism speak in many voices. Thus the richness of the literature of this volume, with vegetarianism understood various-ly as spiritual discipline, respect for journeying souls, mercy toward God's cre-ation, the redemption of our fallen selves, ecstatic affirmation of the identity of all life, compassionate kinship, and the eschatological perfecting of creation.

  Glimpses from each of the traditions follow.

BIRDS AND LEAPING FISH

The ancient writings of the Orphic-Pythagorean tradition evoke a golden age of harmony between nature and humanity, a legendary counterpoint to present violence, wretched pain, and weariness. Described first by the Greek poet Hesiod in the eighth century BCE, this innocent age was marked by the gods' creation of a golden generation of mortals. Life was free of sorrow, hard work, and suffering; nature made abundant provision for human need. In successive generations, as hard work and pain increasingly became the human lot, the gods departed for Olympus, leaving human beings forsaken, defenseless against evil, and turned against both one another and their once benign nature.

  This Orphic vision of the rise and fall of a golden age vividly depicts human violence as time-bound rather than necessary, a characteristic of present blighted generations rather than proof of an essentially broken human nature. Its dim memory of a peaceable harmony with nature expresses the constant hope that violence, both within human communities and toward animals, can be overcome. This hope, combined with the Pythagorean belief in soul trans-migration, provides the twin foundations of Orphic-Pythagorean vegetarian-ism: the conviction that our original nature was nonviolent and at peace with other animals, and a respect for the fluidity of souls that course through small-est worm and fiercest beast. The writings of Hesiod, Porphyry, Ovid, Empedocles, and Philostratus explore these themes of a golden age and soul transmigration in detail. A look at the writings of Empedocles gives a represen-tative sense of the richness of this particular tradition.

  In the few fragments remaining to us, Empedocles speaks of divine decrees, of the birth "under this roofed cave" of human beings, of the pitiless day when first "the wretched deed of eating flesh" occurred, and of the terrible fate—the soul's wandering thrice ten thousand years—imposed by the pollu-tion of bloodshed. The sorrow and groaning of defilement came to be the human lot, even though in the time that once was, no sin or pollution existed. But this defilement isn't inevitable. Empedocles, like all Orphic-Pythagoreans, holds out the possibility of redemption. This possibility presumes an understanding of the cycle of transmigration, its cause as well as strategies for escaping it. The most important of these strategies is forbearance from violence—including the violence of slaughtering animals for their flesh.

Belief in transmigrating souls, from bush to bird to leaping journeying fish, as Empedocles says, evokes the fluidity of all living things and their common embodiment in flesh susceptible to pain and death. Woe to that human who inflicts suffering and death on beasts carrying within them transmigrant souls. "The force of the air pursues [the evil-doer] into the sea, the sea spews him out onto the floor of the earth, the earth casts him into the rays of the blazing sun, and the sun into the eddies of the air; one takes him from the other, but all abhor him." And yet the "far-seeing sun, the serene harmonia, beauty and lovely truth"—the spiritual condition of the legendary golden age:—all these are recoverable if humans cease defiling themselves with blood. The purified father will see in each animal his son, the mother her daughter. No din of slaughter will impede the soul's release.

The Orphic-Pythagorean vision has a pervasive sense of temporality as its mode of understanding violence and affirming hope. Nothing ordains that we must prey on the lives of other animals; nature is not destined to cruelty in the arrangements for its own perpetuation. Whatever is degenerate was once good and shall be—or at least *can* be—once more. A recovery of what once was good, that which is beyond "human sorrows or weariness," always remains a spiritual possibility for humans.

ONE LIFE, ONE WORLD, ONE EXISTENCE

In the *Bhagavad-gītā*, Kṛṣṇa reminds us that every living being possesses a soul. To be free from sin, to escape bondage, delusion, and death, is to practice non-injury (or *ahiṃsā*) to the souls of all life. One who is enlightened realizes this truth: "Knowing and renouncing severally and singly the actions against living beings, in the regions above, below, and on the surface, everywhere and in all ways—a wise man neither gives pain to these bodies, nor assents to others in their doing so." Kṛṣṇa's words express the basic intuition that grounds the Indian spiritual tradition's advocacy of a nonviolent diet.

In the twentieth century, Swami Vivekānanda, monk of the Ramakrishna Order, speaks from the highest ideals of Vedic wisdom to remind us of the spiritual underpinning of Kṛṣṇa's words: that everything is One, that differences between the many orders of life are of degree rather than kind. "The amoeba and I are the same," he asserts; "the difference is only one of degree. . . . A man may see a great deal of difference between grass and a little tree, but if he mounts very high, the grass and the biggest tree will appear much the same."

Vedānta denies both the notion of an essential separation between animals and humans and the belief that animals were created by God to be used for our food. From its perspective, "the lowest animal and the highest man are the same." Were God partial to his human children, Vivekānanda writes, "I would rather die a hundred times than worship such a God." Vivekānanda refuses to reconcile human weakness with holiness. Meat-eating is neither a biological necessity nor a divine ordination. Instead, it is an expression of self-indulgent desire, and we ought not to whitewash this fact. We know the ideal, and know equally well the cruelty involved in not following it. "Let us teach a religion which presents the highest ideal," Vivekānanda pleads, rather than continuing to perpetuate the falsehood that spiritual weakness can be reconciled with holiness. Let us be raised up to God.

This sense of identity among all forms of life and its consequent principle of noninjury to life pervades Indian religious thought and practice. In the ancient *Dharmaśāstras*, of which the Laws of Manu form a part, the religious ideal is expressed early and with absolute clarity: "He who does not seek to cause the sufferings of bonds and death to living creatures, but desires the good of all beings, obtains endless bliss." The spiritual discipline that flows from such principles is made plain in the *Ākarāṅga Sūtra*. The vow of the *Nirgrantha*, the Jain ascetic, is to renounce the killing of any living being, to be careful in walk, to search mind and speech for what might injure living beings, to root out "division, dissension, quarrels, faults and pains."

The poetry of the fifteenth-century Indian Kabīr likewise defends the kindredness between humans and animals. His writings express anger at the unholiness and hypocrisy of animal slaughter and voice the conviction that such bloodshed is an impediment to human salvation. Kabīr mocks the man who ritually purifies himself and worships "according to rules," but whose gluttonous appetite "causes a stream of blood to flow." Animal slaughterers do not realize that "human flesh and the flesh of beasts is similar and their crimson blood is also the same." Nor do flesh-eating humans recognize that the violence they inflict on helpless animals "will certainly take revenge." Their own wickedness commits spiritual violence to themselves, and neither ritualized prayers nor pilgrimages nor alms can wash away the ensuing taint.

Excerpts from Mohandas Gandhi reflect Indian awareness of both the limitations of what is and the idealism of striving for what might be realized in the future. He argues that vegetarianism is a step in the right spiritual direction for both Christians who anticipate the kingdom of God and Hindus who seek the comprehensive *dharma* of nonviolence.

The Indian religious vegetarian tradition, unlike the Orphic-Pythagorean one, invokes no golden age, no distant past of tranquillity and peace among creatures. The path to salvation is conceived differently; the spiritual rhythm moves between the poles of delusion and knowledge, sin and purity. As the ancient Laws of Manu remind us, either we exist in bondage to delusion, or we do not. Either we understand that there is but one Life, one World, one Existence, or we do not. To know the oneness of life, to achieve enlightenment, is to practise noninjury to all life. Such atemporal rhythm—a rhythm more of consciousness than of time or history—pervades Indian writings on vegetarianism. What exists as most real is beyond history, and the self's striving must be directed toward this beyond in an embrace of the oneness of things. This in turn engenders perfect action and nonattachment. To be vegetarian is to acknowledge the truth that there is but one life.

R E L E A S I N G

In Buddhist cosmological visions, world systems, immense in time and space, arise and then dissolve. The karmic trajectories of human beings and animals, the order of their births and rebirths, occur in the realm of desire where humans and animals alike are prodded by ignorance and craving. Life fluidly moves between human and animal forms: Humans have been animals in previous lives and animals have been humans. As a recent commentator on Buddhism puts it, "The concepts of *karma* and rebirth situate one's humanity as provisional, as only a sign of previous good *karma*, and not as a permanent identity. . . . One is not really a human being, nor an animal, but a configuration of parts in a process of flux causing rebirth in different realms according to volition and acts."[1]

In this rebirth system, as in Orphic-Pythagoreanism, compassion for animals is born from a sense of shared, kindred participation in the continuous flow of life. The *Lankāvatāra Sūtra* leaves no room for doubt on this point. "There is not one living being that, having assumed the form of a living being, has not been your mother, or father, or brother, or sister, or son, or daughter, or the one or the other, in various degrees of kinship; and when acquiring another form of life may live as a beast, as a domestic animal, as a bird, or as a womb-born. . . . Let people cherish the thought of kinship with them, and, thinking that all beings are to be loved as if they were an only child, let them refrain from eating meat." This position is reaffirmed by the twentieth-century American-born Zen master Philip Kapleau.

To what extent this compassion is to be construed as forbidding meat eating has been a matter of debate among Buddhist scholars and practitioners. The

Pāli texts of Theravāda (or southern) Buddhism suggest that the Buddha permitted meat eating in cases where the animal slaughter did not occur for that purpose. But the Mahāyāna (or northern) *sūtras* contradict this allowance, claiming that abstinence from all meat eating is an essential expression of compassion and the recognition of the Buddha-nature of all living beings.

According to the Mahāyāna Buddhism of East Asia, the underlying commonality that unites all forms of life consists of the spiritual element *tathāgathahgarbha*, or Buddha-nature. All sentient beings, according to this doctrine of Indian origin, share Buddha-nature. Enlightened perception of *tathāgathahgarbha* had great consequence for the Buddhist practice of vegetarianism and became established doctrine. The latitude that once existed—that animals not killed for one's own purposes could be eaten—no longer remained.

What remains, however, is the need to extinguish craving. Awareness of the Buddha-nature in all sentient beings is frequently clouded by the confusion and suffering born from desire. The Four Noble Truths stress the pervasiveness of craving as well as the insight that an end to suffering is attainable only when craving is destroyed, and nonattachment and compassion for all life embraced. Vegetarianism as *ahiṃsā* exemplifies both these ideals. The world itself will not be changed by the attainment of this enlightened insight; in Buddhism, there is no golden age, no fall, no ultimate restoration of harmony and peace among creatures. But the person who has come to know the Buddha-nature has a deep sense of the liberating promise of compassionate nonviolence, and labors to ease the suffering of all living beings. As Chu-Hung remarks in his eloquent essay, "Releasing life [from suffering] agrees with the teaching of the Buddha." And the karmic reward of such *ahiṃsā* is blessed release from the cycle of transmigration.

NEPHISH CHAYA

Jewish and Christian authors struggle with a religious heritage in which the highest ideals of compassion and love tensely coexist with the violent reality of animal slaughter. The uneasy conscience born of this dissonance is palpable when adherents of the two faith traditions defend vegetarianism. No belief in transmigrating souls or the oneness of all creation makes things easier for them. Their case must be painstakingly pieced together from hints and innuendoes gleaned from tradition and harmonized with scriptural authority. These harmonizations are sometimes obscure—critics may even say forced—but what is abundantly clear is the deep sense Jewish and Christian vegetarians have of the goodness of God's creation, the fullness of God's love for all creatures, the intrinsic value of animals, and the possibility of a peaceable kingdom in which humans and animals might dwell together.

Although Jewish vegetarianism doesn't recognize spiritual equality between humans and animals, it does claim that animals belong to God rather than to humans, and consequently should be treated with reverence and respect: "The earth is the Lord's, and all that dwells therein." This insight prompts Rabbi Everett Gendler to designate beasts as "His"—that is, God's—beasts. The possessive pronoun doesn't suggest that animals are God's property so much as that they reflect something of divine nature and consequently are precious in the eyes of God. The first chapter of Genesis underscores this intuition when it describes both humans and animals as *nephish chaya* or "living souls." Animals are not merely animated lumps of clay whose only purpose is to serve humanity. They are *nephish chaya*, God-created beings of intrinsic worth whose existence testifies to the richness and graciousness of creation.

Jewish vegetarians argue that the primordial couple in Eden recognized the sanctity of animals, and that it was only after the Noachic Flood that fallen humans began to slaughter animals for food. But they also claim that such slaughter is only provisionally approved by God as a concession to human bloodlust. In this spirit Roberta Kalechofsky and Rabbi Abraham Isaac Kook interpret Jewish dietary laws, or *kashrut*. *Kashrut*, they contend, shouldn't be interpreted as an imprimatur for killing animals, but rather as a codified strategy on the part of a supremely patient God to reduce animal slaughter and awaken humans to its savagery. The spirit of *kashrut*, then, harkens back to the Edenic golden age when humans recognized animals as *nephish chaya*. Jewish vegetarianism seeks to recall and live the spiritual and practical implications of that recognition.

FEEDING ON ANIMALS, FEEDING ON GRACE

Sharing as they do a common heritage, Christian defenders of a nonviolent diet are troubled by many of the same ambiguities that vex Jewish vegetarians. Like their Jewish fellow vegetarians, for example, they believe that all life is a holy gift but not metaphysically identical; there exists a "close, vital kinship" between animals and humans, as Tom Regan says, but not the oneness taught in the Indian religious tradition. Moreover, Christian vegetarians agree with Jewish apologists such as Kalechofsky and Kook that carnivorism is not God's original intention, but that God has reluctantly conceded to it—has granted "ambiguous permission," in Andrew Linzey's words—as a provisional measure. Spiritual progress in dietary matters, then, is a matter of going "forward," not "backward," to Genesis.

As we've seen, Jewish defenses of vegetarianism frequently appeal to the Edenic example of peaceful coexistence between beast and person. Christian vegetarians are sympathetic to this approach, but in preaching a nonviolent diet they also invoke the new dispensation that occurs in the Christ event. This event, which for the Christian is *the* exemplary embodiment of God's will, offers a new convenant, one of "grace" rather than "law." Grace reveals the primacy of love and compassion and, according to Christian vegetarians, that love and compassion must extend to all of God's creation. The traditionally presumed right to subjugate and rule the animal world, claims Linzey, does not "fit easily alongside the covenant of grace." At one time physical and historical necessity may have made the slaughter of animals for food a sober fact of life, but for the most part those days are over. Francis Clooney reminds us that the Christian Lord "has always chosen to be found in the context of the [eucharistic] meal." Christian vegetarianism offers the ideal of transfiguring every meal into a sanctified act of reverence and gratitude for God's bounty. Carol Adams puts the matter more starkly: one can feed on grace, or one can feed on animals, but not on both.

What's needed is a systematic rethinking of the spiritual implications of the new dispensation of grace. In Carol Adams's words, we require a "Christology of vegetarianism." Such a Christology would not be concerned with whether the historical Jesus was a vegetarian, but rather with the liberating promise Christlike love extends to humans, animals, society, and nature. Christians can no longer afford to alienate themselves from God by falsely naming sentient animals as mere "meat" and then treating them accordingly. Love is nothing if it fails to encompass all of creation. True *imitatio Christi* requires that we love as deeply and impartially as God does.

EVERY LIFE IS GOD'S

The Islamic tradition at first sight seems even more inhospitable to vegetarianism than Judaism or Christianity. The severity of Arabian desert life at the time of Islam's emergence, the near-absolute dependence on animal flesh for subsistence, and ancient strains in pre-Islamic fatalism of a harsh and unforgiving world order, appear to leave little room in either the *Qur'ān* or later Islamic writings for meditations on the value of animal life. But it would be a mistake to interpret this as an inhospitableness per se to vegetarianism. Infrequent as they may be, writings that recommend compassion and a sense of kindredness with animals are to be found, and they reflect deep undercurrents in Islamic spirituality.

The thirteenth-century Muslim mystic Rūmī speaks of inevitable retribution in his parable of hungry and destitute travelers who, in spite of wise counsel, slaughter and devour an elephant calf. Circling the gorged and sleeping travelers, the avenging mother elephant falls upon them, rending and slaying the murderers one by one. Rūmī points to a moral balance that reestablishes itself after slaughter unsettles it, reflecting belief in a well-ordered universe in which God punishes offenders. Just as belief in karma expresses the devout Hindu's faith in a moral law larger than human action, so the metaphor of the avenging animal expresses Islam's faith in divine retributive justice. Rather than endure violence and death passively at human hands, animals assert power over human salvation, thereby manifesting God's will that all life be recognized as kindred.

Sufi defenses of vegetarianism, represented in this volume by M. R. Bawa Muhaiyaddeen, focus less on retribution than on what the Bawa elsewhere calls the "resplendence of life": the mystical unity of all creation, the compassion and mercy of God, and the dignity and perfect eloquence of even the humblest of animals. Bawa Muhaiyaddeen's interpretation of the meaning of *Qurbān*, the ritual slaughter of animals (which has an obvious resemblance to Judaic *kashrut*) is an illustration. "If a person is to take food for himself," the Bawa says, "he must remember that every life is the sole property of God. And if he would desire a life that is truly the property of God, he must first hand over all responsibility to God in *tawakkal-Allāh* (absolute trust and surrender to God)."

Because humans have forgotten that animal lives are lives like their own, God has laid down certain laws for slaughter. The *Qurbān*, with its emphasis on restraint and empathy with animal suffering, is meant to temper human passions and limit the extravagant sacrifices of pre-Islamic times. Paradoxical as it may seem, the true meaning of *Qurbān*, concludes Bawa Muhaiyaddeen, is the realization of what is right and the wisdom to avoid causing hurt and harm to other lives. As in Jewish and Christian vegetarian writings, God is here understood to give reluctant permission for animal slaughter as a way of conditioning unruly and violent human desire.

Qurbān's check on human bloodthirstiness is a reminder that all life is a sacred sign of God's resplendent creation. As a creature in one of Bawa's parables tells a hunter, "Oh man, God created me and He created you. You are a man. God created you from earth, fire, water, air, and ether. I am an animal, but God created me from these same elements."

The Islamic scholar Al-Ḥāfiz B. A. Masri makes much of the Qur'ānic spirit of compassion toward animals, its hymn to a unified creation. Several striking passages from the *Qur'ān* support Masri's emphasis on human beings and animals as created and equally loved by God. As we read in the *Qur'ān*

(6:38), "There is not an animal on earth, nor a bird that flies on its wings, but they are communities like you." Through both a review of religious laws that mandate responsibility for the welfare of all creatures and an analysis of *Qurbān*, Masri confronts difficult issues in Islamic traditions of animal treatment. He concludes that the weight of passages from the *Qur'ān*, the *Ḥadīth*, and customary law disavows cruelty and exploitation of animals.

"THERE IS A FAULT IN THE CREATION, IT SEEMS"

One of the Indian readings in this volume is a discussion between Swami Prabhupāda, the founder of Krishna Consciousness, and Roman Catholic Cardinal Jean Daniélou. The two religious leaders are speculating about why Christians typically refuse to extend the commandment against killing to animals. At one point in their conversation, Cardinal Daniélou wonders, "But why does [a loving] God create some animals who eat other animals?" His answer to his own question is both haunting and poignant: "There is a fault in the creation, it seems."

Swami Prabhupāda quickly dismisses this possibility. "It is not a fault," he insists. "God is very kind. If you want to eat animals, then He'll give you full facility. God will give you the body of a tiger in your next life so that you can eat flesh very freely. . . . The animal eaters become tigers, wolves, cats, and dogs in their next life." The Swami's point is that if there is a "fault in creation," it originates nowhere but in the devourer of animal flesh and will be reprimanded and redeemed in the working out of karmic necessity. Restless rapacity is the destiny of the meat eater.

And yet the poignancy of Cardinal Daniélou's question remains. If violence in nature and in us is abhorrent, must not creation, entangled in violence despite its beauty and sublimity, be flawed? Animal slaughter is just one of many ways nature is braided through with terror and death. But who can bear this terrible possibility—of a universe in which cruelty and pain exist without meaning, with no divine providence, no escape, no redemption in suffering?

The religious questions that arise so urgently from considerations of animal slaughter and our complicity in it are elemental. Is there nothing but savagery in the entangled web of spirit and of hunger? Is there no eschaton toward which we tend, no end to rebirth, no divine comfort, no stilling of the desire to kill? In response to these somber and bewildering questions, the literature of religious vegetarianism expresses hope that a peaceable kingdom might one day come to pass in which humans, with divine blessing and generous love, exist in harmony with animals and the natural world.

NOTE

1. Knut Jacobsen, "Humankind and Nature in Buddhism," in *A Companion to World Philosophies*, ed. Elliot Deutsch and Ron Bontekoe (Oxford: Blackwell, 1997), p. 384.

THE ORPHIC-PYTHAGOREAN
TRADITION

Feasts of crude flesh I now decline. . .
Never amidst the tombs intrude,
And slay no animal for food.

—Euripides

Almost every world culture appears to have mythopoetic memories of a utopian "golden age" which existed at the beginning of time. These tales of golden ages all have a discernibly religious ring to them. This only makes sense because they purport to harken back to a time when humans were as innocent and pure as the gods intended them, living in peaceful harmony with one another and with nature. But this original innocence was lost, and subsequent generations have been harrowed by strife and violence. Hope remains, however, because the legends of golden ages are forward as well as backward looking: after humans work through the violence and greed that besmirch them and their world, original purity will resurface and paradise will be regained.

The Western world is especially aware of the archetype of a temporarily lost golden age because of the biblical story of the Edenic Fall. But there's another golden age legend that parallels the one in Judaic-Christian memory. It belongs to "pagan" Greek culture, and was first systematically recorded by the eighth-century BCE poet Hesiod. This account was foundational in the development of religious vegetarianism in the ancient world.

According to Hesiod, there have been five "ages" of humankind. The last four, including the one in which Hesiod himself lived, are characterized by various levels of idiocy, selfishness, and violence. But the first was a paradise in which humans neither labored nor worried. The fruits and grains of the earth grew spontaneously, providing regular and rich harvests. Nor was there warfare or hatred in this lost utopian age. People lived peacefully with one another, with animals, and with the gods.

The obvious suggestion in Hesiod's description of the five ages is that the slaughter of animals for food only began in the post–golden age period, and that there is a common and reprehensible link between the taste for animal blood, the urge to slay humans, and the perversion of original innocence. The clear implication is that a life of nonviolence—including nonviolence toward animals—is pleasing to the gods as well as ultimately fulfilling for humans, and that the shattering of the prohibition against bloodshed led to the primordial fall. Thus Hesiod implicitly puts forth a meatless diet as a religious ideal that was swept away when the golden age mutated into its tarnished descendants.

The connection between spiritual purity and vegetarianism that Hesiod's retelling of the golden age legend posited mightily influenced the cult of Orpheus and the school of Pythagoras.[1] Almost nothing is known about the Orphic mysteries. The cult probably originated sometime in the seventh or sixth centuries BCE, and revolved around the semi-legendary figure of Orpheus. Orpheus was believed to have had the power to communicate with animals. But communication with animals is possible (at least to the Orphic mind) only if animals possess a soul, or rational faculty, capable of reason. Although the connections are murky, this belief gradually became associated with the doctrine of metempsychosis, or the transmigration of souls from one body to another.[2] Animals are intelligent because animated by souls previously incarnated in humans. Consequently, the Orphic mysteries sternly condemned carnivorism as a continuation of the violence that brought down the original golden age.

The religious and philosophical school founded by the sixth-century BCE Pythagoras continued the Orphic tradition of vegetarianism. Legends abound concerning this elusive figure and his teachings, but this much at least is clear: Pythagoras accepted the doctrine of soul transmigration, and was acutely aware of the need for humans to repair the damage wrought upon creation by their violence and self-indulgence. He taught his disciples an *ascesis* for purifying themselves and atoning for the evils of the world.

The fifth-century BCE Pythagorean philosopher Empedocles provides us with insight into the urgency of such purifications when he chillingly writes about the consequences of carnivorism: "The father lifts up his own son changed in form and slaughters him with a prayer, blind fool, as he shrieks piteously, beseeching as he sacrifices... In the same way son seizes father and children their mother, and tearing out the life they eat the flesh of those they love." Some six centuries later the sage Apollonius of Tyana would argue on similar grounds against blood offerings, and urge the people of his day to pursue spiritual perfection through the renunciation of violence against their fellows and against animals.

Horrifying as the prospect of devouring one's kin is, the deeper religious message of the Orphic-Pythagorean tradition should not be missed. The practice of violence and the taking of life, whether human or animal, violates the divinely ordained original plan and corrupts the spiritual condition of humans. A merely credal or conceptual renunciation of violence is not enough; one's piety or philosophy must be assimilated into the warp and woof of everyday life. Abstention from the flesh of slaughtered animals was one of the strategies by which devotees in the Orphic-Pythagorean tradition attempted to live their religious convictions.

NOTES

1. This isn't to suggest that Hesiod alone is responsible for the legend. Vestiges of it appear in Homer, who antedated Hesiod by at least a couple of centuries. Nestor (*Iliad* I, 260–69) speaks of ancestors more noble than the men of his generation, and there's some reason to believe that the famous Cyclops story in Book IX of the *Odyssey* is a gloss on the destruction of the golden age. Polyphemus lives in a land which seems innocent of farming or hunting—or violence—until the worldly Odysseus' behavior precipitates a horrible rampage of bloodshed and cannibalism. Moreover, it's certainly the case that Greeks, who were not obvious devotees of the Orphic-Pythagorean mysteries, were influenced by the golden age archetype. The most notable is Plato. In the "Gorgias" (523a, 523c), for example, he compares two of the ages Hesiod wrote about: the "Republic's" famous classification (415a) of the city-state's citizenry into gold, silver, and bronze/iron stock is reminiscent of Hesiod; and in the "Laws" (782), Plato repeats the common belief that the ancients, wiser and nobler than the present generation, were vegetarians. For an impressive study of ancient vegetarianism in general, see Daniel A. Dombrowski's (somewhat mistitled but excellent) *The Philosophy of Vegetarianism* (Amherst, MA: University of Massachusetts Press, 1984).

2. The mythopoetic correlate of Orphism's concept of soul transmigration appears to be one of the stories about Dionysus Zagreus. The story, which falls into the genre of dying and resurrected god stories, has it that the Titans, prompted by a jealous Zeus, sought to slay Dionysus, a child begotten by Zeus out of Semele. Dionysus managed to outwit the Titans for a time by metamorphosing into the shapes of different animals. He

was finally captured and slain while in the form of a bull, although he was later resurrected by a repentant Zeus. But his earlier habitation of a number of animal forms speaks to the metempsychosis doctrine.

The Five Ages

HESIOD

In this selection from his eighth century BCE *Works and Days, Hesiod implies that in the "Golden Age" of humankind a fleshless diet was the norm. Mortals dwelt in peaceful harmony with one another, the gods, and animals; the "fruitful grainland" was their only larder. But the original "golden" age was superseded by corrupt ones whose fallenness is expressed in violence—including the slaughter of animals for food. These subsequent ages were the "silver" one, populated by quarrelsome idiots; the "bronz," a time of violent warriors who "ate no bread"; the age of "hero-men," also violent but noble, who after death once again partook of the "sweet yield" of the "fruitful grainland" in the heavenly islands of the blessed; and the "iron age," populated by the present race of humans, a period characterized by senseless violence, hard work, pain, weariness, and anxiety. Hesiod's description of an aboriginal age of spiritual purity in which a nonviolent diet was natural greatly influenced later Orphic and Pythagorean defences of vegetarianism.*

> In the beginning, the immortals
>> who have their homes on Olympos
> created the golden generation of mortal people.
> These lived in Kronos' time, when he
>> was the king in heaven.
> They lived as if they were gods,
>> their hearts free from all sorrow,
> by themselves, and without hard work or pain;
>> no miserable
> old age came their way; their hands, their feet,
>> did not alter.

They took their pleasure in festivals,
    and lived without troubles.
When they died, it was as if they fell asleep.
    All goods
were theirs. The fruitful grainland
    yielded its harvest to them
of its own accord; this was great and abundant,
    while they at their pleasure
quietly looked after their works,
    in the midst of good things
prosperous in flocks, on friendly terms
    with the blessed immortals.

    Now that the earth has gathered over this generation,
these are called pure and blessed spirits;
    they live upon earth,
and are good, they watch over mortal men
    and defend them from evil;
they keep watch over lawsuits and hard dealings;
    they mantle
themselves in dark mist
    and wander all over the country;
they bestow wealth; for this right
    as of kings was given them.

    Next after these the dwellers upon Olympos created
a second generation, of silver, far worse
    than the other.
They were not like the golden ones either in shape
    or spirit.
A child was a child for a hundred years,
    looked after and playing
by his gracious mother, kept at home,
    a complete booby.
But when it came time for them to grow up
    and gain full measure,
they lived for only a poor short time;
    by their own foolishness
they had troubles, for they were not able
    to keep away from

reckless crime against each other,
    nor would they worship
the gods, nor do sacrifice on the sacred altars
    of the blessed ones,
which is the right thing among the customs of men,
    and therefore
Zeus, son of Kronos, in anger engulfed them,
    for they paid no due
honors to the blessed gods who live on Olympos.

    But when the earth had gathered over this generation
also—and they too are called blessed spirits
    by men, though under
the ground, and secondary, but still
    they have their due worship—
then Zeus the father created the third generation
    of mortals,
the age of bronze. They were not like
    the generation of silver.
They came from ash spears. They were terrible
    and strong, and the ghastly
action of Ares was theirs, and violence.
    They ate no bread,
but maintained an indomitable and adamantine spirit.
None could come near them; their strength was big,
    and from their shoulders
the arms grew irresistible on their ponderous bodies.
The weapons of these men were bronze,
    of bronze their houses,
and they worked as bronzesmiths. There was not yet
    any black iron.
Yet even these, destroyed beneath the hands
    of each other,
went down into the moldering domain of cold Hades;
nameless; for all they were formidable black death
seized them, and they had to forsake
    the shining sunlight.

Now when the earth had gathered over this generation
also, Zeus, son of Kronos, created yet another

fourth generation on the fertile earth,
     and these were better and nobler,
the wonderful generation of hero-men, who are also
called half-gods, the generation before our own
     on this vast earth.
But of these too, evil war and the terrible carnage
took some; some by seven-gated Thebes
     in the land of Kadmos
as they fought together over the flocks of Oedipous;
     others
war had taken in ships over the great gulf
     of the sea,
where they also fought for the sake
     of lovely-haired Helen.
There, for these, the end of death was misted
     about them.
But on others Zeus, son of Kronos, settled a living
     and a country
of their own, apart from human kind,
     at the end of the world.
And there they have their dwelling place,
     and hearts free of sorrow
in the islands of the blessed
     by the deep-swirling stream of the ocean,
prospering heroes, on whom in every year
     three times over
the fruitful grainland bestows its sweet yield.
     These live
far from the immortals, and Kronos
     is kind among them.
For Zeus, father of gods and mortals,
     set him free from his bondage,
although the position and the glory still belong
     to the young gods.

After this, Zeus of the wide brows
     established yet one more
generation of men, the fifth, to be
     on the fertile earth.

And I wish that I were not any part
    of the fifth generation
of men, but had died before it came,
    or been born afterward.
For here now is the age of iron. Never by daytime
will there be an end to hard work and pain,
    nor in the night
to weariness, when the gods will send anxieties
    to trouble us.
Yet here also there shall be some good things
    mixed with the evils.
But Zeus will destroy this generation of mortals
    also,
in the time when children, as they are born,
    grow gray on the temples,
when the father no longer agrees with the children,
    nor children with their father,
when guest is no longer at one with host,
    nor companion to companion,
when your brother is no longer your friend,
    as he was in the old days.
Men will deprive their parents of all rights,
    as they grow old,
and people will mock them too,
    babbling bitter words against them,
harshly, and without shame in the sight of the gods;
    not even
to their aging parents will they give back
    what once was given.
Strong of hand, one man shall seek
    the city of another.
There will be no favor for the man
    who keeps his oath, for the righteous
and the good man, rather men shall give their praise
    to violence
and the doer of evil. Right will be in the arm.
    Shame will
not be. The vile man will crowd his better out,
    and attack him

with twisted accusations and swear an oath
    to his story.
The spirit of Envy, with grim face
    and screaming voice, who delights
in evil, will be the constant companion
    of wretched humanity,
and at last Nemesis and Aidos, Decency and Respect,
    shrouding
their bright forms in pale mantles, shall go
    from the wide-wayed
earth back on their way to Olympos,
    forsaking the whole race
of mortal men, and all that will be left by them
    to mankind
will be wretched pain. And there shall be no defense
    against evil.

The Blessed Life

PORPHYRY

Like his master Plotinus, the third-century Porphyry's vegetarianism was influenced by the Orphic and Pythagorean traditions. In this selection from his On Abstinence from Animal Food, *Porphyry expresses his belief in the ancient legend of a vegetarian golden age when life was peaceful, fulfilled, and blessed. In that "pristine life," humans neither tilled the soil nor slaughtered animals for food. Instead, they ate the fruits of a bountiful earth, free from labor and disease. But eventually humans began to subjugate and slay animals, and the golden age ended. Brutality to animals was the catalyst that opened the door to war and injustice. The identity of the Dicaearchus whom Porphyry cites in this selection is uncertain; many ancient Greek notables bore the name. But the verse about the peace that reigned during the golden age Porphyry quotes without attribution is easily recognized as Hesiod's.*

Among those... therefore, that have concisely, and at the same time accurately, collected an account of the affairs of the Greeks, is the Peripatetic Dicaearchus, who, in narrating the pristine life of the Greeks, says [that] the ancients, being generated with an alliance to the Gods, were naturally most excellent, and led the best life; so that, when compared to us of the present day, who consist of an adulterated and most vile matter, they were thought to be a golden race; and they slew no animal whatever. The truth of this, he also says, is testified by the poets, who denominate these ancients the golden race, and assert that every good was present with them.

> The fertile earth for them spontaneous bore
> Of fruits a copious and unenvy'd store;
> In blissful quiet then, unknown to strife,
> The worthy with the worthy passed their life.

...All things, therefore, are very properly said to have been spontaneously produced; for men did not procure any thing by labor, because they were unacquainted with the agricultural art, and in short, had no knowledge of any other art.

This very thing, likewise, was the cause of their leading a life of leisure, free from labors and care; and if it is proper to assent to the decision of the most skillful and elegant of physicians, it is also the cause of their being liberated from disease. For there is not any precept of physicians which more contributes to health, than that which exhorts us not to make an abundance of excrement, from which those pristine Greeks always preserved their bodies pure. For they neither assumed such food as was stronger than the nature of the body could bear, but such as could be vanquished by the corporeal nature, nor more than was moderate, on account of the facility of procuring it, but for the most part less than was sufficient, on account of its paucity.

Moreover, there were neither any wars among them, nor seditions with each other. For no reward of contention worth mentioning was proposed as an incentive, for the sake of which some one might be induced to engage in such dissensions. So that the principal thing in that life was leisure and rest from necessary occupations, together with health, peace, and friendship. But to those in after times, who, through aspiring after things which greatly exceeded mediocrity, fell into many evils, this pristine life became, as it was reasonable to suppose it would, desirable. The slender and extemporaneous food, however, of these first men, is manifested by the saying which was afterward proverbially used, "enough of the oak;" this adage being probably introduced by him who first changed the ancient mode of living. A pastoral life succeeded to this, in which men procured for themselves superfluous possessions, and meddled with animals. For, perceiving that some of them were innoxious, but others malefic and savage, they tamed the former, but attacked the latter. At the same time, together with this life, war was introduced. And those things, say Dicaearchus, are not asserted by us, but by those who have historically discussed a multitude of particulars. For, as possessions were now of such a magnitude as to merit attention, some ambitiously endeavored to obtain them, by collecting them for their own use, and calling on others to do the same, but others directed their attention to the preservation of them when collected.

Time, therefore, thus gradually proceeding, and men always directing their attention to what appeared to be useful, they at length became conversant with the third, and agricultural form of life. And this is what is said by Dicaearchus, in his narration of the manners of the ancient Greeks, and the blessed life which they then led, to which abstinence from animal food contributed, no less than any other thing.

Hence, at that period there was no war, because injustice was exterminated. But afterward, together with injustice toward animals, war was introduced among men, and the endeavor to surpass each other in amplitude of possessions. On what account also, the audacity of those is wonderful, who say that abstinence from animals is the mother of injustice, since both history and experience testify, that together with the slaughter of animals, war and injustice were introduced.

Pythagoras of Samos:

Spirit Never Perishes

OVID

One of the most eloquent biographers of Pythagoras was the great Roman poet Publius Ovidius Naso (43 BCE–CE 17). Ovid wasn't himself a Pythagorean, but he was a close student of its doctrine. He was also fascinated by the shadowy legends surrounding Pythagoras, and recounts many of them in Book Fifteen of his Metamorphosis, *excerpted here. Ovid's Pythagoras objects to meat eating, or the "storage of flesh in flesh," on two counts: first, because it entails unwarranted violence against living creatures; second, because the slaughtering of food animals has horrifying consequences for anyone who, like Pythagoras, believes in the immortality and transmigration of souls. In the final analysis, it is impious for life to feed on life, and Pythagoras longs for a return to a "pristine age" of spiritual purity in which humans refuse to "defile their lips with blood."*

There was a man, a Samian by birth, but he had fled forth from Samos and its rulers, and through hatred of tyranny was living in voluntary exile. He, though the gods were far away in the heavenly regions, still approached them with his thought, and what Nature denied to his mortal vision he feasted on with his mind's eye. And when he had surveyed all things by reason and wakeful diligence, he would give out to the public ear the things worthy of their learning and would teach the crowds, which listened in wondering silence to his words, the beginnings of the great universe, the causes of things and what their nature is: What God is, whence come the snows, what is the origin of lightning, whether it is Jupiter or the winds that thunder from the riven clouds, what causes the earth to quake, by what law the stars perform their courses, and whatever else is hidden from men's knowledge. He was the first to decry the placing of animal food upon our tables. His lips, learned indeed but not believed in this, he was the first to open in such words as these:

"O mortals, do not pollute your bodies with a food so impious! You have the fruits of the earth, you have apples, bending down the branches with their weight, and grapes swelling to ripeness on the vines; you have also delicious herbs and vegetables which can be mellowed and softened by the help of fire. Nor are you without milk or honey, fragrant with the bloom of thyme. The earth, prodigal of her wealth, supplies you her kindly sustenance and offers you food without bloodshed and slaughter. Flesh is the wild beasts' wherewith they appease their hunger, and yet not all, since the horse, the sheep, and cattle live on grass; but those whose nature is savage and untamed, Armenian tigers, raging lions, bears and wolves, all these delight in bloody food. Oh, how criminal it is for flesh to be stored away in flesh, for one greedy body to grow fat with food gained from another, for one live creature to go on living through the destruction of another living thing! And so in the midst of the wealth of food which Earth, the best of mothers, has produced, it is your pleasure to chew the piteous flesh of slaughtered animals with your savage teeth, and thus to repeat the Cyclops' horrid manners! And you cannot, without destroying other life, appease the cravings of your greedy and insatiable maw!

"But that pristine age, which we have named the golden age, was blessed with the fruit of the trees and the herbs which the ground sends forth, nor did men defile their lips with blood. Then birds plied their wings in safety through the heaven, and the hare loitered all unafraid in the tilled fields, nor did its own guilelessness hang the fish upon the hook. All things were free from treacherous snares, fearing no guile and full of peace. But after someone, an ill exemplar, whoever he was, envied the food of lions, and thrust down flesh as food into his greedy stomach, he opened the way for crime. It may be that, in the first place, with the killing of wild beasts the steel was warmed and stained with blood. This would have been justified, and we admit that creatures which menace our own lives may be killed without impiety. But, while they might be killed, they should never have been eaten.

"Further impiety grew out of that, and it is thought that the sow was first condemned to death as a sacrificial victim because with her broad snout she had rooted up the planted seeds and cut off the season's promised crop. The goat is said to have been slain at the avenging altars because he had browsed the grape vines. These two suffered because of their own offenses! But, ye sheep, what did you ever do to merit death, a peaceful flock, born for man's service, who bring us sweet milk to drink in your full udders, who give us your wool for soft clothing, and who help more by your life than by your death? What have the oxen done, those faithful, guileless beasts, harmless and simple, born to a life of toil? Truly inconsiderate he and not worthy of the gift of grain who could take off the curved plow's heavy weight and in the next moment slay his husbandman; who with his ax could smite that neck which was worn with toil for him, by whose help he had so often renewed the stubborn soil and planted so many crops. Nor is it enough that we commit such infamy: They made the gods themselves partners of their crime and they affected to believe that the heavenly ones took pleasure in the blood of the toiling bullock! A victim without blemish and of perfect form (for beauty proves his bane), marked off with fillets and with gilded horns, is set before the altar, hears the priest's prayer, not knowing what it means, watches the barley meal sprinkled between his horns, barley which he himself labored to produce, and then, smitten to his death, he stains with his blood the knife which he has perchance already seen reflected in the clear pool. Straightway they tear his entrails from his living breast, view them with care, and seek to find revealed in them the purposes of heaven. Thence (so great is man's lust for forbidden food!) do you dare thus to feed, O race of mortals! I pray you, do not do it, but turn your minds to these my words of warning, and when you take the flesh of slaughtered cattle in your mouths, know and realize that you are devouring your own fellow laborers.

"Now, since a god inspires my lips, I will dutifully follow the inspiring god; I'll open Delphi and the heavens themselves and unlock the oracles of the sublime mind. Great matters, never traced out by the minds of former men, things that have long been hidden, I will sing. It is a delight to take one's way along the starry firmament and, leaving the earth and its dull regions behind, to ride on the clouds, to take stand on stout Atlas' shoulders and see far below men wandering aimlessly, devoid of reason, anxious and in fear of the hereafter, thus to exhort them and unroll the book of fate!

"O race of men, stunned with the chilling fear of death, why do you dread the Styx, the shades and empty names, the stuff that poets manufacture, and their fabled sufferings of a world that never was? As for your bodies, whether the burning pyre or long lapse of time with its wasting power shall have consumed them, be sure they cannot suffer any ills. Our souls are deathless, and ever, when they have left their former seat, do they live in new abodes and dwell in the bodies that have received them. I myself (for I well remember it) at the time of the Trojan war was Euphorbus, son of Panthous, in whose breast once hung the heavy spear of Menelaus. Recently, in Juno's temple in Argos, Abas' city, I recognized the shield which I once wore on my left arm! All things are changing; nothing dies. The spirit wanders, comes now here, now there, and occupies whatever frame it pleases. From beasts it passes into human bodies, and from our bodies into beasts, but never perishes. And, as the pliant wax is stamped with new designs, does not remain as it was before nor keep the same form long, but is still the selfsame wax, so do I teach that the soul is ever the same, though it passes into ever-changing bodies. Therefore, lest your piety be overcome by appetite, I warn you as a seer, do not drive out by impious slaughter what may be kindred souls, and let not life be fed on life. . .

"We also change, who are a part of creation, since we are not bodies only but also winged souls, and since we can enter wild beast forms and be lodged in the bodies of cattle. We should permit bodies which may possibly have sheltered the souls of our parents or brothers or those joined to us by some other bond, or of men at least, to be uninjured and respected, and not load our stomachs as with a Thyestean banquet![1] What an evil habit he is forming, how surely is he impiously preparing to shed human blood, who cuts a calf's throat with the knife and listens all unmoved to its piteous cries! Or who can slay a kid which cries just like a little child, or feed on a bird to which he himself has just given food! How much does a deed as that fall short of actual murder? What is the end of such a course? Let the bull plow and let him owe his death to length of days; let the sheep arm you against the rough north wind; let the she-goats give full udders to the milking. Have done with nets and traps, snares and deceptive arts. Catch not the bird with the limed twig; no longer mock the deer with fear-compelling feathers,[2] nor conceal the barbed hook beneath fair-seeming food. Kill creatures that work you harm, but even in the case of these let killing suffice. Make not their flesh your food, but seek a more harmless nourishment."

NOTES

1. A reference to Thyestes, who in Greek legend unwittingly cannibalized his own children.

2. Feather boas were frequently hung from tree branches by ancient hunters to frighten deer into nets.

I Have Been a Leaping

Journeying Fish

EMPEDOCLES

Only fragments survive from the fifth-century BCE *writings of Empedocles, philosopher and Pythagorean. In the selections here, taken from what remains of a manuscript entitled "Purifications," Empedocles announces that he has achieved enlightenment—is "mortal no longer"—and then proceeds to share his insight with others. Bloodshed, he claims, is the sin and pollution that exiles one from the gods and brings the retribution of continuous rebirth: The murderer's soul is forced into a weary, homeless round of transmigrations. Because human souls inhabit the bodies of animals, the slaughter of food animals only continues the violence. But bloodshed was not always the norm. Empedocles, like all other Orphic-Pythagorean vegetarians, recalls a golden age in which Murder, Anger, and Discord did not reign and in which the slaughter of animals, particularly as sacrifices to the gods, was seen as a "defilement." He hints that it is not too late for humans to leave the roofed cave in which they've imprisoned themselves and, Persephone-like, experience spiritual rebirth. But a necessary condition for regaining the lost "height of bliss" is refusal to continue spilling blood, and that of course in part means a return to the peaceful vegetarian diet of the lost golden age. (Ellipses indicate missing or indecipherable portions in the surviving text.)*

Friends, who live in the great city of the yellow Acragas, up on the heights of the citadel, caring for good deeds, I give you greetings. An immortal god, mortal no more, I go about honored by all, as is fitting, crowned with ribbons and fresh garlands; and by all whom I come upon as I enter their prospering towns, by men and women, I am revered. They follow me in their thousands, asking where lies the road to profit, some desiring prophecies, while others ask to hear the word of healing for every kind of illness, long transfixed by harsh pains.

Happy and blessed one, you shall be a god instead of a mortal.

There is an oracle of necessity, ancient decree of the gods, eternal, sealed with broad oaths: when anyone sins and pollutes his own limbs with bloodshed, who by his error makes false the oath he swore—spirits whose portion is long life— for thrice ten thousand years he wanders apart from the blessed, being born throughout that time in all manner of forms of mortal things, exchanging one hard path of life for another. The force of the air pursues him into the sea, the sea spews him out onto the floor of the earth, the earth casts him into the rays of the blazing sun, and the sun into the eddies of the air; one takes him from the other, but all abhor him. Of these I too am now one, an exile from the gods and a wanderer, having put my trust in raving Strife.

I wept and wailed when I saw the unfamiliar place where Murder and Anger and tribes of other Deaths. . . they wander in darkness over the meadow of Doom.

Alas, poor unhappy race of mortals, from what strifes and groanings were you born.

From what high rank and from what a height of bliss. . .

We came under this roofed cave. . .

There were Earth and far-seeing sun, bloody Discord and serene harmonia, Beauty and Ugliness, Haste and Tarrying, lovely Truth and blind Obscurity.

. . . clothing [the soul] in an alien garment of flesh.

Among beasts they are born as lions with lairs in the hills and beds on the ground, and as laurels among fair-tressed trees.

But at the end they come among men on earth as prophets, bards, doctors, and princes; and thence they arise as gods highest in honor, sharing with the other immortals their hearth and their table, without part in human sorrows or weariness.

Those from whom Persephone receives requital for ancient grief, in the ninth year she restores again their souls to the sun above. From them arise noble kings, and those men swift in strength, and greatest in wisdom; and for the rest of time they are called heroes and sanctified by mankind.

———◆◆———

Among them was no war god Ares worshipped nor the battle cry, nor was Zeus their king nor Kronos nor Poseidon, but Cypris [i.e., Aphrodite] was queen. Her they propitiated with holy images, with paintings of living creatures, with perfumes of varied fragrance and sacrifices of pure myrrh and sweet-scented frankincense, throwing to the ground libations of yellow honey. Their altar was not drenched by the unspeakable slaughters of bulls, but this was held among men the greatest defilement—to tear out the life from noble limbs and eat them.

All things were tame and gentle to men, both beasts and birds, and their friendship burned bright.

———◆◆———

But this, the law for all, extends unendingly throughout wide-ruling air and the immense light [of the sun].

Will you not cease from the din of slaughter? Do you not see that you are devouring each other in the heedlessness of your minds?

The father lifts up his own son changed in form and slaughters him with a prayer, blind fool, as he shrieks piteously, beseeching as he sacrifices. But he, deaf to his cries, slaughters him and makes ready in his halls an evil feast. In the same way son seizes father and children their mother, and tearing out the life they eat the flesh of those they love.

Alas that the pitiless day did not destroy me first, before I contrived the wretched deed of eating flesh with my lips.

For I have already been once a boy and a girl, a bush and a bird and a leaping journeying fish.

Apollonious of Tyana:

Sweet Offerings

PHILOSTRATUS

We know almost nothing about Philostratus except that he was born sometime around 170. But his biography of the first-century Apollonius of Tyana is a fascinating account of a neo-Pythagorean sage, ascetic, and reformer. Apollonius, who appears to have died at an advanced age during the reign of Nerva, was a wandering mendicant who tried to reform late classical paganism by turning it away from blood offerings. Renowned for his austerity (he once went five years without speaking), Apollonius emulated Pythagoras by forswearing meat and wine, leather shoes, and clothes made from skins. In this selection from the biography, Apollonius speaks before Egyptian priests in response to the criticisms of someone named Thespesion. He recounts a vision of Wisdom similar to the one that "conquered the soul of Pythagoras" to explain why he adopted a meatless diet.

. . . I long ago made choice of the life which seemed best to myself; and as I am older than any of you, except Thespesion, I myself am better qualified, now I have got here, to advise you how to choose wisdom, if I did not find that you had already made the choice. Being, however, as old as I am, and so far advanced in wisdom as I am, I shall not hesitate as it were to make you the auditors of my life and motives, and teach you that I rightly chose this life of mine, than which no better one has ever suggested itself to me. For I discerned a certain sublimity in the discipline of Pythagoras, and how a certain secret wisdom enabled him to know, not only who he was himself, but also who he had been; and I saw that he approached the altars in purity, and suffered not his belly to be polluted by partaking of the flesh of animals; and that he kept his body pure of all garments woven of dead animal refuse; and that he was the first of mankind to restrain his tongue, inventing a discipline of silence described in the proverbial phrase, "An ox sits upon it." I also saw that his philosophical system was in other respects oracular and true.

So I ran to embrace his teachings, not choosing one form of wisdom rather than another of two presented me, as you, my excellent Thespesion, advise me to do. For philosophy marshaled before me her various points of view, investing them with the adornment proper to each, and she commanded me to look upon them and make a sound choice. Now they were all possessed of an august and divine beauty; and some of them were of such dazzling brightness that you might well have closed your eyes. However I fixed my eyes firmly upon all of them, for they themselves encouraged me to do so by moving toward me, and telling me beforehand how much they would give me.

Well, one of them professed that she would shower upon me a swarm of pleasures without any toil on my part; and another that she would give me rest after toil; and a third that she would mingle mirth and merriment in my toil; and everywhere I had glimpses of pleasures and of unrestrained indulgence in the pleasures of the table; and it seemed that I had only to stretch out my hand to be rich, and that I needed not to set any bridle upon my eyes, but love and loose desire and such like feelings were freely allowed me.

One of them, however, boasted that she would restrain me from such things, but she was bold and abusive and in an unabashed manner elbowed all others aside; and I beheld the ineffable form of wisdom which long ago conquered the soul of Pythagoras; and she stood, I may tell you, not among the many, but kept herself apart and in silence; and when she saw that I ranged not myself with the rest, though as yet I knew not what were her wares, she said: "Young man, I am unpleasing and a lady full of sorrows; for, if anyone betakes himself to my abode, he must of his own choice put away all dishes which contain the flesh of living animals, and he must forget wine, nor make muddy therewith the cup of wisdom which is set in the souls of those that drink no wine; nor shall blanket keep him warm, nor wool shorn from a living animal. But I allow him shoes of bark, and he must sleep anywhere and anyhow, and if I find my votaries yielding to sensual pleasures, I have precipices to which justice that waits upon wisdom carries them and pushes them over; and I am so harsh to those who make choice of my discipline that I have bits ready to restrain their tongues. But learn from me what rewards you shall reap by enduring all this; temperance and justice unsought and at once, and the faculty to regard no man with envy, and to be dreaded by tyrants rather than cringe to them, and to have your humble offerings appear sweeter to the gods than the offerings of those who pour out before them the blood of bulls. And when you are pure I will grant you the faculty of foreknowledge, and I will so fill your eyes with light, that you shall distinguish a god, and recognize a hero, and detect and put to shame the shadowy phantoms which disguise themselves in the form of men."

This was the life I chose, ye wise of the Egyptians; it was a sound choice and in the spirit of Pythagoras, and in making it I neither deceived myself, nor was deceived; for I have become all that a philosopher should become, and all that she promised to bestow upon the philosopher, that is mine. For I have studied profoundly the problem of the rise of the art and whence it draws its first principles; and I have realized that it belongs to men of transcendent religious gifts, who have thoroughly investigated the nature of the soul, the wellsprings of whose existence lie back in the immortal and in the unbegotten.

THE INDIAN
TRADITION

This is the truth:
As from a well-blazing fire, sparks
By the thousand issue forth of like form,
So from the Imperishable, my friend,
Beings manifold
Are produced, and thither also go.

—Muṇḍaka Upaniṣad

The Indian religious and philosophical tradition has proved one of the most hospitable for vegetarian practice. Distinctions between forms of life, especially humans and animals, are rarely conceived as rigid or fixed. Life is a continuum; what differences there are among organisms are ones of degree and not of kind. This belief in the fluidity and commonality of life is closely associated with reincarnation's karmic emphasis on transmutation of forms and malleable embodiment. Gods take animal form, human beings have had past animal lives, animals have had past human lives. Such fluidity of form among living things, conjoined with injunctions to nonviolence and asceticism, has made vegetarianism a significant part of Indian spiritual life.

The origins of Indian religious thought are buried in obscurity. The Vedic Period, the earliest recorded stage of development, is placed by historians somewhere between 2500 and 600 BCE. During that period the four *Vedas (Ṛg, Yajur, Sāma,* and *Atharva)* were composed, comprised of hymns, songs, poems, ritualistic and sacrificial instructions, and philosophical meditations. This earliest literature usually speaks of many gods—of sun, fire, sky, wind, earth, and water—but the *Ṛg Veda's* "Hymn to Creation" describes the origin of the universe as an evolution from an ultimate One who, before desire stirred or life and death existed, breathed amidst darkness and water. In the *Upaniṣads,* the concluding (and historically later) portions of the *Vedas,* this vision of an ultimate One, which is transcendent yet also imminent in all material forms, is well established and leaves its imprint on subsequent Indian religious thought.

In devotional contexts, the divine One is believed capable of infinite manifestations or "descents" *(avatāras).* In the great epics *Mahābhārata* and *Rāmāyana,* as well as in various *pursanas,* the divine manifests itself in male form as Kṛṣṇa or Rāma. As woman, the divine manifests itself as nurturing mother, cosmic energy, fertile creative force, and world-destroyer. But the divine also manifests itself in animal form: as elephant, fish, serpent, boar, or monkey. Human and animal identities, as well as the identities of gods, are conceived as fluid.

What persists—what is most real—is *Brahma,* the ultimate one, the supreme creative principle. The Indian spiritual journey seeks liberation *(mokṣa)* from the constantly changing world of appearance *(māyā)* and a return to *Brahma.* Two necessary conditions for this return are the enlightened awareness that divine essence is in all things and the resolve to treat all things with the reverence that is their due. Thus vegetarianism is consonant with the deepest Indian religious intuitions. Partly spiritual practice, partly commitment to noninjury of living beings, Indian vegetarianism is the obvious corollary of the belief that all forms are manifestations of *Brahma.*

The Laws of Manu, from the Epic Period, the second stage of Indian religious development (600 BCE to 200 CE), are the earliest explicit vegetarian writing from India. They offer an account of the conduct of life and its proper social organization. In the passages anthologized here, spiritual liberation is linked to desiring the good of all beings and vowing noninjury to all creatures. No happiness can be attained by one who causes "the sufferings of bonds and death to living creatures." Nor is just the eating of animal flesh forbidden. "He who permits the slaughter of an animal, he who cuts it up, he who kills it, he who buys or sells meat, he who cooks it, he who serves it up, and he who eats it, must all be considered as the slayers of the animal." Thus the entire social and economic structure of meat eating is condemned as spiritually impure, a judgment that has some affinity with Carol Adams's contemporary Christian analysis of carnivorism as "institutionalized violence" (see her contribution to this volume). The Epic Period saw the rise of both Buddhism and Jainism on the Indian subcontinent. Among the Jains, followers of the sage Mahāvīra, nonviolence *(ahiṃsā)* was elevated as the first principle and rule of life. The *Ākarāṅga Sūtra*, a sacred Jain text, affirms that all animate beings similarly experience pleasure, displeasure, pain, great terror, and unhappiness. This similarity is seen as an indication of the sacred unity of all life, a unity in which accordances are more significant than discordances. Out of reverence for life and the divine One it manifests, the Jain devotee practices self-control and constant awareness in order to refrain from any action that inflicts even the least degree of pain or terror on kindred creatures—and, of course, all creatures are kindred. Thus nonviolence in diet is an essential aspect of "right conduct," which together with "right faith" and "right knowledge" constitute the Jaina threefold path to blessedness.

Although not a Jain, the northern Indian religious poet Kabīr also taught the unity of all life, and his verse frequently decries the human hypocrisy that insists on dismissing animal life as insignificant. "Do not kill living beings, all have life." What heaven can there be, he asks, for those who slaughter a hen at dusk? We share with animals a single flesh and the same crimson blood. No innate superiority, no authority in society, justifies the turning of living soul to a corpse.

In later Indian vegetarianism, represented here by three late nineteenth- and twentieth-century spiritual teachers, the distinctive cast of Indian religious sensibility is unmistakable.

Swami Vivekānanda affirms the oneness of all things and the degradation involved in attempts to reconcile fleshly vanities with highest ideals. Religion must uphold these ideals of reverence for life and not excuse human weakness. "We eat meat not because animals have been given to us for food, but because we want to." Ideals must not be dragged down, argues Vivekānanda, in misguided attempts to defend the practical. We ought to strive instead to realize "the brotherhood of all souls."

Mohandas Gandhi reflects on vegetarianism in two letters, one written in 1896, the other in 1927. Gandhi's thinking is complex and nondogmatic, examining vegetarianism first in a Christian and then in a Hindu context. For both those who seek to live according to the Christian Bible, and for those who seek to live according to *ahiṃsā*, vegetarianism is one important movement, although not the "be-all and end-all," in the direction of spiritual purity

In the final selection, Swami Prabhupāda, founder of Krishna Consciousness, reiterates the Indian theme of fellowship between humans and animals in his argument against Christian tolerance of slaughtering animals for food: "the animal eats, you eat; the animal sleeps, you sleep; the animal mates, you mate; the animal defends, you defend. Where is the difference?"

The Sin of Killing

THE LAWS OF MANU

Attributed to ancient sages or "seers," the most important of whom was Manu, the Dharmaśāstras *constitute a body of precepts related to the three goals* (trivarga) *that a Hindu is enjoined to seek:* dharma *or* righteousness, artha *or* material well-being, *and* kāma *or* pleasure. *The successful pursuit of the* trivarga *is believed necessary for achieving* mokṣa, *final liberation from the cycle of birth and death. In its treatment of lawful and forbidden foods and purity and impurity, the* Laws of Manu *(Mānava* Dharmaśāstra) *emphasize noninjury to living things as well as the importance of refraining from both remote and immediate actions that cause suffering to sentient creatures. Concern for the good of all beings as well as the avoidance of sin is prerequisite to heavenly bliss. The date of the* Laws of Manu *is uncertain but is thought to fall somewhere between 200* BCE *and 100* CE.

— He who injures innoxious beings from a wish to give himself pleasure, never finds happiness, neither living nor dead.

— He who does not seek to cause the sufferings of bonds and death to living creatures, but desires the good of all beings, obtains endless bliss.

— He who does not injure any creature, attains without an effort what he thinks of, what he undertakes, and what he fixes his mind on.

— Meat can never be obtained without injury to living creatures, and injury to sentient beings is detrimental to the attainment of heavenly bliss; let him therefore shun the use of meat.

— Having well considered the disgusting origin of flesh and the cruelty of fettering and slaying corporeal beings, let him entirely abstain from eating flesh.

— He who, disregarding the rule given above, does not eat meat becomes dear to men, and will not be tormented by diseases.

— He who permits the slaughter of an animal, he who cuts it up, he who kills it, he who buys or sells meat, he who cooks it, he who serves it up, and he who eats it, must all be considered as the slayers of the animal.

— There is no greater sinner than that man who, though not worshiping the gods, seeks to increase the bulk of his own flesh by the flesh of other beings.

To Harm No Living Being

ĀKARĀṄGA SŪTRA

The Jaina Sūtras derive from the sacred literature of the Jains, followers of Mahāvīra, founder of the movement in eastern India in the sixth century BCE. Mahāvīra condemned all violence to living beings and taught asceticism, the spiritual benefits of fasting, and the absolute necessity of avoiding injury to life (ahiṃsā). The ideal of ahiṃsā (which Mohandas Gandhi would invoke as the basis of his moral and social thought in the twentieth century; see the pertinent reading in Walters and Portmess, Ethical Vegetarianism *from Pythagoras to Peter Singer, as well as the Gandhi selection in this volume) constitutes the first vow of the Jains and calls for the renunciation of all killing of living beings as well as tolerance, benevolence, and a nonviolent vegetarian diet.*

The Ākarāṅga Sūtra attends not only to action (the ascetic must be careful in his work, must lay down his utensils of begging carefully, must inspect his food and drink so that he doesn't hurt or displace living beings), but to thoughts, intentions, and speech as well. The vow of abstinence from killing embraces divisive and "cutting" speech as much as actual injury and death to living creatures. Vegetarianism is an essential mode of right conduct for the Jain, but always because it's one way of living nonviolently and thus showing reverence for the divine essence in all existence.

Thus I say: there are beings called the animate, viz. those who are produced 1. from eggs (birds, etc.), 2. from a fetus (as elephants, etc.), 3. from a fetus with an enveloping membrane (as cows, buffaloes, etc.), 4. from fluids (as worms, etc.), 5. from sweat (as bugs, lice, etc.), 6. by coagulation (as locusts, ants, etc.), 7. from sprouts (as butterflies, wagtails, etc.), 8. by regeneration (men, gods, hell-beings)... Having well considered it, having well looked at it, I say thus: all beings, those with two, three, four senses, plants, those with five senses, and the rest of creation experience individually pleasure or displeasure, pain, great terror, and unhappiness.

Beings are filled with alarm from all directions and in all directions. See! There the benighted ones cause great pain. See! There are beings individually embodied.

See! There are men who control themselves; others pretend only to be houseless, for one destroys this body of an animal by bad and injurious doings, and many other beings, besides, which he hurts by means of animals, through his doing acts relating to animals. About this the Revered One has taught the truth: for the sake of the splendor, honor, and glory of this life, for the sake of birth, death, and final liberation, for the removal of pain, man acts sinfully toward animals, or causes others to act so, or allows others to act so. This deprives him of happiness and perfect wisdom. About this he is informed, when he has understood, or heard from the Revered One or from the monks, the faith to be coveted. There are some who, of a truth, know this [i.e., injuring] to be the bondage, the delusion, the death, the hell. For this a man is longing, when he injures this body of an animal by bad and injurious doings, and many other beings, besides, which he hurts by means of animals, through acts relating to animals. Thus I say.

Some slay animals for sacrificial purposes, some kill animals for the sake of their skin, some kill them for the sake of their flesh, some kill them for the sake of their blood; thus for the sake of their heart, their bile, the feathers of their tail, their tail, their big or small horns, their teeth, their tusks, their nails, their sinews, their bones; with a purpose or without a purpose. Some kill animals because they have been wounded by them, or are wounded, or will be wounded.

He who injures these animals does not comprehend and renounce the sinful acts; he who does not injure these, comprehends and renounces the sinful acts. Knowing them, a wise man should not act sinfully toward animals, nor cause others to act so, nor allow others to act so. He who knows these causes of sin relating to animals, is called a reward-knowing sage. Thus I say.

Some here are not well instructed as regards the subject of conduct; for desirous of acts, they say: "Kill creatures"; they themselves kill or consent to the killing of others; or they take what has not been given; or they pronounce opinions, e.g., the world exists, the world does not exist, the world is unchangeable, the world is ever changing; the world has a beginning, the world has no beginning; the world has an end, the world has no end; or with regard to the self and actions: this is well done, this is badly done; this is merit, this is demerit; he is a good man, he is not a good man; there is beatitude, there is no beatitude; there is a hell, there is no hell. When they thus differ in their opinions and profess their individual persuasion, know that this is all without reason. Thus they are not well taught, not well instructed in the religion such as it has been declared by the Revered One, who knows and sees with quick discernment. One should either instruct the opponent in the true faith or observe abstinence as regards speech. Thus I say.

Everywhere sins are admitted; but to avoid them is called my distinction. For ye who live in a village or in the forest, or not in a village and not in the forest, know the law as it has been declared. "By the *Brahman*, the wise, three vows have been enjoined [i.e., (1) to kill no living being, (2) to speak no untruth, (3) to abstain from forbidden things such as theft and sexual pleasures]." Noble and tranquil men who are enlightened and exert themselves in these precepts are called free from sinful acts.

Knowing and renouncing severally and singly the actions against living beings, in the regions above, below, and on the surface, everywhere and in all ways—a wise man neither gives pain to these bodies, nor orders others to do so, nor assents to their doing so. Nay, we abhor those who give pain to these bodies. Knowing this, a wise man should not cause this or any other pain to any creatures. Thus I say.

———

The first great vow, Sir, runs thus:

I renounce all killing of living beings, whether subtle or gross, whether movable or immovable. Nor shall I myself kill living beings nor cause others to do it, nor consent to it. As long as I live, I confess and blame, repent and exempt myself of these sins, in the thrice threefold way [i.e., acting, commanding, consenting, either in the past, present, or future, in mind, speech, and body].

There are five clauses.

The first clause runs thus:

A *Nirgrantha* [ascetic] is careful in his walk, not careless. The Kevalin [a reference to Mahāvīra of Kevala, Jain founder] assigns as the reason, that a *Nirgrantha*, careless in his walk, might with his feet hurt or displace or injure or kill living beings. Hence a *Nirgrantha* is careful in his walk, not careless in his walk.

This is the first clause.

Now follows the second clause:

A *Nirgrantha* searches into his mind [i.e., thoughts and intentions]. If his mind is sinful, blamable, intent on works, acting on impulses, produces cutting and splitting or division and dissension, quarrels, faults, and pains, injures living beings, or kills creatures, he should not employ such a mind in action; but if, on the contrary, it is not sinful, etc., then he may put it in action.

This is the second clause.

Now follows the third clause.

A *Nirgrantha* searches into his speech; if his speech is sinful, blamable, intent on works, acting on impulses, produces cutting and splitting or division and dissension, quarrels, faults, and pains, injures living beings, or kills creatures, he should not utter that speech. But if, on the contrary, it is not sinful, etc., then he may utter it.

This is the third clause.

Now follows the fourth clause.

A *Nirgrantha* is careful in laying down his utensils of begging, he is not careless in it. The Kevalin says: A *Nirgrantha* who is careless in laying down his utensils of begging, might hurt or displace or injure or kill all sorts of living beings. Hence a *Nirgrantha* is careful in laying down his utensils of begging, he is not careless in it.

This is the fourth clause.

Now follows the fifth clause:

A *Nirgrantha* eats and drinks after inspecting his food and drink; he does not eat and drink without inspecting his food and drink. The Kevalin says: if a *Nirgrantha* would eat and drink without inspecting his food and drink, he might hurt and displace or injure or kill all sorts of living beings. Hence a *Nirgrantha* eats and drinks after inspecting his food and drink, not without doing so.

This is the fifth clause.

In this way the great vow is correctly practiced, followed, executed, explained, established, effected, according to the precept.

This is, Sir, the first great vow: Abstinence from killing any living beings.

Human Flesh and Beast Flesh

Are the Same

KABĪR

There are few historical figures as religiously ambiguous as the northern Indian poet Kabīr (ca. 1398–1448). Although formally a Muslim, he frequently invoked the holy name of Rāma in his verse, persuaded a Hindu swami to accept him as a student, inspired the founder of the Sikhs, and today is claimed by Hindus as frequently as by Muslims. At the very least it seems that Kabīr was relatively unconcerned with religious demarcations.

What's not at all ambiguous, however, is Kabīr's condemnation of slaughtering animals for food. His poetry is wonderfully direct in its insistence that self-styled religious persons who carefully follow ritualistic formulae while glutting themselves on their fellow creatures are hypocrites. His condemnation of animal sacrifice is reminiscent of the Hebrew prophets: humans make "gods and goddesses of mud," he laments, and offer sacrifices of "living beings" to them. But the hypocrisy of such physical violence begets spiritual decay; "the killed animals will certainly take revenge."

The verses here are taken from the Bījak, *the sacred book of the Hindu sect Kabīr Panth.*

O saints, I have seen both the ways. The Hindus and the Mahomedans could not be restrained; to both the taste [of flesh] is agreeable. The Hindus fast on the eleventh day of the moon and break their fast with milk and water-chestnut. They give up food but cannot restrain their hearts; they finish their fast by eating flesh. The Mahomedan fasts and repeats his prayers and calls out for prayer like the crowing of a cock. They cannot go to heaven as they kill hen at dusk. The Hindus have banished kindness and the Mahomedans compassion from their hearts. The Mahomedans kill as prescribed by their law, the Hindus slaughter by cutting off the head; both have their houses set on fire. The true teacher has pointed out that the [transgression] of the Hindu and the Mahomedan is one. Kabīr says, "Hear, O 'saints,' do not call [on] god."

O saints, the Brahman is a clever butcher. He kills the goat and runs to kill a buffalo; he has no pity in his heart. Having bathed and with the sectarian mark on his forehead he worships the goddess according to the rules. The life is soon destroyed. He causes a stream of blood to flow. He is said to be very holy and of a high family, specially at meetings. Many request him to initiate them in religious observances; O brother, I laugh at him! He preaches the means of destroying sin, but makes the people perform mean acts. I have seen them both drowning; the god of death catching hold of their hands is dragging them. Those who slaughter cows are called Mahomedans; is the Brahman less cruel? Kabīr says, "Hear, O saints, the Brahmans in [this age] are corrupt."

The human flesh and the flesh of beasts is similar and their crimson blood is also the same. The flesh of some beasts all men eat but human flesh is eaten by the jackals. Brahma the potter has filled the earth; many cows have been born and have died. You should not eat fishes and flesh but what grows in the fields. They make gods and goddesses of mud and offer sacrifices of living beasts. If your god is a true one why did he not take the beasts when they were grazing in the field? Kabīr says, "Hear O saints, always repeat the name of Rāma. Whatever you have done for the sake of the tongue, the killed animals will certainly take revenge."

O fools, you have been lost because every moment you do not meditate on Rāma. Forcibly you lay hold of a cow and throw it down on the back and kill it by cutting its throat. The flesh you call holy; O brother, hear its origin. It was generated in the womb impregnated by the semen: the flesh which you eat is not holy. They do not avow their mistake but say that their ancestors practiced it. For the murder you are responsible and those who advised you to do so. The black hairs of your body have changed into white, but your heart has not as yet become white [clean]. What do fasts, prayers and calls to prayer avail; man dies in seclusion. The *paṇḍits* read the Vedas and the *Purāṇas* and the *mulla* reads the *Qur'ān*. Kabīr says that all those who do not meditate on Rāma, every moment, go to hell.

O wretched ones, do not kill living beings, all have life. [Even] if you hear millions of *Purāṇa* scriptures read to you, you shall not escape the punishment for killlling life.

O helpless ones, do not kill living beings, they will in their turn kill you. By going on pilgrimages and giving many diamonds in alms you [still] will not be saved from the punishment of your sin.

Oneness Includes All Animals

SWAMI VIVEKĀNANDA

Although only thirty-five when he died in 1902, Vivekānanda, monk of the Ramakrishna Order, tireless speaker and prolific author, did more than any other individual to popularize Vedānta, the religion of the Vedas, in the West. In this selection from his Jnāna-Yoga, *Vivekānanda argues that from God's standpoint "the lowest animal and the highest man are the same," and that all organic beings are in spiritual fellowship. Ultimately, then, there is no more justification for animal eating than for human eating, and to indulge in it suggests a spiritual somnolence that sacrifices purity for convenience and pleasure.*

You must always remember that the central ideal of Vedānta is Oneness. There are no two in anything—no two lives or even two different kinds of life for the two worlds. You will find the *Vedas* speaking, at first, of heavens and things like that; but later on, when they come to the highest ideas of their philosophy, they brush away all these things. There is but one Life, one World, one Existence. Everything is that One; the differences are of degree and not of kind. The differences between our lives are not of kind. Vedānta entirely denies such ideas as that animals are essentially separate from men and that they were made and created by God to be used for our food.

Some people have been kind enough to start an antivivisection society. I asked a member, "Why do you think, my friend, that it is quite lawful to kill animals for food, and not to kill one or two for scientific experiments?" He replied, "Vivisection is most horrible, but animals have been given to us for food."

Oneness includes all animals. If man is immortal, so also are the animals. The differences are only of degree and not of kind. The amoeba and I are the same; the difference is only one of degree; and from the standpoint of the

50

highest life, all differences vanish. A man may see a great deal of difference between grass and a little tree, but if he mounts very high, the grass and the biggest tree will appear much the same. So, from the standpoint of the highest ideal, the lowest animal and the highest man are the same. If you believe there is a God, then to Him the animals and the highest creatures must be the same. A God who is partial to His children called men, and cruel to His children called brute beasts, is worse than a demon. I would rather die a hundred times than worship such a God. My whole life would be a fight with such a God. But there is no difference from the standpoint of God; and those who say that there is are irresponsible, heartless people, who do not know.

Here, then, is a case of the word *practical* used in a wrong sense. We eat meat not because animals have been given to us for food, but because we want to. I myself may not be a very strict vegetarian, but I understand the ideal. When I eat meat I know it is wrong. Even if I am bound to eat it under certain circumstances, I know it is cruel. I must not drag my ideal down to the actual and give excuses for my weak conduct. The ideal is not to eat flesh, not to injure any being; for all animals are my brothers. If you can think of them as your brothers, you have made a little headway toward the brotherhood of all souls, not to speak of the brotherhood of man! But to carry this out is no child's play. You generally find that this is not very acceptable to many, because it teaches them to give up the actual and go toward the ideal. But if you bring out a theory which can be reconciled with their present conduct, they regard it as entirely practical.

There is a strongly conservative tendency in human nature; we do not like to move one step forward. I think of mankind as being like those I have read about who have become frozen in the snow. All such, they say, want to go to sleep, and if you try to drag them out, they say: "Let me sleep. It is so beautiful to sleep in the snow"; and they die there in that sleep. So is our nature. That is what we are doing all our life—getting frozen from the feet upward and yet wanting to sleep. Therefore you must struggle toward the ideal; and if a man comes who wants to bring that ideal down to your level and teach a religion which does not carry out that highest ideal, do not listen to him. To me that is an impracticable religion. But if a man teaches a religion which presents the highest ideal, I am ready for him.

Beware when anyone is trying to give excuses for sense vanities and sense weaknesses. If anyone wants to preach that way to us—poor, sense-bound clods of earth that we have made ourselves—by following that teaching we shall never progress. I have seen many of these things; I have had some experience of the world; and my country is the land where religious sects grow like mushrooms. Every year new sects arise. But one thing I have marked: that it is only those who never want to reconcile the man of flesh with the man of truth who make progress. Wherever there is this false idea of reconciling fleshly vanities with the highest ideals, of dragging down God to the level of man, there comes decay. Man should not be degraded to worldly slavery, but should be raised up to God.

Diet and Non-Violence

MOHANDAS GANDHI

Mohandas Gandhi (1869–1948), called the Mahātmā *(high-souled person), spent most of his adult life championing the spiritual and ethical principle of* ahiṃsā. *An integral part of his vision was the ideal of a nonviolent diet. Gandhi makes it clear that he doesn't consider vegetarianism to be either an end in itself or a quick (much less exclusive) solution to violence in the world. But he's convinced that sensitivity to the suffering of animals goes hand-in-hand with sensitivity to the suffering of humans, and that the discipline of abstention from flesh draws one closer to* mokṣa *or enlightened liberation.*

The selections here are taken from two of Gandhi's letters. The first, written to "The Natal Mercury" in 1896, argues that carnivorism is "detrimental to the spiritual faculty," and gently chides Christians for not taking more seriously the Genesis suggestion (1:29–30) that God originally decreed a herbivorous diet for humans. In making this case, Gandhi anticipates the biblical exegesis of many contemporary Jewish and Christian vegetarians. The second letter, written in 1927, is in response to a question about diet and violence. In it, Gandhi admits that some degree of violence in eating is unavoidable, but that less harm is inflicted by a vegetarian diet than by a carnivorous one. He also points out that nonviolence is a "comprehensive dharma*" of which vegetarianism is but one aspect, and he reminds his questioner that the spiritual goal of* brahmacharya *or purifying continence, is furthered by a renunciation of meat.*

... [M]ost eminent physiologists declare that fruit is the natural food of man, and... we [also] have the example of Buddha, Pythagoras, Plato, Porphyry, Ray, Daniel, Wesley, Howard, Shelley, Sir Isaac Pitman, Edison, Sir W. B. Richardson, and a host of other eminent men as vegetarians. The Christian vegetarians claim that Jesus was also a vegetarian, and there does not seem to be anything to oppose that view, except the reference to His having eaten broiled fish after the

Resurrection. The most successful missionaries in South Africa (the Trappists) are vegetarians. Looked at from every point of view, vegetarianism has been demonstrated to be far superior to flesh-eating. The Spiritualists hold, and the practice of the religious teachers of all the religions, except, perhaps, the generality of Protestant teachers, shows that nothing is more detrimental to the spiritual faculty of man than the gross feeding on flesh. The most ardent vegetarians attribute the agnosticism, the materialism, and the religious indifference of the present age to too much flesh-eating and wine-drinking, and the consequent disappearance, partial or total, of the spiritual faculty in man...

I submit the following for the consideration of those who believe in the Bible. Before the "Fall" we were vegetarians:

> And God said: Behold, I have given you every herb bearing seed, which is upon the face of all the earth, and every tree in which is the fruit of a tree yielding seed; to you it shall be for meat.
> And to every beast of the earth, and to every fowl of the air, and to every thing that creepeth upon the earth, wherein there is life, I have given every green herb for meat; and it was so.
> [Genesis 1:29–30]

There may be some excuse for the unconverted partaking of meat, but for those who say they are "born again," vegetarian Christians claim, there can be none; because their state surely should be equal, if not superior, to that of the people before the "Fall." Again, in times of Restitution:

> The wolf also shall dwell with the lamb, and the leopard shall lie down with the kid; and the calf and the young lion and the fatling together; and a little child shall lead them... and the lion shall eat straw like the ox ...They shall not hurt nor destroy in all my holy mountain: for the earth shall be full of the knowledge of the Lord, as the waters cover the sea. [Isaiah 11:6, 7, 9]

These times may be far off yet for the whole world. But why cannot those who know and can—the Christians—enact them for themselves at any rate? There can be no harm in anticipating them, and, maybe, thereby their approach may be considerably hastened.

Eating flesh and eating vegetables both involve violence but without the latter man can survive nowhere, while without the former he can ordinarily survive anywhere. If sensitivity to pain differs among creatures, the pain experienced by a cow in the throes of death cannot be experienced by plants. For all living beings, violence in some form is unavoidable. The votary of non-violence will commit the minimum of violence. The other religions do not enjoin flesh-eating; they just do not forbid it. It is well to know the custom in the other religions and even in

Hindu *dharma*, but if our reason considers vegetarianism superior from the moral point of view, we must accept it. The votary of non-violence will progressively restrict himself, even in the use of vegetables. It is difficult, not impossible, to remain a vegetarian in places like Greenland. Even if proved impossible, it cannot establish the necessity of flesh-eating everywhere. Though our acts are seldom without a fault, we abstain from many on the basis of comparative merit. Abstinence is constantly on the increase in the life of a seeker after *mokṣa*, and it is essential too.

...Non-violence is a comprehensive *dharma*. Violence does not consist only in taking life away from the body. Abandoning *brahmacharya* too is violence in my eyes. It is well known that a *brahmachari* must abstain from flesh-diet, eggs and milk too. *Brahmacharya* is more easily attainable with vegetable diet alone.

In conclusion, though the question of diet is very important for a religious man, yet it is not the be-all and end-all of religion or non-violence; nor is it the most vital factor. The observance of religion and non-violence has more to do with the heart. He who does not feel the necessity of abstaining from meat for inner purification need not abstain from it.

Thou Shalt Not Kill

A. C. BHAKTIVEDANTA SWAMI PRABHUPĀDA

This 1973 conversation between Swami Prabhupāda, scholar, mystic, and founder of the Krishna Consciousness movement, and Roman Catholic Cardinal Jean Daniélou, scrutinizes the Biblical Commandment "Thou shalt not kill." At stake is whether only human life is to be considered sacred and worthy of preservation, or the lives of animals as well. Swami Prabhupāda makes several different arguments against Cardinal Daniélou's view that only human life is sacred: (1) that the Bible forbids killing broadly, not just the killing of human beings; (2) that human life can subsist on vegetable food, and is by nature meant to do so; (3) that meat eating can be justified to avoid starvation, but slaughterhouses for the pleasure of appetite cannot; (4) finally (and most distinctively Indian), that animals as well as humans possess souls. Cardinal Daniélou's difficult question, whether there may be a fault in the created order which births violence and bloodshed, is met by Swami Prabhupāda's karmic conclusion that the reincarnation awaiting meat eaters is future punishment for their present rapacity.

ŚRĪLA PRABHUPĀDA: Jesus Christ said, "Thou shalt not kill." So why is it that the Christian people are engaged in animal killing?

CARDINAL DANIÉLOU: Certainly in Christianity it is forbidden to kill, but we believe that there is a difference between the life of a human being and the life of the beasts. The life of a human being is sacred because man is made in the image of God; therefore, to kill a human being is forbidden.

ŚRĪLA PRABHUPĀDA: But the Bible does not simply say, "Do not kill the human being." It says broadly, "Thou shalt not kill."

Cardinal Daniélou: We believe that only human life is sacred.

Śrīla Prabhupāda: That is your interpretation. The commandment is "Thou shalt not kill."

Cardinal Daniélou: It is necessary for man to kill animals in order to have food to eat.

Śrīla Prabhupāda: No. Man can eat grains, vegetables, fruits, and milk.

Cardinal Daniélou: No flesh?

Śrīla Prabhupāda: No. Human beings are meant to eat vegetarian food. The tiger does not come to eat your fruits. His prescribed food is animal flesh. But man's food is vegetables, fruits, grains, and milk products. So how can you say that animal killing is not a sin?

Cardinal Daniélou: We believe it is a question of motivation. If the killing of an animal is for giving food to the hungry, then it is justified.

Śrīla Prabhupāda: But consider the cow: we drink her milk; therefore, she is our mother. Do you agree?

Cardinal Daniélou: Yes, surely.

Śrīla Prabhupāda: So if the cow is your mother, how can you support killing her? You take the milk from her, and when she's old and cannot give you milk, you cut her throat. Is that a very humane proposal? In India those who are meat-eaters are advised to kill some lower animals like goats, pigs, or even buffalo. But cow killing is the greatest sin. In preaching Krishna Consciousness we ask people not to eat any kind of meat, and my disciples strictly follow this principle. But if, under certain circumstances, others are obliged to eat meat, then they should eat the flesh of some lower animal. Don't kill cows. It is the greatest sin. And as long as a man is sinful, he cannot understand God. The human being's main business is to understand God and to love Him. But if you remain sinful, you will never be able to understand God—not to speak of loving Him.

CARDINAL DANIÉLOU: I think that perhaps this is not an essential point. The important thing is to love God. The practical commandments can vary from one religion to another.

ŚRĪLA PRABHUPĀDA: So, in the Bible God's practical commandment is that you cannot kill; therefore killing cows is a sin for you.

CARDINAL DANIÉLOU: God says to the Indians that killing is not good, and he says to the Jews that—

ŚRĪLA PRABHUPĀDA: No, no. Jesus Christ taught, "Thou shalt not kill." Why do you interpret this to suit your own convenience?

CARDINAL DANIÉLOU: But Jesus allowed the sacrifice of the Paschal Lamb.

ŚRĪLA PRABHUPĀDA: But he never maintained a slaughterhouse.

CARDINAL DANIÉLOU: [Laughs.] No, but he did eat meat.

ŚRĪLA PRABHUPĀDA: When there is no other food, someone may eat meat in order to keep from starving. That is another thing. But it is most sinful to regularly maintain slaughterhouses just to satisfy your tongue. Actually, you will not even have a human society until this cruel practice of maintaining slaughterhouses is stopped. And although animal killing may sometimes be necessary for survival, at least the mother animal, the cow, should not be killed. That is simple human decency. In the Krishna Consciousness movement our practice is that we don't allow the killing of any animals. Kṛṣṇa says, *patram puṣpam phalam toyam yo me bhaktyā prayacchati*: "Vegetables, fruits, milk, and grains should be offered to Me in devotion" (*Bhagavad-gītā* 9.26). We take only the remnants of Kṛṣṇa's food (*prasādam*). The trees offer us many varieties of fruits, but the trees are not killed. Of course, one living entity is food for another living entity, but that does not mean you can kill your mother for food. Cows are innocent; they give us milk. You take their milk—and then kill them in the slaughterhouse. This is sinful.

STUDENT: Śrīla Prabhupāda, Christianity's sanction of meat-eating is based on the view that lower species of life do not have a soul like the human being's.

ŚRĪLA PRABHUPĀDA: That is foolishness. First of all, we have to understand the evidence of the soul's presence within the body. Then we can see whether the human being has a soul and the cow does not. What are the different characteristics of the cow and the man? If we find a difference in characteristics, then we can say that in the animal there is no soul. But if we see that the animal and the human being have the same characteristics, then how can you say that the animal has no soul? The general symptoms are that the animal eats, you eat; the animal sleeps, you sleep; the animal mates, you mate; the animal defends, and you defend. Where is the difference?

CARDINAL DANIÉLOU: We admit that in the animal there may be the same type of biological existence as in men, but there is no soul. We believe that the soul is a human soul.

ŚRĪLA PRABHUPĀDA: Our *Bhagavad-gītā* says *sarva-yoniṣu*, "In all species of life the soul exists." The body is like a suit of clothes. You have black clothes; I am dressed in saffron clothes. But within the dress you are a human being, and I am also a human being. Similarly, the bodies of the different species are just like different types of dress. There are 8,400,000 species, or dresses, but within each one is a spirit soul, a part and parcel of God. Suppose a man has two sons, not equally meritorious. One may be a Supreme Court judge and the other may be a common laborer, but the father claims both as his sons. He does not make the distinction that the son who is a judge is very important and the worker-son is not important. And if the judge-son says, "My dear father, your other son is useless; let me cut him up and eat him," will the father allow this?

CARDINAL DANIÉLOU: Certainly not, but the idea that all life is part of the life of God is difficult for us to admit. There is a great difference between human life and animal life.

ŚRĪLA PRABHUPĀDA: That difference is due to the development of consciousness. In the human body there is developed consciousness. Even a tree has a soul, but a tree's consciousness is not very developed. If you cut a tree it does not resist. Actually, it does resist, but only to a very small degree. There is a scientist named Jagadish Chandra Bose who has made a machine which shows that trees and plants are able to feel pain when they are cut. And we can see directly that when someone comes to kill an animal, it resists, it cries, it makes a horrible sound. So it is a matter of the development of consciousness. But the soul is there within all living beings.

CARDINAL DANIÉLOU: But metaphysically, the life of man is sacred. Human beings think on a higher platform than the animals do.

ŚRĪLA PRABHUPĀDA: What is that higher platform? The animal eats to maintain his body, and you also eat in order to maintain your body. The cow eats grass in the field, and the human being eats meat from a huge slaughterhouse full of modern machines. But just because you have big machines and a ghastly scene, while the animal simply eats grass, this does not mean that you are so advanced that only within your body is there a soul and that there is not a soul within the body of the animal. That is illogical. We can see that the basic characteristics are the same in the animal and the human being.

CARDINAL DANIÉLOU: But only in human beings do we find a metaphysical search for the meaning of life.

ŚRĪLA PRABHUPĀDA: Yes. So metaphysically search out why you believe that there is no soul within the animal—that is metaphysics. If you are thinking metaphysically, that's all right. But if you are thinking like an animal, then what is the use of your metaphysical study? "Metaphysical" means "above the physical" or, in other words, "spiritual." In the *Bhagavad-gītā* Kṛṣṇa says, *sarva-yoniṣu kaunteya:* "In every living being there is a spirit soul." That is metaphysical understanding. Now either you accept Kṛṣṇa's teachings as metaphysical, or you'll have to take a third-class fool's opinion as metaphysical. Which do you accept?

CARDINAL DANIÉLOU: But why does God create some animals who eat other animals? There is a fault in the creation, it seems.

ŚRĪLA PRABHUPĀDA: It is not a fault. God is very kind. If you want to eat animals, then He'll give you full facility. God will give you the body of a tiger in your next life so that you can eat flesh very freely. "Why are you maintaining slaughterhouses? I'll give you fangs and claws. Now eat." So the meat-eaters are awaiting such punishment. The animal-eaters become tigers, wolves, cats, and dogs in their next life—to get more facility.

THE BUDDHIST
TRADITION

As a man values his life,
So do animals love theirs.
By releasing life one comes to
realize the truth of no birth.
By releasing life one ends transmigration.

—Chu-hung

B uddhism teaches the continuous flow of life through the realm of rebirth. In that realm the suffering of all beings is believed to arise from desire and craving, conditioned by the karmic effects of both animal and human action. The violence of slaughtering animals for food, and its source in restless craving, reveal flesh eating as one mode in which humans enslave themselves to suffering.

Animals as well as humans suffer. But our kindredness originates not only in our common experience of life as suffering but in our shared cosmic status, a status derived from having experienced many existences in diverse forms. The ethical doctrine of *ahiṃsā* or noninjury to living beings, shared by both Indian and Buddhist religious traditions, derives from the conviction that violence to creatures, whose form and identity over time are fluid, has karmic consequences. For Buddhists, *ahiṃsā* enjoins compassion for animals as well as humans, and is a salvational virtue. Buddhist vegetarianism developed within this context, first in Theravādin and later in Mahāyāna Buddhism.

The Buddha taught that life is a stream of becoming in which no permanent self endures. Individuals are composites of perception, feeling, volition, intelligence, and form, all subject to the law of karma. Hīnayāna or Theravādin Buddhists emphasized the transitoriness of all things and *nirvāṇa* or enlightened liberation as the goal of existence. The saint *(arhat)* is one free from bondage to karma. Among Theravādin devotees vegetarianism was not strict, although meat eating was widely regarded as a fault. Nonattachment to food was generally practiced by Buddhist ascetics in this tradition as one way of withdrawing from the rebirth realm. Compassion and loving kindness were urged in recognition of the shared life of all creatures.

The Mahāyāna tradition emphasizes the phenomenal nature of the world of experience and the Buddha-essence or Buddha-nature *(tathāgathagarbha)* of all sentient beings. Every sentient creature is believed to possess the innate potential of Buddhahood, regardless of its place in the rebirth realm. The one who aspires to Buddhahood, the *bodhisattva*, teaches all sentient beings the emptiness of phenomenal things, and the possibility of attaining *nirvāṇa* by transfigured perception. Mahāyāna's affirmation of spiritual potential or Buddha-nature in all sentient life, coupled with the Theravādin emphasis on compassion and karma, gave rise to the centrality of vegetarianism in Buddhist thought and practice.

In addition to the *Śūraṅgama* and *Laṅkāvatāra Sūtras*, Buddhist defenses of vegetarianism are represented here in the writings of Aśoka, Sir Edwin Arnold, Chu-hung, Philip Kapleau, and the current Dalai Lama.

The emperor Aśoka reigned northern India with the aim of spiritually uplifting his people. "This is my rule—to govern by righteousness, to administer by righteousness, to please my subjects by righteousness, and to protect them by righteousness." Aśoka's invocation of righteousness extended to animals as well as humans; imperial edicts banned animal sacrifice and slaughter in his kingdom. The greatest progress in righteousness, argued Aśoka, comes from "exhortation in favor of non-injury to life and abstinence from killing living beings." Through this respect for life heaven is gained, but Aśoka leaves no doubt that noninjury to life, whatever its merits, is an intrinsic good.

Sir Edwin Arnold focuses more exclusively than Aśoka on the consequences to humans of their treatment of animals. He imagines a scene in which the Buddha appears at a king's hall of sacrificial offering. The Buddha condemns the slaughter, quietly speaking of the preciousness of all life and invoking the cosmic power of karma, "the fixed arithmic of the universe/Which meteth good for good and ill for ill/Measure for measure, unto deeds, words, thoughts/Watchful, aware, implacable, unmoved/Making all futures fruits of all the pasts." The spiritual insight of the Buddha's words convert his auditors: "the priests drew back their garments 'oer the hands/Crimsoned with slaughter, and the King came near/Standing with clasped palms reverencing Buddha."

The notion of rewards also appears in Chu-hung's "Releasing Life." When creatures are set free, released to life rather than killed for food, honor or longer life is bestowed on some humans, others are spared from disasters, some recover from mental illnesses, some achieve rebirth in heaven. But for Chu-hung, the deepest reasons for releasing life are spiritual rather than retributive. "Releasing life accords with the mind of heaven; releasing life agrees with the teaching of the Buddha. . . . By releasing life one comes to realize the truth of no birth."

In our own day, Zen master Philip Kapleau and the Dalai Lama share Chu-hung's insight. Buddhism's primary precept against killing, argues Kapleau, is a reminder of the spiritual truth that harmlessness to living beings is "really a call to creation" that awakens us to the sacredness of all life. The Dalai Lama underscores the primacy of harmlessness by speaking simply and straightforwardly of the sadness of animals slaughtered for food and sport. He recommends compassionate pity, arguing that it is a precious source of strength for creatures gasping in confusion and sorrow at the impermanence that defines reality.

These readings demonstrate that Buddhist defenses of vegetarianism are stamped by the deepest contours of Buddhist religious sensibility. They affirm the central doctrines of impermanence, the fluidity of the animal-human boundary, the kindredness of human beings and animals, and the "deep arithmic" of *karma*. A linear sense of history is absent: worlds rise and worlds fall, and everywhere life is becoming. To escape the cycle of rebirth one must learn the truths of suffering and the cessation of suffering. Recognition of these truths leads the spiritual seeker to compassion for all life as well as disciplined restraint of hunger and desire. In self-discipline, and in pity for all confused and suffering creatures, vegetarianism finds its place in Buddhism.

Prohibition Against Killing

ŚŪRAṄGAMA SŪTRA

The Mahāyāna Sūtras, to which the Śūraṅgama Sūtra belongs, are believed to have been composed in India between the first century BCE *and the sixth century* CE.[1] *Written in Sanskrit, the sutras are largely extant in Chinese and Tibetan translations. The Śūraṅgama Sūtra vividly depicts what awaits flesh eaters who fail to curb their murderous appetites: They corrupt into earth-bound* rākṣasas, *blood-eating and flesh-devouring demons who perversely cling to their rapacity even in the ghostly realm, thereby remaining trapped in the continual cycle of birth and death. Noninjury and nonkilling: these are the teachings of the Buddha defended so vividly by the Śūraṅgama Sūtra. How, the* Sūtra *asks, can those who practice great compassion feed on the flesh and blood of creatures? No liberation, no* Bodhi *enlightenment, is achievable by those who eat the flesh of living beings. Even though the* Sūtra *reluctantly makes a dietary concession to weak-willed novice monks, it expressly forbids the shedding of blood for the sake of food.*

Ānanda [or faithful disciple], if living beings in the six worlds of existence cease to kill they will not be subject to the continual round of births and deaths. Your practice of *Samādhi* [contemplation] should free you from defilements but if your murderous mind is not cut off, they cannot be eliminated. You may acquire much wisdom but if you fail to stop killing, when *dhyāna* [meditation] manifests, you will fall into the way of spirits, in which the high rank is attained by the mighty ghost, the middle one by flying *yakṣas* [demi-gods] and chief ghosts, and the low one by earth-bound *rākṣasas* [blood-drinking, flesh-eating demons]. These have followers and boast that they have attained the Supreme Path. After my *nirvāṇa*, in the *Dharma* ending age, these ghosts will be found throughout in the world, and will boast of how they feed on flesh which leads them to realize *Bodhi* [enlightenment]. *Ānanda*, I permit the *bhikṣus* [monks] to eat only the five kinds of pure flesh which are the product of my transcendental power of transformation and not of animal slaughter.[2] You, *Brahman* [member of the priestly caste], live in a country where vegetables do not grow because it is too damp and hot and because of all the gravel and rock. I use my spiritual power of compassion to provide you with illusory meat to satisfy your appetite. How then, after my *nirvāṇa*, can you eat the flesh of living beings and so pretend to be my disciple? You should know that those who eat meat, though their minds may open and realize a semblance of *Samādhi*, are but great *rākṣasas* who, after this life, will sink back into the bitter ocean of *saṃsāra* and cannot be my disciples. They will kill and devour one another ceaselessly; how then can they escape from the three worlds of existence?

In addition you should teach worldly men who practice *Samādhi* not to kill. This is called the Buddha's profound teaching of the second decisive deed. Therefore, *Ānanda*, if killing is not stopped, the practice of *dhyāna-samādhi* is like shutting one's ears while crying in the hope that people will not hear one's voice, or like trying to hide something that is already exposed to full view. All *bhikṣus* who live purely and all *Bodhisattvas* [enlightened beings] always refrain even from walking on the grass; how can they agree to uproot it? How then can those who practice great compassion feed on the flesh and blood of living beings? If *bhikṣus* do not wear garments made of Chinese silk, boots of local leather and furs, and refrain from consuming milk, cream and butter, they will really be liberated from the worldly; after paying their former debts, they will not transmigrate in the three realms of existence. Why? Because by using animal products, one creates causes (which are always followed by effects), just like a man who eats cereals grown in the soil and whose feet cannot leave the ground. If a man can control his body and mind and thereby refrains from eating animal flesh and wearing animal products, I say he will really be liberated. This teaching of mine is that of the Buddha whereas any other is that of evil demons.

NOTES

1. Some scholars suspect that the *Śūraṅgama Sūtra* in fact is of Chinese origin.

2. The five kinds of pure flesh that may be eaten by a beginner who does not see, hear of, or doubt about the animal having been killed purposely for him to eat, but is certain that it either died naturally or that its flesh had been abandoned by birds of prey.

Cherish Each Being
Like an Only Child

LAṄKĀVATĀRA SŪTRA

The Laṅkāvatāra Sūtra belongs to the sacred writings of the Yogācāra *tradition, that branch of Mahāyāna Buddhism that believes consciousness is inherent in all phenomena and enlightenment potential in all beings. The Sūtra is believed to have been composed prior to 443, although the chapter on meat eating was probably modified in a 513 translation. In the excerpt offered here from that chapter, the Buddha instructs one of his disciples, a* Bodhisattva-Mahāsattva, *about the "vice of meat eating." Out of compassion and for the sake of purity, the wise disciple cherishes all living beings in the way a parent loves an only child. Three stories, one of a king named Simhasaudasa who is excessively fond of meat; another of Indra, who assumed the form of a hawk and ate a pigeon; and a third of a king who sired children from consort with a lioness, teach the difficulty of flesh eaters attaining* nirvāṇa.

At that time Mahāmati the *Bodhisattva-Mahāsattva* [enlightened being] asked the Blessed One in verse and again made a request, saying: Pray tell me, Blessed One, *Tathagata* [the "thus perfected": one of the Buddha's titles], *Arhat* ["worthy one," saint], Fully-Enlightened One regarding the merit and vice of meat-eating; thereby I and other *Bodhisattva-Mahāsattvas* of the present and future may teach the *Dharma* [religious law] to make those beings abandon their greed for meat, who, under the influence of the habit-energy belonging to the carnivorous existence, strongly crave meat-food. These meat-eaters thus abandoning their desire for its taste will seek the *Dharma* for their food and enjoyment, and, regarding all beings with love as if they were an only child, will cherish great compassion toward them. Cherishing great compassion, they will discipline themselves at the stages of *Bodhisattvahood* and will quickly be awakened in supreme enlightenment; or staying a while at the stage of *Śrāvakahood* [holiness] and *Pratyekabuddhahood* ["solitary awakened one": a level of buddhahood], they will finally reach the highest stage of *Tathagatahood*.

Blessed One, even those philosophers who hold erroneous doctrines and are addicted to the views of the *Lokāyata* ["worldly" philosophy] such as the dualism of being and non-being, nihilism, and eternalism, will prohibit meat-eating and will themselves refrain from eating it. How much more, O World Leader, he who promotes one taste for mercy and is the Fully-Enlightened One; why not prohibit in his teachings the eating of flesh not only by himself but by others? Indeed, let the Blessed one who at heart is filled with pity for the entire world, who regards all beings as his only child, and who possesses great compassion in compliance with his sympathetic feelings, teach us as to the merit and vice of meat-eating, so that I and other *Bodhisattva-Mahāsattvas* may teach the *Dharma*.

Said the Blessed One: Then, Mahāmati, listen well and reflect well within yourself; I will tell you.

Certainly, Blessed One; said Mahāmati the *Bodhisattva-Mahāsattva* and gave ear to the Blessed One.

The Blessed One said this to him: For innumerable reasons, Mahāmati, the *Bodhisattva*, whose nature is compassion, is not to eat any meat; I will explain them: Mahāmati, in this long course of transmigration here, there is not one living being that, having assumed the form of a living being, has not been your mother, or father, or brother, or sister, or son, or daughter, or the one or the other, in various degrees of kinship; and when acquiring another form of life may live as a beast, as a domestic animal, as a bird, or as a womb-born, or as something standing in some relationship to you; this being so how can the *Bodhisattva-Mahāsattva* who desires to approach all living beings as if they were himself and to practice the Buddha-truths, eat the flesh of any living being that is of the same nature as himself? Even, Mahāmati, the *Rākṣasa* [a devil], listening to the *Tathagata's* discourse on the highest essence of the *Dharma*, attained the notion of protecting Buddhism, and, feeling pity, refrains from eating flesh; how much more those who love the *Dharma*! Thus, Mahāmati, wherever there is the evolution of living beings, let people cherish the thought of kinship with them, and, thinking that all beings are to be loved as if they were an only child, let them refrain from eating meat. So with *Bodhisattvas* whose nature is compassion, the eating of meat is to be avoided by him. Even in exceptional cases, it is not compassionate of a *Bodhisattva* of good standing to eat meat. The flesh of a god, an ass, a buffalo, a horse, a bull, or man, or any other being, Mahāmati, that is not generally eaten by people, is sold on the roadside as mutton for the sake of money; and therefore, Mahāmati, the *Bodhisattva* should not eat meat.

For the sake of love of purity, Mahāmati, the *Bodhisattva* should refrain from eating flesh which is born of semen, blood, etc. For fear of causing terror to living beings, Mahāmati, let the *Bodhisattva* who is disciplining himself to attain compassion, refrain from eating flesh. To illustrate, Mahāmati: When a dog sees, even from a distance, a hunter, a pariah, a fisherman, etc., whose desires are for meat-eating, he is terrified with fear, thinking, "They are death-dealers, they will even kill me." In the same way, Mahāmati, even those minute animals that are living in the air, on earth, and in water, seeing meat-eaters at a distance, will perceive in them, by their keen sense of smell, the odor of the *Rākṣasa* and will run away from such people as quickly as possible; for they are to them the threat of death. For this reason, Mahāmati, let the *Bodhisattva*, who is disciplining himself, to abide in great compassion, because of its terrifying living beings, refrain from eating meat. Mahāmati, meat which is liked by unwise people is full of bad smell and its eating gives one a bad reputation which turns wise people away; let the *Bodhisattva* refrain from eating meat. The food of the wise, Mahāmati, is what is eaten by the *Rishis* [sages, wise persons]; it does not consist of meat and blood. Therefore, Mahāmati, let the *Bodhisattva* refrain from eating meat.

In order to guard the minds of all people, Mahāmati, let the *Bodhisattva* whose nature is holy and who is desirous of avoiding censure on the teaching of the Buddha, refrain from eating meat. For instance, Mahāmati, there are some in the world who speak ill of the teaching of the Buddha; they would say, "Why are those who are living in the life of a *Śrāmana* [ascetic] or a *Brahman* [member of the priestly caste] reject such food as was enjoyed by the ancient *Rishis*, and like the carnivorous animals, living in the air, on earth, or in the water? Why do they go wandering about in the world thoroughly terrifying living beings, disregarding the life of a *Śrāmana* and destroying the vow of a *Brahman*? There is no *Dharma*, no discipline in them." There are many such adverse-minded people who thus speak ill of the teaching of the Buddha. For this reason, Mahāmati, in order to guard the minds of all people, let the *Bodhisattva* whose nature is full of pity and who is desirous of avoiding censure on the teaching of the Buddha, refrain from eating meat.

Mahāmati, there is generally an offensive odor to a corpse, which goes against nature; therefore, let the *Bodhisattva* refrain from eating meat. Mahāmati, when flesh is burned, whether it be that of a dead man or of some other living creature, there is no distinction in the odor. When flesh of either kind is burned, the odor emitted is equally noxious. Therefore, Mahāmati, let the *Bodhisattva*, who is ever desirous of purity in his discipline, wholly refrain from eating meat.

Mahāmati, when sons or daughters of good family, wishing to exercise themselves in various disciplines such as the attainment of a compassionate heart, the holding of a magical formula, or the perfecting of magical knowledge, or starting on a pilgrimage to the Mahāyāna, retire into a cemetery, or to a wilderness, or a forest, where demons gather or frequently approach; or when they attempt to sit on a couch or a seat for the exercise; they are hindered because of their meat-eating from gaining magical powers or from obtaining emancipation. Mahāmati, seeing that thus there are obstacles to the accomplishing of all the practices, let the *Bodhisattva*, who is desirous of benefiting himself as well as others, wholly refrain from eating meat.

As even the sight of objective forms gives rise to the desire for tasting their delicious flavors, let the *Bodhisattva*, whose nature is pity and who regards all beings as his only child, wholly refrain from eating meat. Recognizing that his mouth smells most obnoxiously, even while living this life, let the *Bodhisattva* whose nature is pity, wholly refrain from eating meat.

The meat-eater sleeps uneasily and when awakened is distressed. He dreams of dreadful events, which makes his hair rise on end. He is left alone in an empty hut; he leads a solitary life; and his spirit is seized by demons. Frequently he is struck with terror, he trembles without knowing why, there is no regularity in his eating, he is never satisfied. In his eating he never knows what is meant by proper taste, digestion, and nourishment. His visceras are filled with worms and other impure creatures and harbor the cause of leprosy. He ceases to entertain any thoughts of aversion toward all diseases. When I teach to regard food as if it were eating the flesh of one's own child, or taking a drug, how can I permit my disciples, Mahāmati, to eat food consisting of flesh and blood, which is gratifying to the unwise but is abhorred by the wise, which brings many evils and keeps away many merits; and which was not offered to the *Rishis* and is altogether unsuitable?

Now, Mahāmati, the food I have permitted my disciples to take is gratifying to all wise people but is avoided by the unwise; it is productive of many merits, it keeps away many evils; and it has been prescribed by the ancient *Rishis*. It comprises rice, barley, wheat, kidney beans, lentils, etc., clarified butter, oil, honey, molasses, treacle, sugar cane, coarse sugar, etc.; food prepared with these is proper food. Mahāmati, there may be some irrational people in the future who will discriminate and establish new rules of moral discipline, and who, under the influence of the habit-energy belonging to the carnivorous races, will greedily desire the taste of meat: it is not for these people that the above food is prescribed. Mahāmati, this is the food I urge for the *Bodhisattva-Mahāsattvas* who have made offerings to the previous Buddhas, who have planted roots of goodness, who are possessed of faith, devoid of discrimination, who are all men and women belonging to the *Śākya* [followers of Buddha] family, who are sons and daughters of good family, who have no attachment to body, life, and property, who do not covet delicacies, are not at all greedy, who being compassionate desire to embrace all living beings as their own person, and who regard all beings with affection as if they were an only child.

Long ago in the past, Mahāmati, there lived a king whose name was Sìmhasaudāsa. His excessive fondness for meat, his greed to be served with it, stimulated his taste for it to the highest degree so that he even ate human flesh. In consequence of this he was alienated from the society of his friends, counselors, kinsmen, relatives, not to speak of his townsmen and countrymen. In consequence he had to renounce his throne and dominion and to suffer great calamities because of his passion for meat.

Mahāmati, even Indra who obtained sovereignty over the gods had once to assume the form of a hawk owing to his habit-energy of eating meat for food in a previous existence; he then chased Visvakarma appearing in the guise of a pigeon, who had thus to place himself on the scale. King Śivi feeling pity for the innocent pigeon had to sacrifice himself to the hawk and thus to suffer great pain. Even a god who became Indra the Powerful, after going through many a birth, Mahāmati, is liable to bring misfortune both upon himself and others; how much more those who are not Indra!

Mahāmati, there was another king who was carried away by his horse into a forest. After wandering about in it, he committed evil deeds with a lioness out of fear for his life, and children were born to her. Because of their descending from the union with a lioness, the royal children were called the Spotted-Feet, etc. On account of their evil habit-energy in the past when their food had been flesh, they ate meat even after becoming king, and, Mahāmati, in this life they lived in a village called *Kuṭīraka* ("seven huts"), and because they were excessively attached and devoted to meat-eating they gave birth to *Dākās* [demons] and *Dākinīs* [demonesses] who were terrible eaters of human flesh. In the life of transmigration, Mahāmati, such ones will fall into the wombs of such excessive flesh-devouring creatures as the lion, tiger, panther, wolf, hyena, wild-cat, jackal, owl, etc.; they will fall into the wombs of still more greedily flesh-devouring and still more terrible *Rākṣasas.* Falling into such, it will be with difficulty that they can ever obtain a human womb; how much more difficult attaining *Nirvāṇa!*

Such as these, Mahāmati, are the evils of meat-eating; how much more numerous evil qualities that are born of the perverted minds of those devoted to meat-eating. And, Mahāmati, the ignorant and the simple-minded are not aware of all this and other evils and merits in connection with meat-eating. I tell you, Mahāmati, that seeing these evils and merits the *Bodhisattva* whose nature is pity should eat no meat.

If, Mahāmati, meat is not eaten by anybody for any reason, there will be no destroyer of life. Mahāmati, in the majority of cases the slaughtering of innocent living beings is done for pride and very rarely for other causes. Though nothing special may be said of eating the flesh of living creatures such as animals and birds, alas, Mahāmati, that one addicted to the love of meat-taste should eat human flesh! Mahāmati, in most cases nets and other devices are prepared in various places by people who have lost their sense on account of their appetite for meat-taste, and thereby many innocent victims [who are moving about in the air, on land, and in water] are destroyed for the sake of the price they bring in... There are even some, Mahāmati, who are like *Rākṣasas* hard-hearted and used to practicing cruelties, who, being so devoid of compassion, would now and then look at living beings as meant for food and destruction— no compassion is awakened in them.

It is not true, Mahāmati, that meat is proper food and permissible for the *Śrāvaka* [holy person] when the victim was not killed by himself, when he did not order others to kill it, when it was not specially meant for him. Again, Mahāmati, there may be some unwitted people in the future time who, beginning to lead the homeless life according to my teaching, are acknowledged as sons of the *Śākya*, and carry the *Kāshāya* robe [worn by a teacher] about them as a badge, but who are in thought evilly affected by erroneous reasonings. They may talk about various discriminations which they make in their moral discipline, being addicted to the view of a personal soul. Being under the influence of the thirst for meat-taste, they will string together in various ways some sophistic arguments to defend meat-eating. They think they are giving me an unprecedented calumny when they discriminate and talk about facts that are capable of various interpretations. Imagining that this fact allows this interpretation, they conclude that the Blessed One permits meat as proper food, and that it is mentioned among permitted foods and that probably the *Tathagata* himself partook of it. But, Mahāmati, nowhere in the sutras is meat permitted as something enjoyable, nor is it referred to as proper among the foods prescribed for the Buddha's followers.

If however, Mahāmati, I had the mind to permit meat-eating, or if I said it was proper for the *Śrāvakas* to eat meat, I would not have forbidden, I would not forbid, all meat-eating for those *Yogins* [disciples], the sons and daughters of good family, who, wishing to cherish the idea that all beings are to them like an only child, are possessed of compassion, practice contemplation, mortification, and are on their way to the Mahāyāna. And, Mahāmati, the interdiction not to eat any kind of meat is here given to all sons and daughters of good family whether they are cemetery-ascetics or forest-ascetics, or *Yogins* who are practicing the exercises, if they wish the *Dharma* and are on the way to the mastery of any vehicle, and being possessed of compassion, conceive the idea of regarding all beings as an only child, in order to accomplish the end of their discipline.

In the canonical texts here and there the process of discipline is developed in orderly sequence like a ladder going up step by step, and one joined to another in a regular and methodical manner. . . Further, a tenfold prohibition is given as regards the flesh of animals found dead by themselves. But in the present sutra all meat-eating in any form, in any manner, and in any place, is unconditionally and once for all, prohibited for all. Thus, Mahāmati, meat-eating I have not permitted to anyone, I do not permit, I will not permit. Meat-eating, I tell you, Mahāmati, is not proper for homeless monks. There may be some, Mahāmati, who would say that meat was eaten by the *Tathagata* thinking this would calumniate him. Such unwitted people as these, Mahāmati, will follow the evil course of their own *karma*-hindrance, and will fall into such regions where long nights are passed without profit and without happiness. Mahāmati, the noble *Śrāvakas* do not eat the food taken properly by ordinary men, how much less the food of flesh and blood, which is altogether improper. Mahāmati, the food for my *Śrāvakas*, *Pratyekabuddhas*, and *Bodhisattvas* is the *Dharma* and not flesh-food; how much more the *Tathagata*! The *Tathagata* is the *Dharmakaya* ["body of the great order": unity of the Buddha with all existence], Mahāmati; he abides in the *Dharma* as food; his is not a body feeding on flesh; he does not abide in any flesh-food. He has ejected the habit-energy of thirst and desire which sustain all existence; he keeps away the habit-energy of all evil passions; he is thoroughly emancipated in mind and knowledge; he is the All-knower; he is All-seer; he regards all beings impartially as an only child; he is a great compassionate heart. Mahāmati, having the thought of an only child for all beings, how can I, such as I am, permit the *Śrāvakas* to eat the flesh of their own child? How much less my eating it! That I have permitted the *Śrāvakas* as well as myself to partake of meat-eating, Mahāmati, has no foundation whatever.

So it is said:

1. Liquor, meat, and onions are to be avoided, Mahāmati, by the *Bodhisattva-Mahāsattvas* and those who are Victor-heroes.

2. Meat is not agreeable to the wise: it has a nauseating odor, it causes a bad reputation, it is food for the carnivorous; I say this, Mahāmati, it is not to be eaten.

3. To those who eat meat there are detrimental effects, to those who do not, merits; Mahāmati, you should know that meat-eaters bring detrimental effects upon themselves.

4. Let the *Yogin* refrain from eating flesh as it is born of himself, as the eating involves transgression, as flesh is produced by semen and blood, and as the killing of animals causes terror to living beings.

5. Let the *Yogin* always refrain from meat, onions, various kinds of liquor, allium, and garlic...

7. From eating meat arrogance is born, from arrogance erroneous imaginations issue, and from imagination is born greed; and for this reason refrain from eating meat.

8. From imagination, greed is born, and by greed the mind is stupefied; there is attachment to stupefaction, and there is no emancipation from birth and death.

9. For profit sentient beings are destroyed, for flesh money is paid out, they are both evil-doers and the deed matures in the hells called *Raurava* (screaming).

10. One who eats flesh, trespassing against the words of the *Muni* [ascetic: probably a reference to Laws of Muni], is evil-minded; he is pointed out in the teachings of the *Śākya* as the destroyer of the welfare of the two worlds.

11. Those evil-doers go to the most horrifying hell; meat-eaters are matured in the terrific hells such as *Raurava*.

12. There is no meat to be regarded as pure in three ways: not premeditated, not asked for, and not impelled; therefore, refrain from meat.

13. Let not the *Yogin* eat meat, it is forbidden by myself as well as by the Buddhas; those sentient beings who feed on one another will be reborn among the carnivorous animals.

14. The meat-eater is ill-smelling, contemptuous, and born deprived of intelligence; he will be born again and again among the families of the *Caṇḍāla*, the *Pukkasa*, and the *Ḍomba* [various classes of outcastes].

15. From the womb of *Dākinī* he will be born in the meat-eaters' family, and then into the womb of a *Rākṣasi* and a cat; he belongs to the lowest class of men.

16. Meat-eating is rejected by me in such *sutras* as the *Hastikakshya*, the *Mahāmegha*, the *Nirvāṇa*, the *Aṅglimālika*, and the *Laṅkāvatāra*.

17. Meat-eating is condemned by the Buddhas, *Bodhisattvas*, and *Śrāvakas*; if one devours meat out of shamelessness he will always be devoid of sense.

18. One who avoids meat, etc., will be born, because of this fact, in the family of the *Brahmans* or of the *Yogins*, endowed with knowledge and wealth.

19. Let one avoid all meat-eating whatever they may say about witnessing, hearing, and suspecting; these theorizers born in a carnivorous family understand not.

20. As greed is the hindrance to emancipation so are meat-eating, liquor, etc., hindrances.

21. There may be in time to come people who make foolish remarks about meat-eating, saying, "Meat is proper to eat, unobjectionable, and permitted by the Buddha."

22. Meat-eating is a medicine; again, it is like a child's flesh; follow the proper measure and be averse to meat, and thus let the *Yogin* go about begging.

23. Meat-eating is forbidden by me everywhere and all the time for those who are abiding in compassion; he who eats meat will be born in the same place as the lion, tiger, wolf, etc.

24. Therefore, do not eat meat which will cause terror among people, because it hinders the truth of emancipation; not to eat meat—this is the mark of the wise.

On Animals I Have Conferred

Many Boons

AŚOKA

Aśoka, king of the Maurya kingdom of northern India, reigned in 373–326 BCE. One of the most important figures in ancient Indian history, Aśoka turned to Buddhism at a time of military crisis and became a lay follower. He then commenced a "reign of dharma" in which he sought to establish virtue and righteousness throughout the country. Weary of cruelties and the depredations of war, Aśoka turned to spiritual conquest. Among his many edicts, which he had inscribed on rocks and stone pillars scattered throughout his kingdom, were teachings affirming generosity, compassion, the need to refrain from killing, and the love of truth. On the basis of this spiritual pacifism, he urged vegetarianism and forbade animal sacrifice.

Thus speaks Aśoka, the Beloved of the Gods. For two and a half years I have been an open follower of the Buddha, though at first I did not make much progress. But for more than a year now I have drawn closer to the Buddhist Order, and have made much progress. In India the gods who formerly did not mix with men now do so. This is the result of great effort, and may be obtained not only by the great, but even by the small, through effort—thus they may even easily win heaven.

Father and mother should be obeyed, teachers should be obeyed; pity... should be felt for all creatures. These virtues of righteousness should be practiced.... This is an ancient rule, conducive to long life.

It is good to give, but there is no gift, no service, like the gift of righteousness. So friends, relatives, and companions should preach it on all occasions.

75

This is duty, this is right; by this heaven may be gained—and what is more important than to gain heaven?

———•+•———

This world and the other are hard to gain without great love of righteousness, great self-examination, great obedience, great circumspection, great effort. Through my instruction respect, love and righteousness daily increase and will increase... For this is my rule—to govern by righteousness, to administer by righteousness, to please my subjects by righteousness, and to protect them by righteousness.

———•+•———

Here no animal is to be killed for sacrifice, and no festivals are to be held, for the king finds much evil in festivals, except for certain festivals which he considers good.

Formerly in the Beloved of the God's kitchen several hundred thousand animals were killed daily for food; but now at the time of writing only three are killed—two peacocks and a deer, though the deer not regularly. Even these three animals will not be killed in future.

———•+•———

On men and animals, birds and fish I have conferred many boons, even to saving their lives; and I have done many other good deeds.

———•+•———

Everywhere in the empire of the Beloved of the Gods, and even beyond his frontiers... the Beloved of the Gods has provided medicines for man and beast. Wherever medicinal plants have not been found they have been sent there and planted. Roots and fruits have also been sent here that did not grow and have been planted. Wells have been dug along the roads for the use of man and beast.

———•+•———

In the past, kings sought to make the people progress in righteousness, but they did not progress... and I asked myself how I might uplift them through progress in righteousness. Thus I decided to have them instructed in righteousness, and to issue ordinances of righteousness, so that by hearing them the people might conform, advance in the progress of righteousness, and themselves make great progress. For that purpose many officials are employed among the people to instruct them in righteousness and to explain it to them.

Moreover I have had banyan trees planted on the roads to give shade to man and beast. I have planted mango groves, and I have had ponds dug and shelters erected along the roads at every eight *kos* [about every sixteen miles]. Everywhere I have had wells dug for the benefit of man and beast. But this benefit is but small, for in many ways the kings of olden time have worked for the welfare of the world; but what I have done has been done that men may conform to righteousness.

All the good deeds that I have done have been accepted and followed by the people. And so obedience to mother and father, obedience to teachers, respect for the aged, kindliness to Brahmans and ascetics, to the poor and weak, and to slaves and servants, have increased and will continue to increase. And this progress of righteousness among men has taken place in two manners, by enforcing conformity to righteousness, and by exhortation. I have enforced the law against killing certain animals and many others, but the greatest progress of righteousness among men comes from exhortation in favor of noninjury to life and abstention from killing living beings.

I have done this that it may endure as long as the moon and sun and that my sons and my great-grandsons may support it; for by supporting it they will gain both this world and the next.

All Life Is Linked

SIR EDWIN ARNOLD

Sir Edwin Arnold, a Buddhist convert born in England in 1832, is best known for his long epic poem "The Light of Asia" (1879), which tells of the life and teaching of the Buddha. Knighted in 1888, Arnold served as principal of the British government college at Poona, India, and later as chief editor of The Daily Telegraph *in London. In one part of his poem, excerpted here, Arnold describes the appearance of the Buddha amidst the flames and bleating victims of a King's atonement sacrifice to the gods. As the priest prays for the king's sins to be laid upon the goat, consuming them as the flesh burns, the Buddha softly speaks of "life, which all can take but none can give, Life, which all creatures love and strive to keep." Moved by the saintly pity of the Buddha and the greatness of his presence, the King henceforth declares that "none shall spill the blood of life nor taste the flesh." Peace, engendered by the Buddha's teaching, spreads among all living creatures.*

The King stood in his hall of offering,
On either hand the white-robed Brahmans ranged
Muttered their *mantras*, feeding still the fire
Which roared upon the midmost altar. There
From scented woods flickered bright tongues of flame,
Hissing and curling as they licked the gifts
Of ghee and spices and the Soma juice,
The joy of Indra. Round about the pile
A slow, thick, scarlet streamlet smoked and ran,
Sucked by the sand, but ever rolling down,
The blood of bleating victims. One such lay,
A spotted goat, long-horned, its head bound back
With *munjua* grass; at its stretched throat the knife

Pressed by a priest, who murmured, "This, dread gods,
Of many *yajnas* cometh as the crown
From Bimbasāra: take ye pleasure in the scent
Of rich flesh roasting 'mid the fragrant flames;
Let the King's sins be laid upon this goat,
And let the fire consume them burning it,
For now I strike."
                 But Buddha softly said,
"Let him not strike, great King!" and therewith loosed
The victim's bonds, none staying him, so great
His presence was. Then, craving leave, he spake
Of life, which all can take but none can give,
Life, which all creatures love and strive to keep,
Wonderful, dear and pleasant unto each,
Even to the meanest; yea, a boon to all
Where pity is, for pity makes the world
Soft to the weak and noble for the strong.
Unto the dumb lips of his flock he lent
Sad pleading words, showing how man, who prays
For mercy to the gods, is merciless,
Being as god to those; albeit all life
Is linked and kin, and what we slay have given
Meek tribute of the milk and wool, and set
Fast trust upon the hands which murder them.
Also he spake of what the holy books
Do surely teach, how that at death some sink
To bird and beast, and these rise up to man
In wanderings of the spark which grows purged flame.
So were the sacrifice new sin, if so
The fated passage of a soul be stayed.
Nor, spake he, shall one wash his spirit clean
By blood; nor gladden gods, being good, with blood;
Nor bribe them, being evil; nay, nor lay
Upon the brow of innocent bound beasts
One hair's weight of that answer all must give
For all things done amiss or wrongfully,
Alone, each for himself, reckoning with that
The fixed arithmic of the universe,
Which meteth good for good and ill for ill,
Measure for measure, unto deeds, words, thoughts;

Watchful, aware, implacable, unmoved;
Making all futures fruits of all the pasts.
Thus spake he, breathing words so piteous
With such high lordliness of truth and right,
The priests drew back their garments o'er the hands
Crimsoned with slaughter, and the King came near,
Standing with clasped palms reverencing Buddha;
While still our Lord went on, teaching how fair
This earth were if all living things be linked
In friendliness and common use of foods,
Bloodless and pure; the golden grain, bright fruits,
Sweet herbs which grow for all, the waters wan,
Sufficient drinks and meats. Which when these heard
The might of gentleness so conquered them,
The priests themselves scattered their altar-flames
And flung away the steel of sacrifice;
And through the land next day passed a decree
Proclaimed by criers, and in this wise graved
On rock and column: "Thus the King's will is:
There hath been slaughter for the sacrifice
And slaying for the meat, but henceforth none
Shall spill the blood of life nor taste the flesh,
Seeing that knowledge grows, and life is one,
And mercy cometh to the merciful."
So ran the edict, and from those days forth
Sweet peace hath spread between all living kind,
Man and the beasts which serve him, and the birds,
On all those banks of Gunga where our Lord
Taught with his saintly pity and soft speech.

Releasing Life

CHU-HUNG

Chu-hung (1535–1615) was a Chinese monk of the Ming Dynasty who proposed a practical path to enlightenment based on a combination of Zen and Pure Land Buddhism. In his meditations on releasing life excerpted here, he teaches the rewards that await one who sets creatures free. Releasing life, Chu-hung argues, accords with the mind of heaven and the teaching of the Buddha, unties the snare of hatred, ends soul transmigration, and above all recognizes the love of every creature for life. Accordingly, Chu-hung condemns the killing of animals for food as well as for ceremonial occasions. Slaughtering animals is justified neither by birthdays, the birth of sons, sacrifices to ancestors, or marriage—much less by entertaining friends, seeking to avert a disaster, or earning a livelihood. The wise person should cultivate compassion and avoid bad karma *by compassionately releasing life rather than causing its suffering and death.*

In my opinion, everyone should buy as many creatures as he can afford and release them whenever he sees them. At the end of a season or at the end of a year, everyone may go to one place, the number he has released can be tabulated, and his merit can be assigned. After this let everyone disperse quickly. Do not waste money to prepare offerings and do not waste time in socializing.

———•◦•———

Of the persons who set creatures free, some receive honor and prestige, some receive added years of life, some are spared from disasters, some recover from mental illnesses, some achieve rebirth in heaven, and some attain enlightenment in the Way. There is clear evidence that as one releases life, he assuredly receives a reward.

———•◦•———

As a man values his life,
So do animals love theirs.
Releasing life accords with the mind of heaven;
Releasing life agrees with the teaching of the Buddha.
Releasing life unties the snare of hatred;
Releasing life purifies the taint of sin.
Releasing life enables one to escape the three disasters[1];
Releasing life enables one to be free from the nine kinds of
    untimely deaths.[2]
Releasing life enables one to live long;
Releasing life enables one to rise high in an official career;
Releasing life enables one to have many children;
Releasing life enables one to have a prosperous household.
Releasing life dispels anxieties and worries;
Releasing life reduces sickness and pain.
Releasing life is the compassion of Kuan-yin;
Releasing life is the deed of P'u-hsien.[3]
By releasing life one comes to realize the truth of no birth.
By releasing life one ends transmigration.

1. On your birthday you should not kill animals. Parents bear the burden of giving birth to you and bringing you up. On the day you are born, your parents have started the slow process of death. Therefore on this day you should do good deeds in order to help the souls of your parents achieve a speedy deliverance from suffering. If you indulge in killing, it will not only be disastrous for yourself, but it will also implicate your parents.

2. When you have a son, you should not kill animals. Since you know that all men are happy to have sons, is it hard to imagine that animals also love their young? If, to celebrate the birth of your son, you take the lives of their sons, can your conscience really be at ease? Furthermore, when your baby is born, you ought to accumulate merit for his sake. If on the contrary, you create bad *karma* by killing: this is stupidity beyond belief.

3. When you sacrifice to your ancestors, you should not kill animals. On the anniversaries of the dead, as well as during the spring and autumn visits to ancestral graves, you ought to observe the precept of nonkilling in order to assist the dead by creating merit. Killing can only bring added bad *karma* upon the dead. For the body in the grave, even the choicest delicacies in the world will not be able to reawaken its sense of taste.

4. For the wedding ceremony, you should not kill animals. From the preliminary rite of asking names, to betrothal, and finally to the wedding, innumerable animals are killed for these ceremonies. But marriage is the beginning of the bringing forth of new life. It is contrary to reason to kill life at the beginning of life. Furthermore, the wedding day is an auspicious day. Therefore it is cruel to perform violent deeds on such a day.

5. In entertaining friends, you should not kill animals. Vegetables, fruits, and plain food are equally conducive to friendly conversation. There is no need for slaughtering animals and procuring extravagant dishes. When you realize that the meat you enjoy came from screaming animals, any person with a heart must feel sad.

6. In praying to avert disaster, you should not kill animals. When a person is sick he often kills animals to sacrifice to the spirits. But to kill another life in order to ask the spirits for the continuity of your own life is contrary to the principle of heaven. Moreover, spirits are upright and just, so how can they be bribed? Therefore not only are you unable to prolong your life, but you incur the evil *karma* of killing.

7. You should not kill animals as a livelihood. It is said that some people have to fish, hunt, or slaughter cows, sheep, pigs, and dogs for the sake of a livelihood. But people who are not engaged in such professions do not necessarily end up starving. To make a living by killing animals is condemned by the spirits, and no one who does this ever achieves prosperity. On the contrary, it will surely lead one to hell and make a person suffer retribution in the next life. Therefore it is imperative for such persons to seek another way of earning a livelihood.

NOTES

1. Fire, water, and wind.

2. The nine "untimely deaths" are (1) death by suffering disease that is not attended to by a doctor; (2) death by doing evil and punished by the law of the land; (3) death by indulging in excessive pleasure that causes one to become careless and thus to give ghosts and spirits the opportunity of stealing one's energy and breath away; (4) death by drowning; (5) death by burning; (6) death through being eaten by ferocious beasts in the forest; (7) death by falling off a cliff; (8) death through being killed by poison or a curse; (9) death from hunger and thirst.

3. Kuan-yin and P'u-hsien are *Bodhisattvas* of Compassion.

Meat Eating and the First Precept

ROSHI PHILIP KAPLEAU

In this selection from his classic To Cherish All Life, *the Venerable Philip Kapleau, American-born Roshi (Zen Master), author, and founder of the Rochester Zen Center, defends a meatless diet as a religious rather than ethical or metaphysical practice. Vegetarianism is mandated by the first precept in Buddhism, the injunction against killing or causing unnecessary harm to living beings. The Buddha-nature shared by all organisms unites them in a sacred harmony. To slay an animal for food (or to be an accomplice after the fact by eating the slain animal's flesh) brutalizes our sensitivity to Buddha-nature and constitutes, as Roshi Kapleau says, a sort of "cannibalism."*

In Buddhism the first precept[1] of not killing, or harmlessness to living beings (*fu-sessho* in Japanese, *ahiṃsā* in Sanskrit) has a religious rather than a moral or metaphysical basis. By this I mean that it is grounded in our Buddha-nature[2]—the matrix of all phenomena—from which arises our sense of compassion and moral goodness. Or to put it another way, this precept is based on the principle of mutual attraction and rightness common to all nature. The same can be said for the other cardinal precepts, each of which can be thought of as an extension or different aspect of the first precept. It is in Buddha-nature that all existences, animate and inanimate, are unified and harmonized. All organisms seek to maintain this unity in terms of their own *karma*. To willfully take life, therefore, means to disrupt and destroy this inherent wholeness and to blunt feelings of reverence and compassion arising from our Buddha-mind. The first precept of not killing is really a call to life and creation even as it is a condemnation of death and destruction.

Deliberately to shoot, knife, strangle, drown, crush, poison, burn, electrocute, or otherwise intentionally take the life of a living being or to purposefully inflict pain on a human being or animal—these are not the only ways to defile this precept. To cause *another* to kill, torture, or harm any living creature likewise offends against the first precept. Thus to put the flesh of an animal into one's belly makes one an accessory after the fact of its slaughter, simply because if cows, pigs, sheep, fowl, and fish, to mention the most common, were not eaten they would not be killed.

Although it is true that in Mahāyāna Buddhism the culpability for taking life involves various considerations, these need not concern us here, for with the exception of hunters, slaughterers, and fishermen, who kill the food they eat, the majority of flesh eaters are only indirectly responsible for the violence to and destruction of animals. This, however, does not make them any less answerable to the first precept.

Yasutani-roshi has pointed out in his book on the precepts why it is important to uphold the precept of not-killing:

> These days many voices proclaim the sanctity of human life. Human life should of course be valued highly, but at the same time the lives of other living beings should also be treasured. Human beings snatch away the lives of other creatures whenever it suits their purposes. The way of thinking that encourages this behavior arises from a specifically human brand of violence that defiles the self-evident laws of the universe, opposes the growth of the myriad things in nature, and destroys feelings of compassion and reverence arising from our Buddha-nature. In view of such needless destruction of life, it is essential that laymen and monks together conscientiously uphold this precept.[3]

The first precept has another religious aspect. Buddhism teaches that there is not a single being that has not been our mother, our father, husband, wife, sister, brother, son or daughter in its ascent and descent of the ladder of cause and effect through countless rebirths—not one being whose kinship with us even while in the animal state has not continued. How then can one who approaches all living things as though they were himself eat the flesh of something that is of the same nature as himself and not be guilty of cannibalism of a sort? Or to put it another way, since our Buddha-nature has endless potential, the creature that is a cow today may in a future rebirth become a human being and from that state realize its innate perfection—that is, achieve buddhahood.[4] Thus we have the fundamental Buddhist teaching that *all* life, human and non-human, is sacred. This does not mean that human beings are to be treated like cows and cows like human beings; clearly each has different capabilities and different needs. What it does mean is that in a just society the rights of non-humans are not ignored or trampled upon.

NOTES

1. The other nine precepts are (2) not to take what is not given, (3) not to engage in improper sexuality, (4) not to lie, (5) not to cause others to use liquors or drugs that confuse or weaken the mind nor to do so oneself, (6) not to speak of the shortcomings of others, (7) not to praise oneself and condemn others, (8) not to withhold material or spiritual aid, (9) not to become angry, and (10) not to revile the three treasures of Buddha, *Dharma*, and *Sangha* (those who follow the Buddha's *Dharma*, or teaching).

2. Buddha-nature: state in which everything is subject to endless transformation; that which is dynamic, devoid of shape, color, and mass; the matrix of all phenomena.

3. Hakuun Yasutani, *Reflections on the Five Ranks, the Three Resolutions, and the Ten Precepts*, 1962, trans. Kenneth Kraft.

4. Buddha: a Sanskrit word used in two senses: (1) ultimate truth or absolute mind, and (2) one awakened or enlightened to the true nature of existence.

Compassion for All Sentient Beings

THE DALAI LAMA

Lhamo Thondup, born in 1935, is the fourteenth Dalai Lama, believed by the faithful to be a reincarnation of the Bodhisattva Avalokiteśvara. Although acknowledged as the spiritual leader of Tibetan Buddhism in general, the Dalai Lama is actually a member of the Gelukpa or "Yellow Hat" sect, one of several Tibetan Buddhist schools.

Tibetan Buddhism does not require strict vegetarianism, in large part, undoubtedly, because the climate and soil of Tibet prohibit large-scale farming. But it does condemn the killing of animals for food. Consequently, butchers in Tibet prior to the Chinese invasion in 1950 tended to be Muslims, many of them from adjoining Kashmir.

The Dalai Lama became a vegetarian in 1965. As he recounts in his autobiography Freedom in Exile *(Hodder & Stoughton, 1990), he one day chanced to see the slaughter of a chicken intended for his lunch. As its neck was wrung, he says, "I thought of how much suffering the poor creature was enduring. The realisation filled me with remorse and I decided it was time to become a vegetarian." To his regret, however, he soon afterward became severely jaundiced and on medical advice returned to meat eating.*

Although no longer a strict vegetarian, the Dalai Lama continues to believe that a meatless diet is one of the practical corollaries of Buddhism's pity for all sentient beings. In the selection below, taken from a series of interviews concerning compassionate action, he reiterates his conviction that Buddhist spirituality entails a concerted forbearance from inflicting harm or pain upon other beings, and concludes that "our basic nature as human beings is to be vegetarian—making every effort not to harm other living beings." Characteristically, however, the Dalai Lama refuses to dogmatize, acknowledging that sometimes meat eating may be unavoidable. The clear message, however, is that it is not the ideal.

QUESTION: Your Holiness, I would like to ask you about [a] situation in which animals suffer a lot—factory farms. In order to change that practice, to reduce the suffering of these fellow species, we need to see their pain. But for many of us, it seems to be too much to bear, and we want to look away. You have described the practice of not turning away from pain, but penetrating into it so that we are not afraid of it. Can you speak more about it, especially in relation to our animal brothers and sisters who are being tortured?

DALAI LAMA: Thousands—millions and billions—of animals are killed for food. That is very sad. We human beings can live without meat, especially in our modern world. We have a great variety of vegetables and other supplementary foods, so we have the capacity and the responsibility to save billions of lives. I have seen many individuals and groups promoting animal rights and following a vegetarian diet. This is excellent.

Certain killing is purely a "luxury." Hunting and fishing as sports, for example, are just nonsense. But other killing, for example commercial fishing for eating, is more understandable. But perhaps the saddest is factory farming. The poor animals there really suffer. I once visited a poultry farm in Japan where they keep 200,000 hens for two years just for their eggs. During those two years, they are prisoners. Then after two years, when they are no longer productive, the hens are sold. That is really shocking, really sad. We must support those who are attempting to reduce that kind of unfair treatment.

An Indian friend told me that his young daughter has been arguing with him that it is better to serve one cow to ten people than to serve chicken or other small animals, since more lives would be involved. In the Indian tradition, beef is always avoided, but I think there is some logic to her argument. Shrimp, for example, are very small. For one plate, many lives must be sacrificed. To me, this is not at all delicious. I find it really awful, and I think it is better to avoid these things. If your body needs meat, it may be better to eat bigger animals. Eventually you may be able to eliminate the need for meat. I think that our basic nature as human beings is to be vegetarian—making every effort not to harm other living beings. If we apply our intelligence, we can create a sound, nutritional program.

It is very dangerous to ignore the suffering of any sentient being. Even in warfare, it is better to be aware of the suffering of others and our own discomfort for causing them pain. Warfare is killing. It is one hundred percent negative. The way it is mechanized today is even worse. Where warfare remains "humanized," I mean where it remains in touch with true human feelings, it is much safer. When the warrior forgets about the suffering of others in order to achieve some small benefit, that is really dangerous. I am thinking here of some Tibetan butchers. Although they make their livelihood as butchers, at the same time they show kindness and love toward the animals. Before the slaughter, they give the animal some pills, and after they finish, they say a prayer. Although it is still killing, I think it is better with that kind of feeling.

...Real compassion comes from seeing the other's suffering. You feel a sense of responsibility, and you want to do something for him or her. There are three types of compassion. The first is a spontaneous wish for other sentient beings to be free of suffering. You find their suffering unbearable and you wish to relieve them of it. The second is not just a wish for their well-being, but a real sense of responsibility, a commitment to relieve their suffering and remove them from their undesirable circumstances. This type of compassion is reinforced by the realization that all sentient beings are impermanent, but because they grasp at the permanence of their identity, they experience confusion and suffering. A genuine sense of compassion generates a spontaneous sense of responsibility to work for the benefit of others, encouraging us to take this responsibility upon ourselves. The third type of compassion is reinforced by the wisdom that although all sentient beings have interdependent natures and no inherent existence, they still grasp at the existence of inherent nature. Compassion accompanied by such an insight is the highest level of compassion.

In order to cultivate and develop genuine compassion within yourself, you need to identify the nature of suffering and the state of suffering that sentient beings are in. Because you want sentient beings to be free from their suffering, first of all you have to identify what suffering is. When Buddha taught the Four Noble Truths, he spoke of three types of suffering: suffering that is obvious and acute, like physical pain; the suffering of change, such as pleasurable experiences that have the potential to turn into suffering; and pervasive suffering, which is the basic fact of conditioned existence. To cultivate compassion, first of all, you have to reflect on suffering and identify suffering as suffering. When reflecting in depth on the nature of suffering, it is always beneficial to search for an alternative—to see whether it is possible to ever get rid of suffering. If there is no way out, just reflecting on suffering will make you feel depressed, and that is not helpful. If there is no possibility of getting rid of the suffering, then it is better to not think about it at all.

After describing the origin of suffering, the Buddha spoke of the cessation of suffering and the path that leads to the cessation. When you realize that it *is* possible to eliminate the root that gives rise to suffering, that awareness will increase your determination to identify and reflect on suffering at all different levels, and that will inspire you to seek liberation.

After reflecting on the nature of suffering and feeling convinced that there is a path that leads to the cessation of suffering, then it is important to see that all sentient beings do not want suffering and do want happiness. Everyone has the right to be happy, to overcome suffering. When reflecting on ourselves, we find that we have a natural desire to be happy and to overcome suffering, and that this desire is just and valid. When we see that all living creatures have the natural right to be happy and overcome suffering and fulfill their wishes, we ourselves have a spontaneous feeling of self-worth.

The only difference between us and others is in number. We are just one individual among infinite others. No matter how important we are, we are just one sentient being, one single self, while others are infinite. But there is a close relationship of interdependence. Our suffering or happiness is very much related with others. That is also reality. Under these circumstances, if, in order to save one finger the other nine fingers are sacrificed, that is foolish. But if, in order to save nine fingers, one finger is sacrificed, it may be worth it. So you see the importance of others' rights and your own rights, and others' welfare and your own welfare. Because of numbers, the infinite numbers of others' rights and welfare naturally become most important. The welfare of others is important not only because of the sheer number, but also if you were to sacrifice the infinite others for your own happiness eventually you will lose. If you think more of others, taking care of others' rights and serving others, ultimately you will gain.

Not only when you are engaging in the meditative practices of the *bodhisattva* path is it harmful to sacrifice the welfare and happiness of infinite others for your own happiness, as it prevents you from making progress in the spiritual path, but if you were to sacrifice the benefit and welfare of infinite others for the sake of your own happiness and welfare in your daily life, you are the one who ultimately will lose and suffer the consequences.

If you want to be selfish, you should be selfish-with-wisdom, rather than with foolishness. If you help others with sincere motivation and sincere concern, that will bring you more fortune, more friends, more smiles, and more success. If you forget about others' rights and neglect others' welfare, ultimately you will be very lonely.

...I myself, as a Buddhist monk who is supposedly a practitioner—although my practice is very lazy and not at all satisfying to myself—even a lazy practitioner with not enough time, step by step, little by little, can change. I can change my own mental attitude, and it brings me some real joy and inner strength. Brothers and sisters, please think along these lines. If you feel you can practice at a certain point, please try to carry it out as a kind of experiment. As time goes on, you may get some benefit. But if you feel it isn't working, don't worry. Don't be concerned at all.

Compassion, or altruistic motivation, is really wonderful. Sometimes I feel a sense of wonder that we human beings can develop such altruism. It is really a precious source of inner strength, happiness, and future success.

THE JUDAIC
TRADITION

*It is forbidden, according to the law of
the Torah, to inflict pain upon any living
creature. On the contrary, it is our
duty to relieve the pain of any creature,
even if it is ownerless or belongs to a
non-Jew.*
—Rabbi Soloman Ganzfreid,
Code of Jewish Laws

The three western "religions of the Book"—Judaism, Christianity, and
Islam—do not espouse vegetarianism as overtly as the Orphic-
Pythagorean, Indian, and Buddhist traditions. For a number of historical reasons
(not the least of which is a climate and geography inhospitable to horticulture),
the faiths that sprang up in Palestine and the Arabian Peninsula did not overtly
forbid the slaughter of food animals. Moreover, it seems pretty clear that the
great spiritual leaders of these three traditions—Moses, Jesus, and
Mohammed—were flesh eaters. Finally, subsequent mainstream theologizing in
the three traditions, not to mention centuries of custom and popular religiosi-
ty, have tended to ignore vegetarianism as a significant spiritual discipline. Even
today, the widespread assumption is that if one is a follower of any of the three
religions of the Book and a vegetarian, there is no necessary connection
between the two. One is a vegetarian *as well as* a Jew or Christian or Muslim,
not *because* one is a Jew or Christian or Muslim.

93

Still, it can hardly be denied that there are good grounds for concluding that a meatless diet is not only compatible with the three religions of the Book, but actually more consistent with their ethical and spiritual teachings than carnivorism is. In recent years especially, Jews, Christians, and Muslims have discovered—or, better, remembered—that concern for the welfare of animals is deeply rooted in their religious traditions.

Judaic vegetarianism, like the classical world's Orphic-Pythagorean tradition, starts from the hypothesis that God's initial intention was that people should be herbivores. The scriptural warrant for this claim is found in the Torah's "golden age" account of the Edenic paradise. On the sixth day of creation, Yahweh created man and woman and gave them stewardship over the fish of the sea, the birds of the air, and the beasts of the earth. The diet of the primordial couple was apparently meatless: "Then God said, 'I give you every seed-bearing plant on the face of the whole earth and every tree that has fruit with seed in it. They will be yours for food' " (Genesis 1:29). In fact, continues the Genesis author in the next verse, the aboriginal diet of *all* creatures was meatless as well: " 'And to all the beasts of the earth and all other birds of the air and all the creatures that move on the ground—everything that has the breath of life in it—I give every green plant for food.' "

But God proposes and humankind disposes. The divinely ordained fellowship between persons and animals (see, e.g., Psalms 104 and 148) was shattered by the willfulness of Adam and Eve. The golden age was lost and with it an appreciation of the sanctity of *all* life. As Rabbi Gendler points out, the expression *nephesh chaya*, "living *souls*," in Genesis (1:20, 21, 24) describes animals. Abel slew animals as sacrifices to the Lord (Genesis 4:4), thereby breaking the taboo against killing (see Rabbi Rosenfeld's contribution) and initiating a slide toward wickedness which eventually led to the Flood. In destroying a human race run amok, Yahweh sought a new beginning, a fresh start. But there is no return to the original purity of creation, for God tells Noah and his sons, "Everything that lives and moves will be food for you. Just as I gave you the green plants, I now give you everything" (Genesis 9:3). On the surface of things, this seems to be a dramatic reversal of the dietary pronouncements in the creation account, and it has been frequently cited as scriptural warrant for carnivorism, animal sacrifice, and (today) medical experimentation on animals.

Jewish vegetarians claim that when read against a broader scriptural and spiritual backdrop, the earlier prohibition against slaughtering animals for food is not superseded by Genesis 9. This was probably the intuition of the first-century Essene sect, which Porphyry, Philo, Josephus, and Pliny the Elder all report as primarily vegetarian.[1] Subsequent Talmudists such as Abraham Isaac Kook argue that Genesis 9 is not a reversal of the divine plan of Genesis 1 so much as a temporary concession to human waywardness. The ideal, intended from the very beginning by Yahweh, is that humans live in compassionate harmony with animals and show reverence for all of God's creation. But the actuality is that humans have proven themselves unable as yet to forswear bloodletting. So God reluctantly allows the killing of animals until such time as we spiritually evolve beyond our sinful urges to act violently.

In defense of this interpretation, vegetarian Talmudists typically appeal to three arguments. In the first place, all of creation, especially living creation, reflects God's glory and goodness and love. It is God's, not ours; as the Psalmist (24:1) puts it, "The earth is the Lord's, and all that is in it, the world and those who dwell therein." Because creation is the Lord's, and because it reflects divine nature, it deserves our respect.

Second, Judaism's respect for God's creation traditionally has expressed itself in compassion for animals as well as humans. The books of Deuteronomy and Leviticus both mandate that animals be treated with concern for their well-being. Oxen should be allowed to eat as they thresh grain (Deuteronomy 25:4), newborn animals ought not to be deprived of their mothers (Leviticus 22:27), lost animals should be located (Deuteronomy 22:1), and owners should tend to their animals' needs before their own (Deuteronomy 11:15). In Exodus (20:8–10), the Hebrews are reminded that the Sabbath is a day of rest for animals as well as humans. Some medieval and modern Talmudists interpreted these and similar texts as proscriptions against hunting,[2] overworking animals,[3] slaying a young animal in sight of its mother (Maimonides comments, "there is no difference in this case between the pain of people and the pain of other living beings, since the love and the tenderness of the mother for her young ones is not produced by reasoning but by feeling, and this faculty exists not only in people but in most living things."[4]), and wearing clothes made of animal fur or hide on Yom Kippur, the most sacred day of the Jewish calendar (the sixteenth-century Rabbi Moses Isserles puts it this way: "How can a man put on shoes, a piece of clothing for which it is necessary to kill a living thing, on Yom Kippur, which is a day of grace and compassion, when it is written 'His tender mercies are over all His works.' "[5]).

Third, Jewish vegetarians argue that the compassion for all living things mandated by a reverence for God's creation is most obviously expressed in *kashrut* (kosher), the tradition's dietary laws. Many commentators, including Roberta Kalechofsky and Rabbi Abraham Isaac Kook, claim that *kashrut's* prohibition against killing all but certain kinds of animals, and even then only in a humane manner, is a codification of the earlier-mentioned divine concession to humankind's bloodlust, a systematized attempt to wean us until we attain the spiritual maturity to forgo flesh entirely. But *kashrut* is not only a remnant of the original divine intention. It's also one obvious way, as Roberta Kalechofsky points out, to integrate the holy into the basic human act of eating.

In light of these claims, it is understandable that Jewish vegetarians argue that a meatless diet is a logical extension of Judaic spiritual tradition. Rabbi Kook even argues that returning to a nonviolent diet is one of the necessary conditions for the Messiah's coming. If it is the case, as the prophet Isaiah (11:6–7) says, that in the kingdom of God the wolf will lie peacefully with the lamb and the lion eat straw with the ox, then a diet that approximates the ideal of peaceful harmony does indeed make straight a way for the Lord.

N O T E S

1. Pliny discusses the Essenes in Book V of his *Natural History*, Porphyry in the fourth book of his *On Abstinence from Animal Food*, Josephus in his *War of the Jews* (Book II) and *Antiquities* (Book XVIII), and Philo of Alexandria in his *On the Contemplative Life*. In this latter work, the ascetic group under scrutiny is referred to by Philo as the "Therapeutae." It's surmised they were a branch of the Essenes.

2. *Avodah Zorah* 18b; *Yorah Deah*, Second Series, 10.

3. *Shulchan Aruch, Yoreh De'ah* 297:2.

4. *Guide for the Perplexed*, 3:48.

5. Quoted in Rabbi Samuel H. Dresner, *The Jewish Dietary Laws: Their Meaning for Our Time* (New York: The Rabbinical Assembly of America, 1983), pp. 33–34.

Kashrut:

A Provegetarian Bias in Torah

ROBERTA KALECHOFSKY

In this essay, widely published advocate of Jewish vegetarianism Roberta Kalechofsky argues that carnivorism is contrary to the basic Judaic value of life affirmation. She argues that reverence for life is the spiritual heart of kashrut, *the Jewish dietary code. Kashrut allows the slaughter and consumption of some animals, but Kalechofsky argues that it's an "uneasy compromise" between the biblically revealed divine injunction to refrain from flesh eating and the rapacity of human appetite. She contends that time and reflection have clarified the "provegetarian bias" of Torah, reawakening us to the fact that the fundamental act of eating properly reflects spiritual awareness just as much as more formal acts of worship do. In discerning a spiritual dimension to food, Kalechofsky is in agreement with Francis Clooney's Christian defense of vegetarianism (later in this volume).*

Vegetarian Judaism rests on five important Jewish mandates which are rooted in Torah and which were expanded by Talmudic and rabbinic commentary: *pikuach nefesh* (the commandment to guard your health and life); *tsa'ar ba'alei chaim* (avoid causing pain to any living creature); *bal tashchit* (the commandment not to waste or destroy anything of value); *tzedakkah* (to help the needy and work for a more just society); and *klal Israel* (to work for the welfare of the Jewish people). These mandates have been developed over millennia in the Talmud and rabbinic responsa, and have guided the Jewish people throughout centuries. But knowledge and implementation of these mandates have declined since the advent of industrial society. Meat and our attitude toward food animals is at the heart of the decline.

The modern meat-based diet has seriously eroded these principles which are not largely and, particularly for most urban Jews, honored merely in sentiment as nostalgic emblems of the Jewish tradition. Rabbis and many knowledgeable Jews can recite the laws concerning Jewish regard for animal life, but in reality these laws have no more application to much of contemporary Jewish life than sitting in the gate of a wall to render judgment. Even worse, the tradition is too often used as a shield against responsibility for contemporary problems concerning animals.

Meat-eating today violates the intentions of historical *kashrut* which, as the rabbis traditionally interpreted the tradition, has two purposes. One purpose was to curb the appetite for meat. In this, *kashrut* has observably failed. . .

The second purpose of *kashrut*, as the rabbis interpreted the tradition, was to refine our sensibilities with respect to animal life and to make us aware of animal pain. Even such an arcane and mysterious commandment that one must not seethe a kid in its mother's milk was given this interpretation in the first century by the Jewish philosopher Philo of Alexandria. He gave the commandment its definitive Jewish cast when he declared that to seethe a kid in its mother's milk was morally repulsive because it is "improper that the matter which sustained the living animal should be used to flavor its meat after its death." Rabbinic commentary declared that the prohibition was intended to refine our appetites with respect to meat, and the commandment became applicable to all meat, as the prohibition underwent expansion from 200–420 CE. The interpretation of this law, as well as of other laws concerning *kashrut*, became ethical and moral: concern for the animal and concern to refine human sensibility with respect to *all* life. Rabbi Samuel Dresner expressed the sentiment succinctly: "Reverence for life. . . is the constant lesson of the laws of *kashrut*."[1] Yet *kashrut*, for most contemporary Jews, has failed in this purpose as well. . .

The historical development of the dietary laws for Jews has been stated many times[2] and is reviewed here briefly. Vegetarianism is conceived in Genesis as the ideal state for human beings. Meat is permitted for the first time after the flood, when Noah set up a slaughter site at his own bidding, with the dire divine foresight that human beings will now know war and will be separated from other animals who will flee from them (Genesis 9:3). Permission to eat meat is also given with the proviso that the human race is not to bite into the living animal or eat its blood (the law of *ever min hadai*, Genesis 9:4). Isaiah called this commandment "the ancient covenant" and regarded violations of it with intense aversion:

> The earth is withered, sere;
> The world languishes, it is sere;

The most exalted people of the earth languish.
For the earth is defiled
Under its inhabitants;
Because they transgressed teachings,
Violated laws,
Broke the ancient covenant.
That is why a curse consumes the earth,
And its inhabitants pay the penalty. (24:4–12)

The law of *ever min hahai* singles out the human race from other predatory animals. It is considered applicable to the whole human race as one of the Noachic laws: we are not to take our meat as predatory animals do. Hunting, which was considered essential to all great empire-building states in the identification of hunter and warrior and in the training of the warrior, was prohibited to the Jewish people. Jews had permission to eat meat, but not to be predators. The meat they ate was to be chosen from their flock and was to be properly sacrificed before it could be eaten. There is no commandment to eat meat, but there are strict commandments regarding the kind of meat to be eaten and how the animal was to be sacrificed before it could be eaten. Walter Burkett's observation in his book *Homo Necans*, that "For the ancient world, hunting, sacrifice, and war were symbolically interchangeable,"[3] was not true for the Jewish people, who broke that connection for themselves. By prohibiting hunting, Judaism severed an historic relationship between hunting and the consumption of meat, and between hunting and war. Judaism does not know the camaraderie of the hunt. What remained was the sacrificial system which gave to Judaism the association of eating meat with holidays and festivals. This association was later denied by the Talmud, after the fall of the Temple. Furthermore, as Burkett states, Judaism in the diaspora could spread precisely because sacrifice was concentrated in the Temple in Jerusalem. Diaspora Judaism had been "a religion without animal sacrifice." After the fall of the Temple, the Jewish association with a meat-centered diet was not inevitable, but developed in the West with the same response pattern of other Western or Westernized people. It is essentially a response of cultural assimilation.

Observant Jews limited their meat to those animals who were vegetarian animals, in accordance with traditional *kashrut*, which mandated that not only were Jews not to take their meat as predators do, but they were not to eat predatory animals. . .

The Bible tells us that there were "food riots" during the forty years in the desert, tensions caused by the lack of meat. It relates that these conflicts were caused by "the riff-raff": "The mixed multitude, or the riff-raff, that was among them, began to lust [for meat]; and the Children of Israel also cried out, 'Would that we had flesh to eat!' " (Numbers 11:4).

The reference to "the riff-raff" suggests derision, a derision we meet elsewhere in reference to meat. Upon entering Canaan, the Israelites are given permission to eat "the meat of lust." As Rabbi Dresner points out, the reference is derisive,[4] and has been traditionally interpreted as such by the rabbis. Rashi's comment on the food riots, "It was right for the Jews to cry for bread, but not for meat, for one can live without meat," reflects the derisive sentiment toward "meat of lust." We see a similar derision toward meat in the incident in Numbers 11:4 in the designation of the grave in which the "meat-eaters" were buried as *Kibroth-hataavah*, or "graves of lust."[5] The entire description of this incident is told in the language of anger and derision. After the Hebrews stuffed their mouths with quail so that "the meat was still between their teeth, unchewed... the anger of God blazed out against the camp and struck it with plague" (Numbers 11:33).

There was indeed contention about the eating of meat in the formation of the Hebrew nation, and compromises were struck. In Deuteronomy 12:20, God promises to allow meat to be eaten once the Hebrew nation enters Canaan, "because your appetite craves eating meat" (Deuteronomy 12:20). In the passage in Numbers 11:4, we gather from Moses' words the strain which the argument put upon him: "Moses was distressed and said to the Lord, 'Why have you dealt ill with your servant... and laid the burden of all this people upon me.... Where am I to get meat to give them when they whine before me and say, "give us meat to eat!" ' "

...Eating meat poses a problem in many societies. Meat of one kind or another is the most universally tabooed, controlled, or ritually eaten food, suggesting discomfort with the eating of meat in many societies. For Jews ...meat remained... without the status which the seven sacred species have. These are figs, dates, pomegranates, wheat, barley, olives, and grapes. Later discussions in the Talmud indicate that though the rabbis believed meat to have nutritional value, they regarded it negatively and contrived to circumvent its consumption: "Man should not eat meat unless he has a special craving for it, and then shall eat it only occasionally and sparingly" and "A man should not teach his son to eat meat" (*Chulin* 84a).

There is a "provegetarian bias in Torah," as Rabbi Arthur Green has discerned,[6] which time has clarified. The original instincts of *kashrut* sought to limit the consumption of meat; the general rabbinic judgment in the Talmud reflects an uneasy compromise with the human lust for it. After the fall of the Temple and the end of the sacrificial system (which at the least lent dignity to the consumption of meat) the rabbis were even less comfortable with the idea of eating meat. Since eating meat was historically embedded in the sacrificial system, after the Temple fell there was much discussion in the Talmud about what the status of meat would now be. The association of eating meat with the festivals bequeathed to Jews the tradition that joyous occasions (*simchat yom tov*) should be celebrated with meat and wine. This association with meat was declared no longer to be in effect after the sacrifices ended. *Beit Yoseph* states: "In the days when the Temple was in existence, there was no rejoicing without meat... but now that there is no longer the Temple, there is no rejoicing without wine." Jews are commanded to celebrate the holidays and Shabbat with wine and with joy, but there is no *halachic* requirement to celebrate them with meat...

After the fall of the Temple, the focus of Jewish celebration shifted from the Temple to the synagogue and the home which, we should remember, was the focus for all Diaspora Jews—which was the majority of Jews at the time. The table in one's home, prepared properly for Shabbat and the holidays, was to be considered as an altar. The shift in religious concept testifies to the flexibility of the rabbis who were able to take command of the historic hour, as we should be able to do with ours.

> Today we have no Temple in Jerusalem, no altar there, no sacrifices, no priests to minister. But in their stead we have something even greater. For every home can be a Temple, every table an altar, every meal a sacrifice and every Jew a priest. And what was formerly an animal function, a meaningless, mechanical behavior, is suddenly transformed into an elaborate ritual full of mystery and meaning.[7]

This is the way eating was intended to be for Jews, for whom food has always been holy. In *Berakhot Talmud*, the rabbis laid out a scheme for the blessing of food in order of importance in values: (1) it must be pleasurable; (2) it should be one of the seven species, subject to the obligation of first fruits; (3) it should be offered on the altar; (4) it should have food value; (5) it should have dignity. This last requirement is noteworthy, because it arose in the context of whether there should be a blessing for eating poultry (39a–b). It was decided that poultry had the same status as a vegetable in terms of pleasure and nourishment, but that it lacked dignity. Eating should also be done in an orderly fashion, as the word *seder* (order) means. It is not only what we eat, but how we eat that matters. In addition to our nutritional needs, there is a spiritual dimension to food...

Why did the Talmudic rabbis feel that the consumption of poultry lacked dignity, why did they withhold a special blessing from the consumption of meat, such as bread and wine have, and yet not denounce meat altogether? The key to the situation seems to be that they took a position of neither encouraging nor discouraging vegetarianism, but of definitely discouraging meat. The explanation must lie in problems in Talmudic times: that the rabbis felt that open encouragement of vegetarianism might be regarded as a break with the tradition of animal sacrifice; they were also concerned about advocating vegetarianism because most vegetarian practice at the time was associated with non-Jewish values such as celibacy and the condemnation of creation and matter.[8] Such ideas have always been perceived to rupture the affirmative impulses of Judaism: Choose life, be fruitful and multiply. As John Cooper observes, the vegetarian bias in the Bible is strongly implicative: "During the wanderings of the children of Israel in the wilderness the Torah continued to hold meat eating in low esteem. . . . Despite these concessions to human weakness, the Torah and the prophets came down firmly in favor of a vegetarian diet."[9] Jewish vegetarianism today arises out of the life-affirming impulses of guarding one's health, protecting the environment, and reverence for all life. As Rabbi Green has written:

> If Jews have to be associated with killing at all in our time, let it be only for the defense of human life. Life has become too precious in this era for us to be involved in the shedding of blood, even that of animals, when we can survive without it. This is not an ascetic choice, we should note, but rather a life-affirming one. A vegetarian Judaism would be more whole in its ability to embrace the presence of God in all of Creation.[10]

This early uneasiness with meat consumption exhibited itself at a time when biblical Jews ate very little meat. Since the consumption of meat for Jews was originally embedded in the sacrificial system, it had the effect of limiting the amount of meat most biblical Jews ate. The main diet of biblical Jews, as of the Greeks and the Romans, was vegetarian. The restriction against eating meat, as Elijah Schocet points out in *Animal Life in Jewish Tradition*, is underscored by the law in Leviticus (17:3–4) which "condemns as murder the slaughter of animals outside the precinct of the altar of the sanctuary."[11] This suggests that God-fearing Jews in the Diaspora ate no meat except for the three occasions of pilgrimage to Jerusalem.[12] The exhortation of the prophets not to permit a temple in Judea other than the one in Jerusalem may have been motivated by the desire to minimize the consumption of meat, as much as by any other reason.[13]

. . . The Jewish arguments for a vegetarian Judaism are those of our five mandates: human health, compassion for animal life, environmental health, charity, and concern for the community. A Jewish vegetarianism grows out of Jewish values. It is . . . reverence for life, not ascetic denials of the world, of the body, or of life. . .

A vegetarian Judaism returns us to the biblical mandate; it gives us a relationship and harmony with the earth and with the other creatures. A vegetarian

Judaism contains a moral symmetry in its concern for human health, for animal life, for nature. It reaches down into the deepest level of moral insight that what is good for human health is good for the health of the planet and for other life on it. A vegetarian Judaism does not negate the past, nor pass judgment on the Temple or on the conduct of our patriarchs and matriarchs. . . . We do not judge the past in becoming vegetarians. Rather, like Noah who was righteous in his generation, we accept the imperatives of our generation, and seek a renewed covenant with the earth. As Andrea Cohen-Kiener observes, the lesson of that interesting qualifier "righteous in his generation" is that "the exact 'medicine' for world repair is subtly unique for each generation." The medicine for our generation is vegetarianism. Unlike Noah, we do not begin the new age with the construction of a slaughter site, recognizing with Ecclesiastes that "Unto each thing there is a season." Now is the time to heal and to build up. History has prepared the Jew for vegetarianism and the arguments for it today are imperative. If not now, then when?

NOTES

1. Rabbi Samuel Dresner, *The Jewish Dietary Laws: Their Meaning for Our Time* (The Rabbinical Assembly of America, 1982), 27. It should also be stated that explanations of the dietary laws as either "hygienic" or "ethical" have been challenged by anthropologists such as Mary Douglas, who regards the dietary laws as part of an intricate system related to a "cognitive ordering of the universe," involving other rituals, such as the purity rituals, etc. A good short view of this matter is in Everett Fox's translation, *The Five Books of Moses, Vol. 1* (Schocken, 1995), 445–555.

2. Most recently in the introduction to *The Jewish Vegetarian Year Cookbook* by Roberta Kalechofsky and Rosa Rasiel (Micah Publications, 1997).

3. Walter Burkett, *Homo Necans*, trans. P. Bing (University of California Press, 1983).

4. Ibid., 25.

5. Everett Fox's translation is "Burial-Places of the Craving." The episode is rendered in his translation [of *The Five Books of Moses*] with great drama, 713-718.

6. See Rabbi Arthur Green's articles, "To Work It and Guard It: Preserving God's World," and "Vegetarianism, A *Kashrut* for Our Time," in *Seek My Face, Speak My Name* (Jason Aronson, 1992).

7. Dresner, *Jewish Vegetarian Dietary Laws*, 40.

8. Robert Eisenmann, *James the Brother of Jesus* (Viking, 1996), examines the twin advocacy of celibacy and vegetarianism in James and first century "Jewish Christians."

9. John Cooper, *Eat and Be Satisfied: A Social History of Jewish Food* (Jason Aronson, 1993), 19, 21.

10. In *Rabbis and Vegetarianism: An Evolving Tradition*, ed. Roberta Kalechofsky (Micah Publications, 1995), 27.

11. Elijah Judah Schochet, *Animal Life in Jewish Tradition: Attitudes and Relationships* (Ktav, 1984), 47.

12. However, note that Deuteronomy 12:21 states that if there is no Temple available for proper sacrifice, "you may slaughter animals from among your herds and your flocks." Nevertheless, this would not affect most Diaspora Jews who lived in cities and did not have access to herds and flocks.

13. We know of only one other place in the Diaspora in which a temple for animal sacrifice was built. This was by a Jewish garrison on the island of Elephantis in Egypt.

The Life of His Beast

EVERETT E. GENDLER

In this essay, Rabbi Gendler argues that respect for animals is inseparable from a reverence for life. The Hebrew Bible makes plain the relatedness of humans and beasts as well as the former's religious duty to care for the latter. Animals are not really our possessions. Like everything in the world, they are God's; they are "His" beasts. In treating them with compassion and respect, we do honor to the Creator of all life. But when we slaughter them for food, and especially when we subject them to the brutalities of factory farming, we mistreat a part of the creation that God has loved into being. Gendler also suggests that the manner in which we treat "His" beasts is tied to "the issue of the treatment of other human beings and ourselves."

Charles Darwin was not the first human being to posit a close relation between man and the other animals. He may have put this particular notion to new theoretical use, he may have made our sense of kinship with other animals function differently in this particular age from the way it did in the centuries preceding. But the fact is that man's sense of relatedness to other living creatures is a very ancient inheritance of the human species. The 104th Psalm and the 148th Psalm express clearly the Psalmist's close identification not only with human life but also with the entire life of the Universe, even as it expresses itself in the lives of the beasts of the field, the monsters of the deep, and the birds of the air.

Nor is this simply an accident of the Book of Psalms. Those of you who are familiar with the creation story in Genesis have perhaps noticed that the sea animals and the birds which fly receive the same blessings as men: "be fruitful and multiply" (Genesis 1:22). One notices also that beasts of the earth as well as men are invited to the banquet provided by the herbs, fruits, and growths of the earth's surfaces (Genesis 1:30). One notices even that the important Hebrew term *nephesh chaya*—which means "a living being" or "a living soul"—is applied

105

both to animals and to man in the creation story in Genesis (Genesis 1:20, 21, 24). Granted, man in some respects, surpasses the capacities of the animals; Genesis is explicit about this. But the basic relatedness is not lost sight of even with the awareness of difference.

Nor is this sense of kinship confined simply to sentiments for singing on occasions of worship. The five Books of Moses include a number of specific laws dealing with proper treatment of the other animals, for they too are creatures of the Divine and objects of His express concern. To mention a few of them briefly: "you may not muzzle an ox as it threshes the grain" (Deuteronomy 25:4). The grain looks good to it? Let it eat! It must not be subjected to the frustration of facing food while it works and is itself muzzled. "*Lo tachsom.*" Don't muzzle the ox as it threshes. And this was extended by rabbinic interpretation to other animals, even birds, working within sight of food.[1]

Another example: Even at the time when the sacrificial cult was practiced, it was forbidden to take a newborn ox, sheep, or goat from the mother until it had at least seven days of warmth and nourishment directly from its mother (Leviticus 22:27). The idea that a newborn sacrifice is superior was rejected by the Bible lest there be the immediate theft of the offspring from the warm suckling of the mother.

There are other provisions, including the commandment that we're all familiar with: "Remember the Sabbath day and keep it holy. Six days you shall labor and do all your work, but the seventh day is a Sabbath of the Lord your God: you shall not do any work—you, your son or daughter, your male or female slave, or your cattle, or the stranger who is within your settlements" (Exodus 20:8–10). Less famous but even more significant is the provision in Exodus 23:12. "Six days you shall do your work, but on the seventh day you shall cease from labor, in order that your ox and your ass may rest, and that your bondsman and the stranger may be refreshed." Here the Sabbath is proclaimed not only for the sake of man but for the sake of animals as well!

All of this could be summed up in the saying in Proverbs: *vo-de-a tza-dik ne-fesh b'hem-to,* "the decent man considers the life of the beast" (12:10).

Nor is the notion confined in the West only to the Jewish tradition. One of the great figures of Western culture is surely Francisca of Assisi, called St. Francis by the Church. Many of you are undoubtedly familiar with St. Francis' great friendship with other creatures, and you probably recall that St. Bonaventure, in *The Life of St. Francis,* mentions that when Francis "bethought himself of the first beginning of all things, he was filled with a yet more overflowing charity, and would call the dumb animals, howsoever small, by the names of brother and sister, forasmuch as he recognized in them the same origin as in himself."[2] And many of you, I'm sure, also are aware of the provision in *The Mirror of Perfection* which St. Francis urges upon the emperor: "to make a law that men should make a good provision for birds and oxen and asses and the poor at Christmas time," with a specification thereof.[3]

It is against this background of biblical and traditional Western religious concern for all living creatures, then, that I want briefly to view this new development: so-called factory farming or intensive rearing. What do the terms mean? Not simply the use of machines in farming, nor the striving for efficiency as such, but rather the uncritical application of technology to animal rearing so that animals, admittedly useful to man, are not regarded as fellow creatures.

It's an enterprise with which many of you are surely more familiar than I, but the effect on the observer is quite shocking. My own awareness of the development dates from a couple of years ago when my wife and I were in Maine, driving along a country road at night, and discovered time and again buildings, multistoried, with light shining from them, looking very much like urban apartment dwellings. Yet there was no signs of any other habitations around, no sizable towns on the map, and it was very puzzling. A couple of days later, walking along a country road, we came upon one such building by daylight and discovered that a door was open. There was netting across the opening, making sure that none of the "contents" of the structure would spill out, and we saw crowded against the netting, piled on top of one another, countless numbers of chickens. From an elevated vantage point we were able to discern that this particular structure contained tens of hundreds of chickens, most of them in a semigloom, barely visible, obviously enclosed permanently. We were rather horrified by this forcible enclosure of beings who, however "low" on the evolutionary scale, presumably are gifted with flesh, blood, and at least a rudimentary sensory apparatus. For it is now the case that millions of animals spend their entire lives in darkness or semidarkness, without any free exposure to the natural elements, crowded together in pitiless fashion, subsisting but hardly living.

"... Day-old chicks are installed, eight or ten thousand at a time, sometimes more, in long, windowless houses punctuated only with extractor fans in surried rows along the ridge of the roofs, and air intake vents along the side walls... Inside a house the impression is of a long, wide, dark tunnel disappearing into the gloom, the floor covered with chickens as far as the eye can see."[4]

And the results? "The battery chickens I have observed seem to lose their minds about the time they would normally be weaned by their mothers and off in the weeds chasing grasshoppers on their own account. Yes, literally, the battery becomes a gallinaceous madhouse. The eyes of these chickens through the bars gleam like those of maniacs. Let your hand get within reach and it receives a dozen vicious pecks—not the love peck or the tentative peck of idle curiosity bestowed by the normal chicken, but a peck that means business, a peck for flesh and blood, for which in their madness they are thirsting. They eat feathers out of each other's backs or, rather, pull out each other's feathers and nibble voraciously at the roots of the same for tiny blocks of flesh and blood that may adhere thereto."5

Thus feather-pecking and cannibalism replace the normal "pecking order" of the farmyard. And the "solutions" to these technologically created problems? Not the establishment of conditions of life considerate of the instinctual needs of these creatures, but rather debeaking, reduced light, the fitting of opaque "specs" which prevent the chicken from seeing directly in front of it, cages, etc.

Please notice that I am not raising the issue of a few technological improvements, nor am I raising the issue of food production, though that is a consideration. Neither am I raising the question of the ultimate end of these animals, slaughter for human food, though that also is a question. I am rather asking that in the light of our religious heritage we face the question posed by Ruth Harrison in *Animal Machines*: "How far have we the right to take our domination of the animal world? Have we the right to rob them of all pleasures in life simply to make more money more quickly out of their carcasses? Have we the right to treat living creatures solely as food converting machines? At what point do we acknowledge cruelty?"6 In the words of St. Francis, even while they live, how in fact are we treating our "brothers and sisters" who help sustain us? In the words of Proverbs, how are we regarding the lives of our beasts?

Listen to the terms we use now. As Ruth Harrison points out, the animal terms "hens" and "chickens" have become changed to such terms as "capons," a marketably profitable result of hormonal distortion, or "broilers," a term descriptive of the end result of creatures whose living identity no longer matters to us.

Listen to this quotation from a technical journal: "The modern layer is, after all, only a very efficient converting machine, changing the raw materials—feeding stuffs—into the finished produce—the egg—less, of course, maintenance requirements."7

And such examples can be brought in relation to veal calves, milk cows, and other animals whose very animality is disregarded in this one-dimensional viewing of them as mere food machines.

And please let's dispel a certain kind of technological provincialism. Technology has never before on this planet been developed to its present heights. But there was awareness long ago of the fact that if you let an animal run around, part of the energy which could go into eggs or milk or flesh for consumption is dissipated. It's interesting that there is a discussion by a medieval Jewish commentator in which he asks whether the provisions for resting the beast on the Sabbath mean that you simply rest the beast while being permitted to keep it enclosed, or whether this requires that the beast be permitted to graze freely on the farmland, nibbling the grass, etc. And the opinion of the commentator is that because the Bible uses the term "that your beast enjoy," it is required that it be permitted free grazing.[8] All of which suggests that the calculations we make and can act on with greater efficiency in our age are not unique to our age. The most significant difference between previous ages and our own may be that while they to some extent regarded the lives of their beasts, we seemingly manage to ignore them almost completely.

"To some extent, as the [Agricultural] Minister is so fond of telling us, farm animals have always been exploited by man in that he rears them specifically for food. But until recently they were individuals, allowed their birthright of green fields, sunlight, and fresh air; they were allowed to forage, to exercise, to watch the world go by, in fact to live. Even at its worst, with insufficient protection against inclement weather or poor supplementation of natural food, the animal had some enjoyment in life before it died. Today the exploitation has been taken to a degree which involves not only the elimination of all enjoyment, the frustration of almost all natural instincts, but its replacement with acute discomfort, boredom, and the actual denial of health. It has been taken to a degree where the animal is not allowed to live before it dies."[9]

Let me briefly suggest also that if we were to look closely at the issue, it might even occur to us that the issue of respect for animals is really the issue of respect for life as such. Great seers such as Gandhi and Schweitzer also suggest that life is a continuum, and that one cannot make arbitrary cuts anywhere in the chain without doing injury at all levels. The least that Darwinism should mean for rational man is that, in a continuum, orientation toward one level of life will affect orientation toward all other levels of life. The issue of treatment of His beasts is, I suspect, in a subtle way also the issue of the treatment of other human beings and ourselves as well. There are those who have noticed that the sound of the planet is somewhat different now from what it used to be. St. Francis heard the songs of the beasts in praise of the Lord, and the psalmist recites his extravagant poetry with the accompanying sounds of all Creation praising Him, the Creator of all life. Our own ears seem to hear only the whir of machinery, not only as once in cities and factories, but now increasingly in the mangers of the beasts and the nests of the feathered ones, and this, I think, poses yet another part of the grave problem for us.

I want to conclude with a story about one of the Hasidic rabbis, Reb Zusya.

Once Rabbi Zusya traveled cross-country collecting money to ransom prisoners. He came to an inn at a time when the innkeeper was not at home. He went through the rooms, according to his custom, and in one saw a large cage with all kinds of birds. And Zusya saw that the caged creatures wanted to fly through the spaces of the world and be free birds again. He burned with pity for them and said to himself: "Here you are, Zusya, walking your feet off to ransom prisoners. But what greater ransoming of prisoners can there be than to free these birds from their prison?" Then he opened the cage, and the birds flew out into freedom.

When the innkeeper returned and saw the empty cage, he was very angry, and asked the people in the house who had done this to him. They answered: "A man is loitering about here and he looks like a fool. No one but he can have done this thing." The innkeeper shouted at Zusya: "You fool! How could you have the impudence to rob me of my birds and make worthless the good money I paid for them?" Zusya replied: "You have often read and repeated these words in the psalm: 'His tender mercies are over all His works.'" Then the innkeeper beat him until his hand grew tired and finally threw him out of the house. And Zusya went his way serenely.10

The conditions of captivity are different and the requirement for freeing the birds and other animals perhaps less radical. But their captors today will not initially smile at any attempt to reopen the cages, and those so concerned will seem, like Reb Zusya and St. Francis, rather strange and somewhat queer creatures. There will be verbal beatings, and out of many an agricultural establishment and academic department we are likely to be tossed unceremoniously. But I would nonetheless suggest that if ever again on this anguished planet we are to realize that His tender mercies do indeed extend over all His works, even human creatures; and if ever again we are to sing a full hymn of praise to the Creator of all Life, then somehow all of us must ourselves regain, and help our society itself regain, some considerable regard for the lives of our beasts.

NOTES

1. Rashi, citing *Talmud Baba Metziah* 94b in support.

2. Ch. VIII, Sec. 6.

3. Sec. XII, Ch. CXIV.

4. Ruth Harrison, *Animal Machines* (London: Vincent Street Ltd., 1964), 12.

5. *Ibid.*, 154–44.

6. *Ibid.*, 3.

7. *Ibid.*, 50.

8. Rashi on Exodus 23:12.

9. Harrison, op., *Animal Machines,* cit., p. 3.

10. *Tales of the Hasidim* by Martin Buber, vol. I, 249.

The Religious Justification

for Vegetarianism

JOSEPH ROSENFELD

Joseph Rosenfeld, Jerusalem-born and for many years Minister of London's Sinai Synagogue, offers here a reading of the familiar story of Cain and Abel that is fascinatingly original. Patiently probing the text in the best tradition of Talmudic exegesis, Rabbi Rosenfeld asks why it is that God did not follow the law and put Cain immediately to death for slaying his brother Abel. Rosenfeld's subtle answer to this question is a uniquely Judaic justification of vegetarianism in which Abel, who offered butchered animals as a sacrifice unto the Lord, and not Cain, is seen as the first transgressor of the ancient prohibition against killing. The conclusion, in Rosenfeld's judgment, is that the commandment against killing extends to animals as well as humans.

Those who study the Bible do not need a Rabbi to prove to them that there is religious justification for vegetarianism and those who are ideally convinced of the soundness of the philosophy of vegetarianism as a way of life will continue to practice that ideal whether it is religiously justified or not. Accordingly I have jotted down some biblical and Talmudic references and will be indebted for any sources I fail to quote. And so I had better start, like all things, at the beginning.

All creatures are endowed with two irresistible instincts, self-preservation and procreation, and the latter can surely be said to be complementary to the first. When Adam and Eve first roamed the hills and plains that surrounded them they were ignorant of everything, and like all creatures were following their instincts; they did not know how to cohabit or perform all the other functions of life. Each species adopted its own way of life according to its structure and environment; one copied the others and man copied much of his behavior from them. Unfortunately the baser instincts of animal behavior have not yet been eradicated from us and become more manifest when these two main instincts are faced with opposition and in danger of remaining unsatisfied. Civilization has not altered much of our behavior in our efforts to satisfy these instincts, and later on I will attempt to give you the reasons and humbly suggest the remedy.

For ten generations from Adam to Noah, no flesh of any creature was permitted to be eaten. Genesis 1:29 is quite explicit. "Behold I have given you every herb yielding seed which is upon the face of all the earth, and every tree, in which is the fruit of the tree yielding seed—to you it shall be for food." And not only was the instruction directed to man but also to all creatures as stated in verse 30. "And to every beast of the earth, and to every fowl of the air, and to every thing that creepeth upon the earth, wherein there is a living soul, I have given every green herb for food. And it was so." It is on these verses that Rabbi Judah bases his statements in *Tractate Sanhedrin* 59:2. Up to Noah the eating of flesh was prohibited.

At this stage I would like to pass before you a problem and I cannot trace that it has been raised by any of the known and renowned commentators.

Everyone knows the story of Cain and Abel, as related in Genesis, chapter 4, but it would be instructive to review it in order to show what is so puzzling about the sequence of events. Cain devoted himself to tilling the ground and the produce of the land while Abel became a shepherd of sheep. Cain brought an offering to God of the fruit of the land, apparently not of the best, and God did not show favor. Abel brought his offering from the fullest and choicest of his sheep, to which God showed favor. Cain was angry and God told him if he would do better he would be forgiven. Then Cain said something to Abel and when they were in the field Cain arose and killed his brother Abel.

There are several questions which present themselves to us. What was wrong with Cain's offering? True, it was not of the choicest of the fruit, still it was an offering and after all it was he who first thought of the idea of a thanks-offering. So why was he slighted? The second question is: what was it that Cain said to Abel before he killed him? The Bible does not tell us. The third and most potent question is: why was Cain not sentenced to death for the capital crime he committed? His only punishment was banishment from society and what is more puzzling is Cain's plea, "Is then my sin too great to be forgiven? Anyone who will find me will kill me." God presented him with a sign to save him from being assassinated. An amazing plea from the lips of a murderer and an even more surprising response from the judge of all things on earth. Seven generations later, Cain's great-great-grandson was out hunting and as his sight was failing him, his boy accompanied him to pin-point the position of any animal. Cain was mistaken for an animal and was killed by Lemech. On discovering his mistake, Lemech clapped his hands in remorse and killed his own son in the process. These questions troubled me very much and I failed to find the answers until a little while ago when another very curious question came to my mind. The question which perplexed me was why Abel was killed, and I had an irresistible desire to delve deeper until I found a satisfactory explanation.

We know that no one was punished unless something had been done to deserve it, especially when it concerned capital offense. Now what did Abel do to deserve death? Nowhere in the Bible or anywhere else is there any hint that he sinned against the Lord or man, certainly not to deserve death. Then why was he murdered? The answer came like a flash and I realized that this would answer the other questions. For ten generations up to Noah no creature was allowed to eat flesh. No living creature was to be killed by either man or beast for any purpose whatsoever. Although the purpose for which Abel killed the fattest and choicest of his sheep was an offering to God, it did not alter the fact that he shed the blood of an innocent sheep, albeit for a selfless motive. The answer to my first question as to why Cain's offering was not accepted is simple. Here is the first lesson of how to shape our characters. When we make an offering it should be of the best. God accepted Abel's offering rather than Cain's not because the one was of a living creature and the other was of the fruit of the land. Does then the Lord require animal sacrifices? Isaiah 1:11: "To what purpose is the multitude of your sacrifices unto me?" said the Lord. "I am full of the burnt-offerings of rams and the fat of the fed beasts and I delight not in the blood of bullocks or of the lambs or he-goats"; and 22:13: "And behold joy and gladness, slaying oxen and killing sheep, eating flesh and drinking wine—let us eat and drink for tomorrow we shall die. Surely this iniquity shall not be expiated by you till ye die."

We can now understand what Cain said to Abel before he killed him. "Why did you slay those innocent lambs? If you desired to bring a thank-offering to the Lord then you should have brought him from the toil of your hands and not at the expense of the lives of others." This also explains why Cain was not sentenced to die immediately but was postponed for seven generations. Cain, and this is my own personal opinion, thought that in killing his brother he was carrying out the commandment of the Lord. Did not God say, Genesis 9:5: "But the blood of your souls I will demand. I will demand it from the hand of every beast and from the hand of man."

I am no longer puzzled and perplexed why Abel died. He was the first to break the law of God. Cain was not the first man to kill, it was Abel who first shed the blood and took the life of a living creature and so had to die in consequence of his deed. There is no difference between depriving the life and soul of man and that of an animal. Does not King Solomon tell us [in] Ecclesiastes 3:21: "Who knows whether the spirit of the sons of man ascends above, or the spirit of the cattle descends down into the earth?"

In my contact with many vegetarians I detect that the greater majority have forsaken a carnivorous diet for health reasons rather than for the lofty ideal itself that it is wrong in principle to be carnivorous. It is, of course, right and proper that we should look after our health and adhere to a diet which preserves and prolongs life, which surely a vegetarian diet does. But if you reduce the ethical values of vegetarianism to the pursuit of health then you are just as likely to revert to your former habits of flesh eating when someone will cite the example of a number of people who live to the age of ninety and even to one hundred and who have been eating flesh all their lives. To think of vegetarianism in terms of health only is equating our lives with that of the animal. I have always wondered what Solomon, the cleverest of all men, meant when he said [in] Ecc. 3:19: "And the pre-eminence of man over beast is naught for all is vanity." Surely a man and especially men like Solomon himself could not be said that they are not of greater eminence than the animal. It is inconceivable that man with all his apparent superiority, thought, design and deeds, could be classified on the same level as the beast. Yet this is what Solomon seems to tell us. On reflection, however, I came to the conclusion, and incidentally this is my own opinion, that the translators have all erred in their interpretation of the last part of this verse. The mistake lies in the translation of the word *Kee*; this word has several meanings and in this context the only sensible and correct translation would be *when*. The whole verse assumes now quite a different aspect and meaning thus: "and the pre-eminence of man over beast is naught *when* all is vanity."

If man is occupied throughout his life in the pursuit of his basic instincts, eating, drinking and the seeking of pleasures, in this sense there is no advantage of man over beast. The animal likewise is preoccupied all its life in the pursuit of satisfying its basic instincts. It too has its pleasures, limited though they may be; the coolness of water, the shade of a tree, the warmth of the sun. This is why I am not impressed with vegetarians who are concerned only with their state of health. Far better to adopt a vegetarian way of life as an ideal, only then will you be a good and convincing example to others.

Admittedly it is difficult for Jewish people to discard their carnivorous way of life; to provide for Sabbaths and festivals the expensive delicacies of meat and fish. But the Talmud (*Pessachim* 109a) states "Rabbi Yehuda who said that there is no *Simcha* [occasion for rejoicing] only with meat, agrees that this only applied at the time when the Temple was in existence." We also find in *Tracte Babba Bathra* 608, Rabbi Yishmael said "from the day that the Holy Temple was destroyed it would have been right to have imposed on ourselves the law prohibiting the eating of flesh." But the Rabbis have laid down a wise and logical ruling that the authorities must not impose any decree unless the majority of the members of the Community are able to abide by it. Otherwise the law and those who administer it get into disrepute.

That is why ten generations after Adam man was so corrupt that, like the ferocious animal, he would tear a limb from a living creature, eat it and drink its blood. The Torah, realizing that it would take many generations of special training before man's soul would become completely refined, permitted the eating of flesh after Noah but with many reservations and restrictions. Hence the humane laws of *Shechita* [ritual slaughter] and the dietary laws of *Kashrut*: for example, the soaking for an hour or half an hour and salting of Kosher meat before we are allowed to cook it, in order to extract the maximum amount of blood of which we are not allowed to partake. "For blood is the soul." Life, thought, character, behavior, are all contained in the chemicals comprised in the blood. The less of the animal blood in man, the purer his soul becomes, the nearer he gets to the Divine being. When the Israelites were near the *Mishcon*, the Sanctuary, the eating of flesh was forbidden to them (*Orlah* 2, *Mishnah* 17). It is true, therefore, that the eating of flesh is looked upon as a lust and Jewish law aims to restrict and arrest that diet. Thousands of years of adhering to these traditional dietary laws have resulted in a gradual process of purification to the soul, and there is no doubt that these teachings had a profound effect upon the civilized nature of the Jew who as a rule is rarely found guilty of wanton cruelty, either to animals or man.

The best story I have heard which illustrates this lack of cruelty for the sake of sport or revenge is the following: Yankel and Mendel were in the habit of discussing aspects of the law every morning after the service at the Synagogue. One morning they became involved in a very heated argument when Yankel called Mendel a swindler. The latter was enraged and he told Yankel that the only way to settle the matter was by duel with guns. It was accordingly arranged to meet the next morning at 6 A.M. in the local park. Mendel and his seconds arrived punctually at six o'clock and it was nearing seven and Yankel had still not arrived. Mendel was about to depart calling his opponent a coward when he saw Yankel's second running toward him. They came to apologize on behalf of Yankel who forgot that he had *Yahrzeit* (Memorial Service) and could not come before eight o'clock but in the meantime he had no objection if Mendel started shooting.

These estimable characteristics of mercy, kindness, compassion, and charitableness so much pronounced among the Jewish people is a result of following for generations the laws of the Torah and the instructions of the Prophets. David said in Psalm 145:9: "God is good to all and his tender mercies are over all His works." Force of habit leads us to think that we cannot or must not do without flesh, but the Torah does not say you must or should eat flesh. Knowing the weakness of man it permitted only certain animals, and then only after *Shechita* had been performed, which was the humane way of ending the life of a creature. But we must train ourselves to discard that habit which has been ingrained in us for generations. Every creature has a right to live and no one has a right to destroy life.

A Firm and Joyous Voice of Life

ABRAHAM ISAAC KOOK

First Askenazic chief rabbi of Palestine after the British mandate, prolific writer, and mystic, Rabbi Kook (1865–1935) was also an influential defender of religious vegetarianism. The signature characteristic of his approach is the claim that a moral and spiritual evolutionism is at work in history, one that is gradually moving us toward love and justice for all life, animal as well as human. According to Kook, human compassion and concern for animals is natural. But after the Fall, self-centeredness and a will to violence induced forgetfulness of our original awareness of the sacred nature of life. Kashrut, or kosher laws, are institutionalized attempts, inspired by God, to reawaken in us a "firm and joyous" reaffirmation of life. They provide the "moral therapy" humans need to progress to higher stages of spiritual development.

The free movement of the moral impulse to establish justice for animals generally and the claim of their rights from mankind are hidden in a natural psychic sensibility in the deeper layers of the Torah. In the ancient value system of humanity, while the spiritual illumination (which later found its bastion in Israel) was diffused among individuals without involvement in a national framework, before nations were differentiated into distinct speech forms, the moral sense had risen to a point of demanding justice for animals. "The first man had not been allowed to eat meat" (*Sanhed.* 59b), as is implied in God's instruction to Adam: "I have given you every herb yielding seed which is on the face of all the earth, and every tree in which is the fruit of a tree yielding seed—it shall be to you for food" (Genesis 1:29). But when humanity, in the course of its development, suffered a setback and was unable to bear the great light of its illumination, its receptive capacity being impaired, it was withdrawn from the fellowship with other creatures, whom it excelled with firm spiritual superiority. Now it became necessary to confine the concern with justice and equity to mankind, so that divine fire, burning with a very dim light, might be able to warm the heart of man, which had cooled off as a result of the many pressures of life. The changes in thought and disposition, in the ways of particularized developments, required that moral duty be concentrated on the plane of humanity alone. But the thrust of the ideals in the course of their development will not always remain confined. Just as the democratic aspiration will reach outward through the general intellectual and moral perfection, "when man shall no longer teach his brother to know the Lord, for they will all know Me, small and great alike" (Jeremiah 31:34), so will the hidden yearning to act justly toward animals emerge at the proper time. What prepares the ground for this state is the commandments, those intended specifically for this area of concern.

There is indeed a hidden reprimand between the lines of the Torah in the sanction to eat meat, for it is only after "you will say, I will eat meat, because you lust after eating meat—then you may slaughter and eat" (Deuteronomy 12:20, 12:15). The only way you would be able to overcome your inclination would be through a moral struggle, but the time for this conquest is not yet. It is necessary for you to wage it in areas closer to yourself. The long road of development, after man's fall, also needs physical exertion, which will at times require a meat diet, which is a tax for passage to a more enlightened epoch, from which animals are not exempt. Human beings also acted thus in their most justified wars, which were incumbent on them as a transition to a higher general state.

This is the advantage of the moral sense when it is linked to its divine source. It knows the proper timing for each objective, and it will sometimes suppress its flow in order to gather up its strength for future epochs, something that the impatient kind of morality that is detached from its source would be unable to tolerate. When the animal lust for meat became overpowering, if the flesh of all living beings had been forbidden, then the moral destructiveness, which will always appear at such times, would not have differentiated between man and animal, beast and fowl and every creeping thing on the earth. The knife, the axe, the guillotine, the electric current, would have felled them all alike in order to satisfy the vulgar craving of so-called cultured humanity.

The commandments, therefore, came to regulate the eating of meat, in steps that will take us to the higher purpose. The living beings we are permitted to eat are limited to those that are most suitable to the nature of man. The commandment to cover the blood of an animal or bird captured while hunting focuses on a most apparent and conspicuous inequity. These creatures are not fed by man, they impose no burden on him to raise them and develop them. The verse "If anyone ... captures by hunting any beast or bird that may be eaten, he must pour out its blood, covering the earth" (Leviticus 17:13) involves an acknowledgment of a shameful act. This is the beginning of moral therapy, as is suggested in the verse, "...that you may remember and be ashamed... when I forgive you" (Ezekiel 16:63). It means: Cover the blood! Hide your shame! These efforts will bear fruit; in the course of time people will be educated. The silent protest will in time be transformed into a mighty shout and it will triumph in its objective. The regulations of slaughter, in special prescriptions, to reduce the pain of the animal registers a reminder that we are not dealing with things outside the law, that they are not automatons devoid of life, but with living things. What is inscribed in such letters on rolls of parchment will be read in the future, when the human heart will be conditioned for it. The feelings of the animal, the sensitivity to its family attachment implied in the rule not to slaughter an ox or a sheep "with its young on the same day" (Leviticus 22:28), and, on the other hand, the caution against callous violation of the moral sense in an act of cruelty shown particularly in the breakup of the family implied in the directive concerning a bird's nest, to let the mother bird go before taking the young (Deuteronomy 22:26–27)—all these join in a mighty demonstration against the general inequity that stirs every heart, and renews vitality even to souls that have strayed, whose hearts have grown dull because of sickness and anger. The divine protest could not extend to man's right over the animal raised by him, until a much later time. Then concern will even be shown for the taste of the food eaten by the tilling animal, expressing a permanent spirit of compassion and an explicit sense of justice. "Oxen and asses that till the soil will eat their fodder savored with spices, and winnowed with shovel and fan to remove the chaff" (Isaiah 30:24).

The prohibition of eating the fat comes to us, on the other hand, in a subdued call. If, by necessity, to strengthen your prowess, you slaughter the animal, which you raised by your exertion, do not indulge in this to satisfy the vulgar craving that lusts for fat, especially in the primitive stages of man. When the savage luxury of eating fat and blood—one can always find room for a delicacy—is forbidden, it takes away the worst element of this cruel gluttony. The impact of this provision will become apparent in the full maturing of culture that is due to come in the future.

The legal inequity in the ownership of property is registered in the prohibition of wearing a mixed garment of wool and linen. We are inhibited from the free mixing of wool, which was taken by robbery from the innocent sheep, with flax, which was acquired by equitable, pleasant and cultured labor. The animal will yet rise in cultural status through the control of a higher moral sense, so that its readiness for idealistic participation with man will not be strange or far away. Therefore we are directed to add to the fringe on a linen garment a woolen thread of blue [as a reminder of God and of the divine law ordained in

Numbers 15:38], and similarly to mix freely a mixture of wool and linen in the garment of the priests (Exodus 28:5,8) [the priestly vestments were to be made of "blue, purple and scarlet" yarn, which is of wool and twined linen].

The mixing of meat and milk is a grave offense, an act that is pervaded altogether with the oppression of life, an oppression of a living being—and of property. Milk, which serves so naturally to feed the tender child, that he might enjoy the mother's breast, was not created so as to stuff with it the stomach, when you are so hard and cruel as to eat meat. The tender child has a prior and more natural right than you.

Just as the rule to cover the blood extends the sway of "You shall not murder" to the domain of the animal, and the prohibition of mixing meat and milk and the banning of linen and wool in a garment extends the injunctions, "You shall not rob" and "You shall not oppress," so does the rule against eating the meat of an animal killed by another animal or one that died by itself extend the duty to offer help and visit the sick to the animal kingdom: be compassionate at least on the unfortunate ones, if your heart is insensitive to the healthy and the strong.

When this seed is planted in the thick earth of the field blessed by the Lord, it will bear its fruit. It is necessary for its cultivation to join all these sensibilities into a national center so that the echo released by the moral voice shall not be the voice of weaklings, of ascetics and timid spirits, but the firm and joyous voice of life.

THE CHRISTIAN
TRADITION

*The Saints are exceedingly loving
and gentle to mankind, and even to
brute beasts. . . Surely we ought
to show [animals] great kindness
and gentleness for many reasons,
but, above all, because they are of
the same origin as ourselves.*

—St. John Chrysostom, *Homilies*

C hristianity and vegetarianism have had an uncomfortable relationship
with one another over the centuries. Individual Christians and a few
Christian sects (e.g., the tenth-century Slavic Bogomils, the eleventh-century
Cathars, and contemporary Seventh Day Adventists[1]) have championed a meatless diet, but mainstream Christianity generally has not viewed vegetarianism as
a spiritual goal. Even today, when more and more Christians agree with the theologian and animal rights advocate Carol Adams that it's impossible to feed on
both grace and animals, the attitude of the broader Christian community to
vegetarianism is at best ambivalent.

This ambivalence stems in part from Christianity's Judaic roots. As we saw
in the preceding section, Judaism traditionally teaches compassion and reverence for all life, but at the same time allows the slaughter, *kashrut*-regulated
though it is, of animals for food (and, in ancient times, for sacrifice). Christianity

inherited this tension. On the one hand, the early church believed (as did devout Jews) that God's original Edenic intention was that humans and animals should live together in peace, and many early Christians refused to partake of flesh. Tradition has it that James, brother of Jesus and leader of the Jerusalem church, never ate animal food, and that late in life the apostle Peter also lived on grain and fruit. According to legend, the gospelist Matthew was also an herbivore. But on the other hand, there's no oral or scriptural evidence to suggest that Jesus of Nazareth adopted a vegetable diet. Scripture records, in fact, that he definitely partook of fish (Luke 24:43), and it's incredible to suppose that a first century, non-Essene Jew would not also have eaten meat on holy days such as Passover.

As a further complication, the early church was confronted with a number of competing heretical or pagan movements that espoused a meatless diet. Both gnostics and Manicheans, primarily because of their repugnance for the corporeal, advocated vegetarianism on the grounds that the human soul, striving for union with God, was weighed down by a diet of corpses. In fulminating against such heretics, the church fathers typically condemned their eating habits as well. Moreover, the fact that flesh consumption was a sign of social and economic status, which many early Christians were eager to attain, only served to push the church farther away from taking vegetarianism as a serious spiritual discipline.

The upshot is that for centuries, through the Middle Ages and Renaissance right up to the modern era, conventional Christian wisdom held that the slaughter of animals for food was permissible. Even those occasional voices of dissent—Tertullian and Clement of Alexandria in the third century, Saints Jerome and John Chrysostom in the fourth, the fifth century's desert fathers and mothers, St. Benedict in the sixth, St. Francis in the thirteenth, Erasmus and Thomas More in the sixteenth—objected to the eating of animals primarily on ascetic grounds: to gorge oneself on flesh (or any other food, for that matter) was to become enslaved to carnal appetite. Little concern was shown for the well-being of animals, or the detrimental spiritual consequences for humans of shedding animal blood. The standard view was that humans were given dominion over birds of the air, fish of the seas, and beasts of the earth. This frequently translated, particularly after the scientific and industrial revolutions of the seventeenth and eighteenth centuries, into the presumption that God's sole reason for creating animals was so they could service and feed humanity.

This sentiment in the Christian community has undergone radical changes in recent years. Many theologians and laypersons now realize that the stewardship of nature given to humans by God shouldn't be understood as one of conquest and domination. Instead, the call to Christian stewardship entails an *imitatio* of the compassion, nonviolence, and shepherdlike nurturing of Jesus Christ. Andrew Linzey, for example, argues that we are called to share Jesus' special concern for the powerless and oppressed. Because animals in a flesh-eating culture are especially vulnerable to suffering and slaughter, Linzey concludes that a vegetarian diet is not only compatible with but essential to the Christian message of compassionate love. Similarly, Carol Adams denounces meat eating as institutionalized violence that is as antithetical to the Christian spirit as any other form of "officially" sanctioned violence. We can feed on violently slain animals, she says, or we can feed on the compassionate love offered us by divine grace. But we cannot partake of both.

If the spiritual life is a seamless garment, then what we do in our ordinary, everyday lives both influences and is influenced by our religious beliefs. If we affirm a religion that preaches nonviolence and compassion for all living creatures, that commitment should be exemplified in how we live from day to day. As Francis Clooney writes, refusing to participate, even indirectly, in the slaughter of food animals is one way for Christians to bridge conviction and practice. The sanctification of our meals that occurs when we expunge them of violence is particularly appropriate to a faith tradition in which the act of eating, exemplified in the Eucharist, has always been seen as holy. Forbearance also provides an opportunity, as philosopher Tom Regan reminds us in his essay, to celebrate in word as well as deed the intrinsic goodness of divine creation. Animals possess independent rather than merely instrumental or utilitarian value. They are living expressions of God's creative love. When we treat them compassionately, we not only honor God. We also help to co-create the universal fullness God intends for reality.

NOTES

1. For an interesting discussion of "heretical" Christian sects that have advocated vegetarianism as a spiritual discipline, see Colin Spencer, *The Heretic's Feast: A History of Vegetarianism* (Hanover: University Press of New England, 1995), 108–200.

Vegetarianism as a Biblical Ideal

ANDREW LINZEY

In this selection from his book Animal Theology, *Andrew Linzey, Anglican priest, author, professor, and leading proponent of Christian vegetarianism, argues that a careful examination of passages in Genesis and Isaiah suggests that the Judaic-Christian prohibition against killing originally extended to animals as well as humans, and that the future Kingdom of God will reinstate the pre-Fall ideal of nonaggression. Linzey allows that in certain historical and geographical contexts the slaughter of animals for food may have been an unhappy necessity. Jesus, for example, who lived in a land with scarce vegetable sources of protein, probably ate fish and perhaps meat as well. Moreover, Linzey agrees with Jewish vegetarians such as Roberta Kalechofsky and Rabbi Abraham Isaac Kook that God reluctantly tolerates animal slaughter as a concession to human weakness. But Jesus' special affinity for the weak, powerless, and oppressed, as well as his teachings on nonviolence, make it clear that where it is possible for the Christian to abstain from killing animals for food, he or she is called upon to do so.*

Of all the ethical challenges arising from animal theology, vegetarianism can arguably claim to have the strongest biblical support. Even the acceptance of the minimalist principle of avoiding injury to sentients wherever possible renders killing for gastronomic pleasure unacceptable. In this chapter, I chart the outline of the argument drawn from Genesis and Isaiah while also taking account of the fact that Jesus is not depicted as a vegetarian in the canonical Gospels. Even if we accept that Genesis 9 permits meat-eating as a special concession to human sinfulness, it still remains an open question as to whether carnivorousness can be justified as a matter of principle.

FOOD OF PARADISE

> And God said, "Behold, I have given you every plant yielding seed which is upon the face of all the earth, and every tree with seed in its fruit; you shall have them for food. And to every beast of the earth, and to every bird of the air, and to everything that creeps on the earth, everything that has the breath of life, I have given every green plant for food." (Genesis 1:29–30, RSV)

> And God blessed Noah and his sons, and said to them, "...Every moving thing that lives shall be food for you; as I gave you the green plants, I give you everything." (Genesis 9:1–4, RSV)

At first glance, these two passages may be taken as epitomizing the difficulty of appealing to scripture in the contemporary debate about animal rights. The sheer contradictoriness of these statements presses itself upon us. Genesis 1 clearly depicts vegetarianism as divine command. Indeed "everything" that has the breath of life in it, is given "green plant for food." Genesis 9, however, reverses this command quite specifically. "[A]s I gave you the green plants, I give you everything" (9:3). In the light of this, the question might not unreasonably be posed: Cannot both vegetarians and carnivores appeal to scripture for justification and both with *equal* support?

In order to unravel this conundrum we have first of all to appreciate that the community whose spokesperson wrote Genesis 1 were not themselves vegetarians. Few appreciate that Genesis 1 and 2 are each the products of much later reflection by the biblical writers themselves. How is it then that the very people who were not vegetarian imagined a beginning of time when all who lived were vegetarian (herbivore to be precise) by divine command?

To appreciate this perspective we need to recall the major elements of the first creation saga. God creates a world of great diversity and fertility. Every living creature is given life and space (Genesis 1:9–10, 24–25), earth to live on and blessing to enable life itself (1:22). Living creatures are pronounced good (1:25). Humans are made in God's image (1:27), given dominion (1:26–29), and then prescribed a vegetarian diet (1:29–30). God then pronounces that everything was "very good" (1:31). Together the whole creation rests on the sabbath with God (2:2–3). When examined in this way, we should see immediately that Genesis 1 describes a state of paradisal existence. There is no hint of violence between or among different species. Dominion, so often interpreted as justifying killing, actually precedes the command to be vegetarian. Herb-eating dominion is hardly a license for tyranny. The answer seems to be then that even though the early Hebrews were neither pacifists nor vegetarians, they were deeply convinced of the view that violence between humans and animals, and indeed between animal species themselves, was not God's original will for creation.

But if this is true, how are we to reconcile Genesis 1 with Genesis 9, the vision of original peacefulness with the apparent legitimacy of killing for food? The answer seems to be that as the Hebrews began to construct the story of early human beginnings, they were struck by the prevalence and enormity of human wickedness. The stories of Adam and Eve, Cain and Abel, Noah and his descendants are testimonies to the inability of humankind to fulfill the providential purposes of God in creation. The issue is made explicit in the story of Noah:

> Now the earth was corrupt in God's sight, and the earth was filled with violence. And God saw the earth, and behold, it was corrupt; for all flesh had corrupted their way upon the earth. And God said to Noah, "I have determined to make an end of all flesh; for the earth is filled with violence through them." (Genesis 6:11–14, RSV)

The radical message of the Noah story (often overlooked by commentators) is that God would rather not have us be at all if we must be violent. It is violence itself within every part of creation that is the preeminent mark of corruption and sinfulness. It is not for nothing that God concludes that: "I am sorry that I have made them." (Genesis 6:7)

AMBIGUOUS PERMISSION

It is in *this* context—subsequent to the Fall and the Flood—that we need to understand the permission to kill for food in Genesis 9. It reflects entirely the situation of the biblical writers at the time they were writing. Killing—of both humans as well as animals—was simply inevitable given the world as it is and human nature as it is. Corruption and wickedness had made a mess of God's highest hopes for creation. There just had to be some accommodation to human sinfulness. "Every moving thing shall be food for you; and as I gave you the green plants, I give you everything." (Genesis 9:3) For many students of the Bible this seems to have settled the matter of whether humans can be justified in killing animals for food. In the end, it has been thought, God allows it. And there can be no doubt that throughout the centuries this view has prevailed. Meat eating has become the norm. Vegetarians, especially Christian vegetarians, have survived from century to century to find themselves a rather beleagued minority. The majority view can be summed up in this beautifully prosaic line of Calvin:

> For it is an insupportable tyranny, when God, the Creator of all
> things, has laid open to us the earth and the air, in order that we may
> thence take food as from his storehouse, for these to be shut up from
> us by mortal man, who is not able to create even a snail or a fly.[1]

What Calvin appears to overlook, however, as do many in the Christian tradition, is that the permission to kill for food in Genesis 9 is far from uncondi-
tional or absolute:

> Only you shall not eat flesh with its life, that is, its blood. For your
> lifeblood I will surely require a reckoning; of every beast I will
> require it and of man... (Genesis 9:4–5, RSV)

Understanding these lines is far from straightforward. At first sight these quali-
ficatory lines might be seen as obliterating the permission itself. After all, who
can take animal life without the shedding of blood? Who can kill without the
taking of blood, that is, the life itself? In asking these questions we move to the
heart of the problem. For the early Hebrews life was symbolized by, even constituted by, blood itself. To kill *was* to take blood. And yet it is precisely *this* permission which is denied.

It is not surprising then that commentators have simply passed over these
verses suggesting that some ritual, symbolic significance was here entertained
but one which in no way substantially affected the divine allowance to kill. But
this, I suggest, is to minimize the significance of these verses. Rereading these
verses in the light of their original context should go rather like this: The world
in which you live has been corrupted. And yet God has not given up on you.
God has signified a new relationship—a covenant with you—despite all your
violence and unworthiness. Part of this covenant involves a new regulation concerning diet. What was previously forbidden can now—in the present circumstances—be allowed. You may kill for food. But you may kill only on the understanding that you remember that the life you kill is not your own—it belongs
to God. You must not misappropriate what is not your own. As you kill what is
not your own—either animal or human life—so you need to remember that for
every life you kill you are personally accountable to God.[2]

If this reading is correct, and I believe few scholars would now dissent
from this interpretation, it will be seen immediately that Genesis 9 does not
grant humankind some absolute right to kill animals for food. Indeed, properly speaking, there is no *right* to kill. God allows it only under the conditions of
necessity. A recent statement by the Union of Liberal and Progressive
Synagogues expresses it this way: "Only after the Flood (contends Genesis 9:3)
was human consumption of animals permitted and that was later understood as
a concession, both to human weakness and to the supposed scarcity of edible

vegetation."[3] John Austin Baker similarly concludes: "The Old Testament
. . . does nothing to justify the charge that it represents an exploitative, human-
ly egoistical attitude to nature. Although it recognizes man's preying on nature
as a fact, it characterizes that fact as a mark of man's decline from the first perfect intentions of God for him."[4]

To give a more complete account of biblical themes requires us to move
on from Genesis 1 and 2, to Isaiah 11. We need to appreciate that while killing
was sometimes thought to be justifiable in the present time, biblical writers were
also insistent that there would come another time when such killing was unnecessary. This is the time variously known as the "future hope of Israel" or the
"Messianic Age." Isaiah speaks of the one who will establish justice and equity
and universal peace. One of the characteristics of this future age is the return to
the existence envisaged by Genesis 1 before the Fall and the Flood:

> The wolf shall dwell with the lamb, and the leopard shall lie down
> with the kid, and the calf and the lion and the fatling together, and
> a little child shall lead them. The cow and the bear shall feed; their
> young shall lie down together; and the lion shall eat straw like the
> ox. The sucking child shall play over the hole of the asp, and the
> weaned child shall put his hand on the adder's den. They shall not
> hurt or destroy in all my holy mountain; for the earth shall be full
> of the knowledge of the Lord as the waters cover the sea. (Isaiah
> 11:6–9, RSV)

It seems therefore that while the early Hebrews were neither vegetarians nor
pacifists, the ideal of the peaceable kingdom was never lost sight of. In the end,
it was believed, the world would one day be restored according to God's original will for all creation. Note, for example, how the vision of peaceable living
also extends to relations between animals themselves. Not only, it seems, are
humans to live peaceably with animals, but also formerly aggressive animals are
to live peaceably with other animals.

We may sum up the main elements as follows: Killing for food appears
essential in the world as we know it influenced as it is by corruption and
wickedness. But such a state of affairs is not as God originally willed it. Even
when we kill under situations of necessity we have to remember that the lives
we kill do not belong to us and that we are accountable to God. Moreover,
God's ultimate will for creation shall prevail. Whatever the present circumstances, one day all creation, human and animal, shall live in peace. As Anthony
Phillips writes: "While the Old Testament recognizes that this is not an ideal
world, and makes concessions until the messianic kingdom comes, it remains
man's duty to do all in his power to reverence animal life."[5]

LIVING WITHOUT VIOLENCE

It should now be seen that far from being confused and contradictory, biblical narratives on killing for food have not only internal integrity but also relevance to the contemporary debate about animal rights and vegetarianism. There are three challenges in particular that we should grapple with.

The first thing that should be noted is that these biblical perspectives do not minimize the gravity of the act of killing animals. So often in our heavily industrialized societies we think of animals, especially farm animals, as merely food machines or commodities that are to be bought or sold for human consumption. This presumed, institutionalized *right* does not fit easily alongside the covenant of grace. Genesis 1 specifically speaks of animal life as that which "has the breath of life." (1:30) This life is a gift from God. It does not belong to human beings. It may be used only with the greatest reserve and in remembrance of the One from whose creative hands it comes. Those who wish to use animals frivolously or with no regard for their God-given worth cannot easily claim Genesis in support.

Karl Barth is instructive on this point and deserves to be read in full:

> If there is a freedom of man to kill animals, this signifies in any case the adoption of a qualified and in some sense enhanced responsibility. If that of his lordship over the living beast is serious enough, it takes on a new gravity when he sees himself compelled to express his lordship by depriving it of its life. He obviously cannot do this except under the pressure of necessity. Far less than all the other things which he dares to do in relation to animals, may this be ventured unthinkingly and as though it were self-evident. He must never treat this need for defensive and offensive action against the animal world as a natural one, nor include it as a normal element in his thinking or conduct. He must always shrink from this possibility even when he makes use of it. It always contains the sharp counter-question: Who are you, man, to claim that you must venture this to maintain, support, enrich and beautify your own life? What is there in your life that you feel compelled to take this aggressive step in its favour? We cannot but be reminded of the perversion from which the whole historical existence of the creature suffers and the guilt of which does not really reside in the beast but ultimately in man himself.[6]

The second challenge is that we have no biblical warrant for claiming killing as God's will. God's will is for peace. We need to remember that even though Genesis 9 gives permission to kill for food it does so only on the basis that we do not misappropriate God-given life. Genesis 9 posits divine reckoning for the life of every beast taken even under this new dispensation (9:5). The question may not unnaturally be asked: How long can this divine permission last? Karl Barth writes that "it is not only understandable but necessary that the affirmation of this whole possibility (of killing for food) should always have been accompanied by a radical protest against it." And yet he concludes: "It may well be objected against a vegetarianism which presses in this direction that it represents a wanton anticipation of what is described by Isaiah 11 and Roman 8 as existence in the new aeon for which we hope."7 Whatever may be the merits of Barth's arguments here, it should be clear that Barth cannot and does not claim that killing is God's will. On the contrary it stands in direct contrast to the "new aeon for which we hope" or, as he puts it elsewhere, "under a caveat."8 In short: even though killing may be sometimes permissible, God will not tolerate it forever.

In this respect it is interesting that one highly regarded Talmudic scholar, Abraham Isaac Kook, maintains that the most spiritually satisfying way of reading the practical biblical injunctions concerning killing is in terms of preparation for a new dawn of justice for animals. "The free movement of the moral impulse to establish justice for animals generally and the claim for their rights from mankind," he argues, "are hidden in a natural psychic sensibility in the deeper layers of the Torah." Given the corruption of humankind, it was natural and inevitable that moral attention had first to be paid to the regulation of human conduct toward other humans. But in Kook's view the various injunctions concerning the selection and preparation of meat (in for example Leviticus 17:13; Ezekiel 16:63; Leviticus 22:28 and Deuteronomy 22:26–27) were commandments "to regulate the eating of meat, in steps that will take us to the higher purpose." And what is this higher purpose? None other it seems than universal peace and justice. Kook maintains that just as the embracing of democratic ideals came late within religious thinking "so will the hidden yearning to act justly towards animals emerge at the proper time."9

The third challenge to be grasped is that those who wish now to adopt a vegetarian or vegan lifestyle have solid biblical support. Biblical vegetarians will not say, "It has *never been* justifiable to kill animals." Rather they should say, "It is *not now* necessary to kill for food as it was once thought necessary." The biblical case for vegetarianism does not rest on the view that killing may never be allowable in the eyes of God, rather on the view that killing is always a grave matter. When we have to kill to live we may do so, but when we do not, we should live otherwise. It is vital to appreciate the force of this argument. In past ages many—including undoubtedly the biblical writers themselves—have thought that killing for food was essential in order to live. But we now know that—at least for those now living in the rich West—it is perfectly possible to sustain a healthy diet without any recourse to flesh products. This may not have always been true in the past. Until comparatively recently conventional wisdom was always that meat was essential to live well.

Those individuals who opt for vegetarianism can do so in the knowledge that they are living closer to the biblical ideal of peaceableness than their carnivorous contemporaries. The point should not be minimized. In many ways it is difficult to know how we can live more peaceably in a world striven by violence and greed and consumerism. Individuals often feel powerless in the face of great social forces beyond even democratic control. To opt for a vegetarian lifestyle is to take one practical step toward living in peace with the rest of creation. One step toward reducing the rate of institutionalized killing in the world today. One less chicken eaten is one less chicken killed.

Nevertheless, we do well to appreciate the biblical perspective that we do not live in an ideal world. The truth is that even if we adopt a vegetarian or vegan lifestyle, we are still not free of killing either directly or indirectly. Even if we eat only beans and nuts and lentils, we have to reckon with the fact that competing animals are killed because of the crops we want to eat. Even if we decide not to wear dead animal skins, we have to face the fact that alternative substances have frequently been tested for their toxicity on laboratory animals. Even if we only eat soya beans we do well to remember that these have been forced fed to animals in painful experiments. As I have written elsewhere, there is no pure land.[10] If we embark on vegetarianism, as I think we should, we must do so on the understanding that for all its compelling logic, it is only one very small step toward the vision of a peaceful world.

PRINCE   OF   PEACE

There is, however, one major—and some would say conclusive—objection to my pro-vegetarian thesis that should be considered. We have previously encountered it: Jesus was no vegan and probably no vegetarian. There are no recorded examples of Jesus eating meat in the Gospels. The only possible exception is the Passover itself, but it is not entirely clear that Jesus ate the traditional passover meal.[11] Jesus did, however, eat fish if the Gospel narratives are to be believed. How are we to reconcile this to the established Christian view of Jesus as the Prince of Peace? There are four possible answers to this question.

The first is that the canonical Gospels are mistaken and Jesus was actually a vegetarian. However implausible this view may appear, among those who are pro-animals there have always been a number who have never believed that Jesus ate the flesh of other living creatures.[12] Those who take this view argue that "fish" in the New Testament did not actually mean fish as we know it today.[13] Moreover it has been argued that Jesus was really an Essene, albeit an unusual one, a member of the sect who were strict vegetarians.[14] Indeed there are various "Essene gospels" in which Jesus is depicted as a vegetarian but all of these are, I think, of comparatively modern invention.[15] However there are some fragments of some early gospels, such as the Gospel of the Ebionites, which do depict Jesus as a vegetarian though one suspects for reasons of their own.[16] What I think is much more interesting is the quantity of apocryphal material which in various ways does describe Jesus as having a special concern for, and affinity with, the animal world.[17] How much, if any, of this material is historically reliable is highly questionable but in an area where we know so little it is probably unwise to be dogmatic. It is just conceivable that some of this material does contain genuine historical reminiscence of some kind but that has to be a remote possibility. What may be significant is that this material, historical or not, exhibits a sensitivity to animals which some in the Christian community felt at one stage or another was—or rather should be—characteristic of the historical Jesus.

There is one other question which should perhaps be pondered and it is this: What would it have *meant* for Jesus to have been a vegetarian in first-century Palestine? In context, it could well have meant associating himself with a Manichean philosophy of asceticism which would have been inimical to his teaching as a whole. Since the Manichaeans were almost all vegetarians—largely on ascetical grounds—it may be pondered whether Jesus was ever confronted with ethical vegetarianism such as we know it today.

The second possible answer is that Jesus was not perfect in every conceivable way. Jews and Muslims would, of course, have no difficulty with this proposition but orthodox Christians would surely find this idea difficult. After all, traditional Christian belief has always been that Jesus Christ was truly God and truly human. Most Christians would hold that being sinless was an essential part of being God incarnate. Those who argue that Jesus was not wholly perfect, however, are not, of course, wholly without biblical support. The question of Jesus: "Why do you call me good?" and his answer: "No one is good but God alone" is recorded in all three Synoptic Gospels (Luke 18:19; Matthew 19:17; Mark 10:18).

Moreover, it is not inconceivable that Jesus could have been *both* God incarnate and less than morally perfect in every way. Some scholars, such as John Robinson, have maintained this.[18] Perhaps it could be argued that while Jesus committed no sins of commission (deliberate wrongdoing), of necessity every human being commits some sins of omission (things left undone). However, such a view falls short of traditional Christian doctrine and biblical texts such as Hebrews 4:15, which argues that Jesus "was tempted as we are, yet without sin." Though, even here, it is possible that Hebrews is describing ritual purity rather than ethical perfection.

The third answer is that the killing of fish is not a morally significant matter or, at least, not as significant as the killing of animals. There is something to be said for this view. Even those who argue rigorously for animal rights sometimes do so on the basis that animals as God's creatures are "subjects of a life"— that is they have sensitivity and consciousness and the ability to suffer—but it is not clear that *all* fish do actually possess *all* these characteristics. In many cases we simply do not know. This must mean, I think, that their moral status is somewhat different from those animals where self-consciousness and sentiency can reasonably be taken for granted. Nevertheless, do not fish merit some benefit of the doubt? Are they not also fellow creatures with some God-given life and individuality which means that wherever possible their lives should be respected?

APPROXIMATING THE PEACEABLE KINGDOM

The fourth answer is that sometimes it can be justifiable to kill fish for food in situations of necessity. Such a situation, we may assume, was present in first-century Palestine where geographical factors alone seem to suggest a scarcity of protein. Such a view would on the whole be more consistent with the biblical perspective that we may kill but only in circumstances of real need. Hence we may have to face the possibility that Jesus did indeed participate in the killing of some life forms in order to live. Indeed we may say that part of his being a human being at a particular state and time in history necessitated that response in order to have lived at all.

Of all the four possible responses, I find this one the most convincing. As I have indicated before, the biblical view is not that killing can never be justified and ought to be avoided at all costs. There are times, for example, when euthanasia may well be the most compassionate response to an individual being undergoing unrelievable suffering. But even if we accept that killing for food may be justified in those situations of real necessity for human survival, such as may be argued in the case of Jesus himself, this in no way exonerates us from the burden of justifying what we now do to animals in circumstances substantially different. This last point is centrally important and must not be obscured. There may have been times in the past or even now in the present where we have difficulty imagining a life without killing for food. But *where we do have the moral freedom* to live without recourse to violence, there is a prima facie case to do so. To kill without the strict conditions of necessity is to live a life with insufficient generosity.

It would be wrong, however, to give the impression that the life and teaching of Jesus is a disappointment as far as the enlightened treatment of animals is concerned. While it is true that there is a great deal we do not know about Jesus' precise attitudes to animals, there is a powerful strand in his ethical teaching about the primacy of mercy to the weak, the powerless and the oppressed. Without misappropriation, it is legitimate to ask: Who is more deserving of this special compassion than the animals so commonly exploited in our world today? Moreover, it is often overlooked that in the canonical Gospels Jesus is frequently presented as identifying himself with the world of animals. As I have written elsewhere:

> His birth, if tradition is to be believed, takes place in the home of sheep and oxen. His ministry begins, according to Mark, in the wilderness "with the wild beasts" (1:13). His triumphal entry into Jerusalem involves riding on a "humble ass" (see Matthew 21:6). According to Jesus it is lawful to 'do good' on the Sabbath, which includes the rescuing of an animal fallen into a pit (see Matthew 12:10–12). Even the sparrows, literally sold for a few pennies in his day, are not "forgotten before God." God's providence extends to the entire created order, and the glory of Solomon and all his works cannot be compared to that of the lilies of the field (Luke 12:27). God so cares for his creation that even "foxes have holes, and birds of the air have nests; but the Son of man has nowhere to lay his head" (Luke 9:58).[19]

The significance of these and other verses may be much more than had previously been thought. One small example must suffice. Mark describes Jesus' ministry as taking place firstly within the context of wild animals (1:13). Richard Bauckham has recently argued that the context in which this verse should be understood is messianic in orientation. Jesus is shown to be in continuity with the Isaianic tradition in seeing the messianic age as bringing about a reconciliation between nature and humanity.[20] If this is true, it may be that Mark is seeking to demonstrate how the gospel of Jesus has implications for the whole of the created world and harmony within the animal world in particular. Those who follow Jesus might argue that in seeking to realize what can now be realized in our own time and space of the messianic age is to live now in conformity with the Spirit of Jesus itself.

In conclusion, reference has already been made to how vegetarians have formed a rather beleagued minority in times past. But it is worth recalling that not a few of the great figures in Christendom have adopted a vegetarian diet. Among these should not go unnoticed the wide variety of saints who have expressed a particular regard for animals and opposed their destruction. "Poor innocent little creatures," exclaimed St. Richard of Chichester when confronted with animals bound for slaughter. "If you were reasoning beings and could speak you would curse us. For we are the cause of your death, and what have you done to deserve it?"[21] There has always been an ascetical strand within Christianity which has insisted that humans should live gently on the earth and avoid luxury food. The rule of life penned by St. Benedict for his religious community, for example, expressly forbade the eating of meat. "Except the sick who are very weak, let all abstain entirely from the flesh of four-footed animals."[22] Moreover, it often comes as a surprise for Christians to realize that the modern vegetarian movement was strongly biblical in origin. Inspired by the original command in Genesis 1, an Anglican priest, William Cowherd, founded the Bible Christian Church in 1809 and made vegetarianism compulsory among its members. The founding of this church in the United Kingdom and its sister church in the United States by William Metcalfe, effectively heralded the beginning of the modern vegetarian movement.[23]

The subsequent, if rather slow, growth of vegetarianism from 1809 to 1970, and its rapid and astonishing growth from 1970 to the present day is testimony that Cowherd may have been right in his view that mainstream biblical theology has overlooked something of importance in Genesis 1. It may be that when the history of twentieth-century cuisine is finally written, the radical changes in diet which we are currently witnessing will be found to be due more to the rediscovery—by Cowherd and his modern descendants—of two biblical verses (Genesis 1:29–30) than anything else. These two verses, we may recall, came into existence by people imagining possibilities in the light of their belief in God the Creator. By rekindling the same vision in our own time, we may be enabled to realize—at least in part—those possibilities which our forebears could only imagine. Forward, we may say, not backward to Genesis.

NOTES

1. John Calvin, *Commentaries on the First Book of Moses*, Vol. 1 (Edinburgh: Calvin Translation Society, 1847), 291–292, extract in Andrew Linzey and Tom Regan, eds., *Animals and Christianity* (New York: Crossroad, 1989), 199–200.

2. This argument is developed at length in Andrew Linzey, *Christianity and the Rights of Animals* (New York: Crossroad, 1987), 141–149.

3. *Where We Stand on Animal Welfare*, Rabbinic Conference of the Union of Liberal and Progressive Synogogues, London, May 1990, 1.

4. John Austin Baker, "Biblical Attitudes to Nature," in Hugh Montefiore, ed., *Man and Nature* (London: Collins, 1975), 96; see also pp. 93–94.

5. Anthony Phillips, "Respect for Life in the Old Testament," *King's Theological Review* (Autumn 1983), 32. I am indebted to this article, though I am perplexed by the subsequent line: "While animals, like all God's creation, *were made for man*, he must still order that creation in accordance with God's will" (my emphasis, p. 32). I think a fundamental distinction must be drawn between our dominion over creation and the notion that it was made for our use.

6. Karl Barth, *Church Dogmatics: The Doctrine of Creation* 111/4, trans. G. W. Bromiley and T. F. Torrance (New York: Scribners, 1958–1961), 352; extract in *Animals and Christianity*, pp. 191–193.

7. *Ibid.*, 353 n.

8. *Ibid.*, 354.

9. Abraham Isaac Kook, *The Lights of Penitence, the Moral Principles, Lights of Holiness, Essays, Lectures, and Poems* (New York: Paulist Press, 1979), pp. 317–323. I am grateful to Jonathan Sacks for this reference.

10. See, Linzey, *Christianity and the Rights of Animals*, 148.

11. See, the discussion in J. Jeremias, *The Eucharistic Words of Jesus* (London: SCM Press, 1966).

12. See Geoffrey L. Rudd, *Why Kill for Food?* (London: The Vegetarian Society, 1970), 78–90, and Steven Rosen, *Food for the Spirit: Vegetarianism and the World Religions* (New York: Bala Books, 1987), 33–39.

13. See V. A. Holmes-Gore, *These We Have Not Loved* (London: C. W. Daniel, 1946), 86–9.

14. See J. Todd Ferrier, *On Behalf of the Creatures* (The Order of the Cross, 1983), 111f.

15. See *The Gospel of the Holy Twelve and The Essene Humane Gospel of Jesus*, cited and discussed in Rosen, *Food for the Spirit*.

16. "The Gospel of the Ebionites," in Montague R. James, ed., *The Aprocryphal New Testament* (London: Oxford University Press, 1955), 8–10.

17. See "The Gospel of Thomas," 49–56; "The Acts of Thomas," 396–402; and "The Acts of Philip," 446–448, all in James, Ibid. See also "The Acts of Peter," in E. Hennecke, ed., *New Testament Apocrypha*, Vol. II, *Apostolic and Early Church Writings* (London: SCM Press, 1974), 294–297.

18. J. A. T. Robinson, "Need Jesus Have Been Perfect?" in S. W. Sykes and J. P. Clayton, eds., *Christ, Faith and History* (Cambridge: Cambridge University Press, 1972), 39–52.

19. Introduction to Linzey and Regan, eds., *Compassion for Animals*, xv.

20. I am grateful to Richard Bauckham for a lecture at Essex University on this theme and for bringing to my attention the significance of this verse. I understand that his work will be published as *Jesus and the Greening of Christianity*.

21. St. Richard of Chichester, cited in Alban Butler, *Lives of the Saints*, revised by Herbert Thurston and Donald Attwater (New York: P. J. Kennedy & Sons, 1946), 157; also extract in *Compassion for Animals*, 66.

22. *Rule of St. Benedict*, ch. 39, 46.

23. See Richard D. Ryder, *Animal Revolution: Changing Attitudes towards Speciesism* (London: Blackwell, 1946), 96. For a history of the Church in America see *The History of the Philadelphia Bible-Christian Church, 1817–1917* (Philadelphia: J.B. Lippincott, 1922). I am grateful to Bernard Unti for this last reference.

In the Fullness of God's Creation

TOM REGAN

Philosopher Tom Regan argues here that the Genesis account of creation suggests a "close, vital kinship" between animals and humans. Whether the story is read literally or symbolically, its description of the Edenic paradise is a revelation of the divine plan for fulfillment. In that plan, animals are not intended to be used by humans for food, tools, ornamentation, entertainment or sport. Instead, argues Regan, they are independently good expressions of divine love and creativity. To see their only value as a utilitarian one is contrary to "God's original hope," conveyed in the biblical image of Eden, for the maximal flourishing of all life.

I take the opening account of creation in Genesis seriously, but not, I hasten to add, literally (for example, a day, I assume, is not to be understood as twenty-four hours). I take it seriously because I believe that this is the point from which our spiritual understanding of God's plans in and hopes for creation must begin and against which our well-considered judgments about the value of creation finally must be tested. It is therefore predictable that I should find significance in the fact that God is said to find each part of creation "good" before humans came upon the scene and that humans were created by God (or came upon the scene) on the same day as the nonhuman animals... —those whose limbs are severed, whose organs are brutally removed, and whose brains are ground up for purposes of scientific research, for example. I read in this representation of the order of creation a prescient recognition of the close, vital kinship humans share with these other animals, a kinship I earlier endeavored to explicate in terms of our shared *biological* presence and one, quite apart from anything the Bible teaches, supported both by common sense and our best science. If I may be pardoned even the appearance of hubris, I may say, in the language of St. Thomas, that this fact of our common biographical presence is both a "truth of reason" and a "truth of faith."

But I find in the opening saga of creation an even deeper, more profound message regarding God's plans in and hopes for creation. For I find in that account the unmistakable message that God did not create nonhuman animals for the use of humans—not in science, not for the purpose of vanity products, not for our entertainment, not for sport or recreation, not even for our bodily sustenance. On the contrary, the nonhuman animals currently exploited by these human practices were created to be just what they are—*independently good* expressions of the divine love which, in ways that are likely always to remain to some degree mysterious to us, was expressed in God's creative activity.

The issue of bodily sustenance, of food, is perhaps the most noteworthy of the practices I have mentioned since, while humans from "the beginning" were in need of bodily sustenance and had a ready supply of edible nonhuman animal food sources available, there were no rodeos or circuses, no leg-hold traps or dynamite harpoons in the original creation. Had it been a part of God's hopes in and plans for creation that humans use nonhuman animals as food, therefore, it would have been open to God to let this be known. And yet what we find in the opening saga of creation is just the opposite. The food we are given by God is not the flesh of animals, it is "all plants that bear seed everywhere on the earth, and every tree bearing fruit which yields seed: they shall be yours for food" (Genesis 1:29, NEB).

Now I do not believe the message regarding what was to serve as food for humans in the most perfect state of creation could be any clearer. Genesis clearly presents a picture of veganism; that is, not only is the flesh of animals excluded from the menu God provides for us, even animal products—milk and cheese, for example—are excluded. And so I believe that, if, as I am strongly inclined to do, we look to the biblical account of "the beginning" as an absolutely essential source of spiritual insight into God's hopes for and plans in creation, then—like it or not—we are obliged to find there a menu of divinely approved bodily sustenance that differs quite markedly from the steaks and chops, roasts and stews most people, in the Western world at least, are accustomed to devouring.

To a less than optimal or scholarly degree I am aware of some of the chapters and verses of the subsequent biblical record: the fall, the expulsion from the garden, the flood, and so on. There is no debate about *the details* of the subsequent account I could win if paired against an even modestly astute and retentive young person preparing for first communion. I wear my lack of biblical (and theological) sophistication on my sleeve—although even I cannot forbear noting, in passing, that the covenant into which God enters with humanity after the flood is significant for its inclusion of nonhuman animals. The meaning of this covenant aside, I believe that the essential moral and spiritual truth any openminded, literate reader of the first chapter of Genesis *must* find is the one I already have mentioned; namely, that the purpose of nonhuman animals in God's creation, given the original hopes and plans of God-in-creation, was not that humans roast, fry, stew, broil, bake, and barbecue their rotting corpses (what people today call meat).

In this reading of God's creative activity, therefore, I find a spiritual lesson that is unmistakably at odds with both the letter and the spirit of speciesism. That lesson, as I understand it, does not represent the nonhuman animals to whom I have been referring as having no or less inherent value than humans. On the contrary, by unmistakably excluding these animals from the menu of food freely available to us, as granted by God's beneficence, I infer that we are called upon by God to recognize the independent value of these animals. They are not put here to be utilized by us. At least this was not God's original hope. If anything we are put here to protect them, especially against those humans who would reduce these animals to objects for human use. As you might imagine, the message we find in Genesis 1 is celestial music to the ears of one who, like myself, is not embarrassed or silenced by the "extremism" of the animal rights position.

I am aware that some theologians take a different view than I do of Genesis's opening saga of creation. Eden never was, they opine; the perfection of creation is something we are to work to bring about, not something that once existed only to be lost. I do not know how to prove which vision of Eden, if either, is the true one. What I do believe is that, when viewed in the present context, this question is entirely moot. For what is clear—clear beyond any doubt, as I read the scriptures—is that human beings simply do not eat nonhuman animals in that fullness of God's creation that the image of Eden represents. And this is true whether Eden once was (but was shattered), or is yet to be (if, by the grace of God, we will but create it).

Vegetarianism and Religion

FRANCIS X. CLOONEY

Francis Clooney, a Jesuit priest, reminds us in this essay that there's frequently a rupture between theological convictions and everyday piety. He suggests that vegetarianism is one way of helping Christians integrate the two into a coherent, living spirituality. Many Christians view diet as peripheral to their faith, but Clooney disagrees. On the contrary, he argues, what and how one eats are statements and actions that are fundamentally religious. After all, the Christian Lord "has always chosen to be found in the context of the meal." Commitment to a nonviolent, meatless diet is one way of showing regular and concrete fidelity to the gospel message of peace, justice, and concern for the oppressed.

Vegetarianism is no longer simply a fad in our country. While men and women who refrain from eating meat and fish (ovo-lacto vegetarians) and those who refrain from eating cheese, milk and eggs (vegans) are still rare enough to be of interest or concern when met at dinner parties, in restaurants or on airplanes, it is nevertheless true, as one newspaper reported last summer, that vegetarians are no longer "oddballs" or vaguely "un-American." We are fast becoming used to the variety of meatless and vegetable cookbooks, and are not surprised to discover meatless entrees on the menus of fashionable restaurants. Yet, we may feel, the issue of what one eats is in the final analysis peripheral: It is what one does that really counts.

There are good reasons, however, for further consideration of the religious significance of vegetarianism, the choice of a diet that does not include meat and fish products. Looking back into our tradition, we are aware today that since Vatican II we have dismantled significant portions of an older, somewhat dated spirituality and practice; gone are many of the devotions and prayers, the fasts and abstinences that characterized an earlier Catholicism. With them, too, there has fallen into disuse a whole theology and ecclesiology which had served well for centuries. While we do not wish to look back with yearning to that age, we must admit that we have not yet been able to put back together theology and the lived piety of the church; we have yet to construct sufficiently coherent and comprehensive models that can nourish everyday, routine Christian life, and we are still looking for a new, organic unity of mind and heart that can be lived "in ordinary times."

Looking to the future, we are more and more aware of the vast social issues of peace and justice facing us. As we live more clearly in a "global village," and attend more seriously to structural injustices that oppress and degrade whole groups of people and nations, we are seeking a kind of spirituality that can enable us to internalize and experience affectively these apparently vague and general concerns. Both for those who work with the poor and need a spirituality to support them in the strenuous and often unrewarding efforts involved, and for those of us who rarely see that oppression firsthand, we are seeking a kind of asceticism that unites us more deeply to the world and its people and helps us to embody the Gospel as a source of social, institutional change in the world.

It is my suggestion here that vegetarianism offers one plausible, effective way in which the contemporary Christian can again integrate the more speculative and general concerns of the church with a concrete personal piety. The experiment with vegetarianism, when undertaken prudently and with sufficient reflection, can offer a solid contribution toward the development of new and dynamic forms of spirituality. To understand how this can be so, it is helpful to examine some of the reasons usually given for becoming a vegetarian.

Vegetarianism is good for your health.

The point is made here that we Americans eat too much meat, and would do ourselves good by becoming vegetarians. While it is true that we do eat too much meat, and while a good and nourishing diet need not include meat at all, the argument in itself is not entirely convincing. On the one hand, what is called for concerning good health need only be moderation in the consumption of meat, not abstention; on the other, it is well known that nonmeat diets can be seriously deficient in necessary vitamins and proteins, and in the long run at least as detrimental to health as an excessive consumption of meat.

Vegetarianism offers us as a simpler lifestyle.

According to this argument, our lives are too complicated, too "consumerized," removed from the natural and addicted to the rich, the expensive and the novel; vegetarianism would be a serious step toward a more gentle, cleaner and purer way of living. The restriction of diet involved would teach us to value more fully what we do choose to eat. Akin to this, of course, is the movement toward natural and organic foods, the rejection of the artificial and synthetic. To some extent, there is thus involved an ambivalence about the value of technological society, a yearning for an earlier simplicity and closeness to nature. Therein lie both the value and the weakness of this argument. Our consumption of meat and the attitudes thereby implied can indeed be taken as appropriate symbols for a society increasingly bound to various artificial and commercial values, and vegetarianism can offer a constructive and wholesome critique of that tendency. However, not only is vegetarianism liable to the same commercialized packaging (as can be demonstrated by the proliferation of natural food emporiums, expensive and gourmet "countercultural" cookbooks, etc.), but it can easily be reduced to a fairly comfortable substitute for any more complicated, more urgent efforts to understand and respond to the problems of a technological age.

VEGETARIANISM RESPONDS TO AN UNJUST ECONOMIC SYSTEM.

Even those of us who have not traveled to Third World countries or into our own inner city areas are becoming aware that in many ways meat is a luxury, a rare treat for many families who must otherwise subsist on vegetable products. Moreover, there is a greater awareness today that the production of animal protein is an inefficient and costly process, requiring a far greater proportion of energy and feed than would an equivalent amount of vegetable/grain protein. Thus, for example, if ten people can be nourished for a certain period of time on the meat of one cow, a hundred people could be nourished for the same time period on the grain used to feed and fatten that cow for market. It is often the case, too, that economic profits induce poor countries to use valuable land to graze cattle and/or grow grain for feed, often for export to this country—rather than using the same resources more efficiently and justly to feed their own malnourished people. Responding to this systematized inequity, the vegetarian chooses to refrain from eating meat as a kind of personal reminder and protest, to live voluntarily according to the diet forced upon many people by the realities of prices and economic systems. Involved is a kind of consciousness-raising, reminding the vegetarian that meat even once a day is a luxury, one gained at the expense of many people who are not even adequately nourished. This kind of effort, which can also be seen as a kind of traditional "penance" for the sinful effects of an economic system, is worthwhile on a personal basis and makes concrete for the vegetarian otherwise abstract issues. It is most worthwhile when it becomes a group effort, either as a community decision or project, or in conjunction with constructive efforts to change the system, e.g., by joining Bread for the World or some similar organization.

VEGETARIANISM EMBODIES A RESPECT FOR LIFE.

From this point of view, vegetarianism is a further, clearer effort to remind the person that all life is precious and should not be taken except in urgent necessity, and that when there is such necessity, when we have to eat, higher forms of life deserve more respect. Thus, the refusal to eat meat and fish includes both a respect for these animals, which in some ways share life as we do, and a preference to gain sustenance from those forms of life that are more rhythmically, seasonally renewable. When the vegetarian admits that he or she does in fact "kill" plant life for food, we are all relieved of a kind of absolutism which would say that no life can be taken for any reason. Like everyone else, the vegetarian recognizes that choices must be made, that there is a qualitative difference between plant and animal and between animal and human being; the vegetarian does not, however, see human life as utterly distinct from and above all other kinds of life. Similarly, the vegetarian can admit that there are extreme circumstances when the eating of meat or fish is called for, yet also concludes that to make meat-eating a daily necessity is unrealistic and an unnecessary form of violence. The respect for life thus emphasized so simply on a daily basis heightens the vegetarian's appreciation and reverence for all life, calls him or her to a deeper sense of stewardship and truly humane dominion over a world of nature and offers a more acute awareness of all kinds of violence and disrespect for human life woven into the fabric of everyday social patterns.

VEGETARIANISM MAKES MANIFEST THE UNITY OF CREATION.

There is a story about St. Francis of Assisi to the effect that one cold winter's day, Brother Leo came into his small hut to light a fire for the shivering and frail ascetic. Francis stopped him, saying: "No, let me be cold; if I cannot bring warmth to so many of my brothers and sisters who are cold today, then at least I can join them by being as cold as they are." We are very aware today of the darkness of life, the suffering woven into existence, the loneliness and fear that surround the lives of so many people. In a small yet significant way, the vegetarian chooses to be like St. Francis, to step in the direction of that darkness and be closer to those who are trapped there. There is fostered the awareness that we are all truly one, and that only in a togetherness that accepts and does not flee our common plight can any of us find happiness. Nor are the limits of this unity closely restricted, for as St. Francis and many of the saints have seen, we are one with the animals too, and with all life, and do ourselves a great disservice in forgetting that unity. Vegetarianism reminds us, very quietly and persistently, of this reality before us.

Should one become a vegetarian? While the responses presented are not wholly compelling, the least that can be said is that the choice to become a vegetarian can be a prudent and religious one, founded in values not alien to our tradition. In the years to come, as our awareness of social issues grows sharper and as we enter into a deeper and more familiar dialogue with the religions of the East, wherein the practice of vegetarianism has a somewhat broader and more popularly accepted currency, the possibilities and values of vegetarianism will perhaps become even clearer and more easily available to the Christian community as a whole.

In conclusion, two aspects of the choice may be noted. First, the decision to become a vegetarian may begin on a variety of levels, more or less profound, but inevitably the whole person will be involved, as an individual and member of society. The former, because what we eat is so fundamentally characteristic of who we are, and because vegetarianism as a change of diet often leads to a much quieter, gentler experience of life; the latter, because even as a private choice vegetarianism is acted out within the context of the meal, a basic milieu of human society and discourse, and inevitably leads to reflection and discussion within the given community as to the reasons for the decision, the values, etc. So, too, the heightened awareness of social realities and injustices afforded by vegetarianism may very well lead to broader, more visible decisions about lifestyle, position within American society and a larger global community.

The second aspect of the choice to be noted is the manner in which the decision is made. For many, it has begun as a very tentative decision, an experiment for a short period of time. For some, a broader leap is made and found to be easier. The decision may be a strong and positive response to a suddenly realized understanding of the world about us, with its virtues and faults, or it may be simply the manifestation of an inner experience, an interiority that is also a kind of cosmic unity. Whatever the specifics of the manner, however, the Christian may discover one fundamental dynamic: the heartfelt desire to discover anew in our age the Lord who has always chosen to be found in the context of the meal.

Feeding on Grace:

Institutional Violence, Christianity,

and Vegetarianism

CAROL J. ADAMS

Carol Adams, groundbreaking author of The Sexual Politics of Meat *(1990), argues here that Christianity traditionally has sanctioned institutionalized violence against animals by appealing to a conquest-and-dominion model of human stewardship. But in fact such an understanding is contrary to the spirit of Christianity, contributing as it does to an ethos of violence and exploitation (of humans as well as animals) rather than one of compassion and love. "One cannot," she tells us, "feed on grace and eat animals." Consequently, Adams calls for a "Christology of vegetarianism," in which the spiritual and ethical implications of Jesus' gospel message are consciously extended to our relationship with animals.*

The day after I arrived home from my first year at Yale Divinity School, an urgent knocking summoned me from my task of unpacking. It was a distressed neighbor reporting that someone had just shot one of our horses. We ran through the pasture to discover that indeed, one of my horses was lying dead, a small amount of blood trickling from his mouth. Shots from the nearby woods could still be heard. One horse lay dead and the other frantically pranced around him.

That night, upset and depressed, I sat down to a dinner of hamburger. Suddenly I flashed on the image of Jimmy's dead body in the upper pasture, awaiting a formal burial by backhoe in the morning. One dead body had a name, a past that included my sense of his subjectivity, and was soon to be

148

respectfully buried. The other dead body was invisible, objectified, nameless, except in its current state as hamburger, and was to be buried in my stomach. At the time I realized the hypocrisy of my actions. The question confronting me was: "If Jimmy were meat would I, could I, be his meat eater?" And the answer was "of course not." Having recognized his individuality, his subjectivity, having been in relationship with him, I could not render him beingless. So why could I do this to another animal, whom, if I had known her, would surely have revealed her individuality and subjectivity? The invisible became visible: I became aware of how I objectified others and what it means to make animals into meat. I also recognized my ability to change myself: realizing what meat actually is, I also realized I need not be a meat eater.

This experience in 1973 catalyzed the process by which I became a vegetarian slightly more than a year later. It also catalyzed a theoretical and theological search to understand why our society invests so many economic, environmental, and cultural resources into protecting the eating of animals. It is my position that the eating of animals is a form of institutional violence. The corporate ritual that characterizes institutional violence deflects or redefines the fact that the eating of animals is exploitative. This is why conscientious and ethical individuals do not see meat as a problem. It is fair to say that the most frequent relationship the majority of Christians have with the other animals is with dead animals whom they eat. Because of institutional violence, meat eating is conceived of neither as a relationship nor as the consuming of dead animals. It is not often while eating meat that one thinks: "I am now interacting with an animal." We do not see our meat eating as contact with animals because it has been renamed as contact with food. We require an analysis of institutional violence to identify just why it is that Christians ought to reconceptualize meat eating. This essay offers such an analysis and reconceptualization.

THE INSTITUTIONAL VIOLENCE OF EATING ANIMALS

Through an understanding of institutional violence we will come to see the dynamics of exploitation vis-à-vis the other animals, and begin to recognize their suffering as morally relevant in determining our own actions.

For something to be *institutional* violence it must be a significant, widespread, unethical practice in a society. As an industry, meat production is the second largest in this country. It is both widespread and vitally important to our economy. Though meat eating is now the normative expression of our relationship with other animals, a close examination of the functioning of institutional violence will reveal why I call it unethical.

Institutional violence is characterized by:

1. An infringement on or failure to acknowledge another's inviolability.

2. Treatment or physical force that injures or abuses.

3. A series of denial mechanisms which deflect attention from the violence.

4. The targeting of "appropriate" victims.

5. Detrimental effects on society as a whole.

6. The manipulation of the public (e.g., consumers) into passivity.

Meat eating fits this definition of institutional violence. In fact, the word *meat* itself illustrates several of these components. It renders animals appropriate victims by naming them as edible and deflects our attention from the violence inherent to killing them for food. Because the word *meat* contributes to minimizing the implications of institutional violence, it will be enclosed in quotation marks in this essay. At times the more accurate term "flesh" will be used.

Institutional violence toward animals at its core denies their inviolability. Its function is to uphold and act upon the violability of animals. It works at the individual level by wrenching any notion of inviolability from one's sense of Christian ethics. Even if many children object to eating animals upon learning where "meat" comes from, this objection is rarely respected. And even if adults are discomforted by some form of flesh—whether it be because of the animal it is stolen from, a dog, a horse, a rat, or the part of the animal being consumed, the brain, the liver—they have no Christian ethical framework into which these objections might be placed. The absence of such a framework means that any reminders that animals have to be killed to be consumed, experienced by children explicitly and by adults implicitly, remain unassimilated and repressed. Institutional violence interposes an ethics of exploitation for any burgeoning ethic of inviolability.

We become firmly and persuasively convinced that the eating of animals is not only acceptable but necessary for survival. This deviates from the representation of our corporate beginning in Genesis as vegetarians, when God/ess[1] says in Genesis 1:29: "Behold, I have given you every plant yielding seed which is upon the face of all the earth, and every tree with seed in its fruit; you shall have them for food." This corporate and personal beginning as vegetarians seems to be confirmed by anthropological sources that indicate that our earliest hominid ancestors had vegetarian bodies. In the records of their bones, dental impressions, and tools, these anonymous ancestors reveal the fact that "meat," as a substantial part of the diet, became a fixture in human life only recently—in the past 40,000 years. Indeed, it was not until the past two hundred years that most people in the Western world had the opportunity to consume "meat" daily.

Our bodies appear better suited to digesting seeds and fruits than muscle and blood, suggesting again our personal origins as vegetarians. From this perspective, ingesting flesh is an act against our own body as well as against another animal's body, a double violation.

We have fallen from this state of grace with the other animals represented in Genesis 1:29 and substituted institutional violence for respect for their inviolability.

THE INSTITUTIONAL VIOLENCE OF EATING ANIMALS IS AN INFRINGEMENT ON OR FAILURE TO ACKNOWLEDGE ANOTHER'S INVIOLABILITY.

Some individuals recognize the inviolability of animals. In other words, they believe that animals are not ours to use, abuse, or consume. They believe that if animals could talk, farmed animals, vivisected animals, fur-bearing animals, circus, zoo, and rodeo animals, hunted animals, would all say the same thing: "Don't touch me!" In the absence of a language that animals can speak that proclaims their inviolability, some human beings are searching for a language that speaks this on their behalf. So far most of these efforts could be grouped under the general heading of animal rights theory. . . . [T]he notion of animals' inviolability is a deep belief in search of a language. Because we have no adequate language for emotions or intuitions, we have no framework into which our misgivings about animals' current violability can be fit. In the absence of such language, it is important that we widen Christian ethical discourse to address the problem of the use of animals.

I believe that flesh eating is an unjust use of another for one's own profit or advantage. It is unjust because it is *unnecessary* (people do not need to eat animals to survive), *cruel*, and perpetuates inauthentic relationships among people and between people and the other animals. As such, it enacts the first component of institutional violence—the failure to honor another's wholeness and the interposition of your will against another's self-determination. Through the term "inviolability" I am claiming "Don't touch me" on behalf of animals, or to put it otherwise, "Animals should be inviolable!" Institutional violence tramples these claims and arrogates to humans the right to dominate and violate animals' bodies.

INSTITUTIONAL VIOLENCE INVOLVES TREATMENT OR PHYSICAL FORCE
THAT INJURES OR ABUSES.

By treatment I mean *ongoing* conditions that are abusive or injurious. Factory
farming involves such treatment. Intensively farmed animals fare poorly, being
raised in enclosed, darkened, or dimly lit buildings. Their lives are characterized
by little external stimulus; restriction of movement; no freedom to choose social
interactions; intense and unpleasant fumes; little contact with human beings;
ingestion of subtherapeutic doses of antibiotics to prevent diseases that could
tear through an entire population of imprisoned animals, sometimes 70,000 in
one building. Laying hens live with two to four others in cages slightly larger
than this opened book. When being cooked in an oven, the chicken has four or
five times more space than when she was alive. "Veal" calves are kept in crates
that measure 22 inches wide by 54 long, where they cannot turn around, since
exercise would increase muscle development, toughen the flesh, and slow
weight gain. Standing on slatted floors causes a constant strain. Diarrhea, a frequent problem because of their improper diet which is meant to keep their flesh
pale, causes the slats to become slippery and wet; the calves often fall, getting leg
injuries. When taken to slaughter, many of them can hardly walk.

Factory farming is inevitable in a "meat" advocating culture, because it is
the only way to maintain and meet the demand for flesh products. Thus, those
who argue that factory farming is immoral but alternatives to obtaining animal
flesh are acceptable, are attempting to deny the historical reality that has brought
us to this time and place. Moreover, no matter where the animals to be slaughtered have been raised, it is the custom to withhold feed for the last twenty four
hours of their life. As the authors of *Raising Pigs Successfully* reveal: "Withholding
feed is usually done for the sake of the butcher (less mess when the intestines
and stomach are empty) and to save wasted feed. Some raisers don't do it
because they say that it upsets the animal to miss feedings and adds to the stress
level on butchering day." (Kellogg, 110)

This is clearly abusive treatment.

By physical force, I mean *specific* actions that cause injuries, in this case death
by violence. While raising an animal in a loving family farm situation may mean
that the conditions described above are not present, this condition—that of force
that injures or abuses—will always be present, for an animal does not become
"meat" without being violently deprived of his or her life. This violence can
come in one of three ways: death at the hands of the family farmer, death by a
hired gun who comes to the farm, or, as with animals intensively farmed, death
at a slaughterhouse. This last option requires the transporting of the animals—
often the only time that an animal will travel—a strange, sometimes uncomfort-

able, and perplexing if not alarming experience. At the slaughterhouse, smells and sounds alert the animal that something frightening is happening.

Clearly, animals prefer to live rather than to die, and when given the opportunity they tell us so.

As a child growing up in a small village, I lived down the street from the town butcher. We were allowed to watch him kill and butcher the animals. These animals did not go merrily to their deaths. Several times, rather than face his rifle, cows escaped from the truck and went running down the street. Pigs let out high squeals, moved frantically, and upon having their throats slashed, continued to toss and turn until yanked heavenward so that bleed-out would begin.

The killing of animals is physical force that injures and abuses animals against their will.

INSTITUTIONAL VIOLENCE REQUIRES A SERIES OF DENIAL MECHANISMS.

Denial of the extent and nature of violence is an important protective device for maintaining institutional violence. It communicates that the violence that is an integral part of the existence of some commodity, some benefit, is neither troublesome nor severe. In the language of "meat" and "meat eater" the issues of animal suffering and killing are neutralized. This language reveals that we have difficulty *naming the violence*. Why are we unable truthfully to name the eating of animals as such? Why do we eat animals and yet, through language, deny that this is what we are doing? Adrienne Rich offers one answer: "Whatever is named, undepicted in images . . . whatever is misnamed as something else, made difficult-to-come-by, whatever is buried in the memory by the collapse of meaning under an inadequate or lying language—this will become, not merely unspoken, but unspeakable."

The truth about raising and slaughtering animals is both unspoken and unspeakable. We are especially not to discuss it when animals' bodies are being consumed. As a consequence *false naming* is a major component of institutional violence. Indeed, false naming begins with the living animals. Whether they are to be found on family farms or in factory farms, the advice is the same: Do not give animals to be eaten by human beings any names that bestow individuality. Family farmers advise: "If you're going to eat it [sic], don't give it [sic] a pet name. Try something like 'Porky' or 'Chops' or 'Spareribs' if the urge to name is too strong." (Kellogg, 13)

Factory farmers advise: "Forget the pig [or a cow, a chicken, etc.] is an 'animal.' Instead, view them as 'a machine in a factory.' " (Byrnes in Mason and Singer, 1)

Do not name animals you are going to consume; don't call them Mary, Martha, or Paul, or even a pig, chicken, or cow, but a food-producing unit, a protein harvester, a computerized unit in a factory environment, an egg-producing machine, a converting machine, a biomachine, a crop, a grain-consuming animal unit.

False naming means that we can avoid responsibility. False naming creates false consciousness. We communicate something different about our relationship to animals when we speak about "meat" than when we speak either about living animals who enjoy relationships or about the eating of slaughtered, cooked, and seasoned severed animal muscle and blood.

False naming means that "meat" eaters are people of the lie. They are lying about their actions, which they do not see as actions. Through language, we lose sight of the fact that someone must be acting as a perpetrator of violence for there to be something else called "meat."

Language removes agency and cloaks violence: "Someone kills animals so that I can eat their corpses as meat" becomes "Animals are killed to be eaten as meat" then "Animals are meat" and finally "Meat animals" thus "Meat." Something *we do to animals* has become instead something that is a part of animals' nature and we lose consideration of our role as eaters of animals entirely. False naming about "meat" is an integral aspect of eating animals.

False naming enacts what I have called the structure of the absent referent. In *The Sexual Politics of Meat* I argue that animals in name and body are made absent as animals for "meat" to exist. If animals are alive they cannot be "meat." Thus a dead body replaces the live animal and animals become absent referents. Without animals there would be no flesh eating, yet they are absent from the act of eating flesh because they have been transformed into food. Animals are also made absent through language that renames dead bodies before consumers eat them. The absent referent permits us to forget about the animal as an independent entity and enables us to resist efforts to make animals present.[2] False naming and the structure of the absent referent create the permission for institutional violence and announce that *there is no call to accountability* for the eating of animals. In the absence of accountability, abuse continues.

The lack of any direct involvement with or consciousness of the violence of the slaughterhouse keeps us unaccountable. Again, as the family farmers reveal: "We usually send our hogs out to be slaughtered simply because we don't want the work of preparing the meat ourselves and because, emotionally, we tend to grow attached to the porkers. It is far easier to pat them good-bye as they leave in the truck and welcome them back in white paper wrappers. The act of killing something [sic] you have raised from a baby is not an easy task." (Kellogg, 109)

Killing, except for the ritual of the hunt, remains distasteful to most consumers. Since the institutional violence of meat eating requires killing, at the rate of some 15 million a day, a cloud of denial surrounds this.

Denial is enacted at the financial level as well. "Meat" eaters do not have to pay the true costs for the "meat" that they eat. The cheapness of a diet based on grain-fed terminal animals exists because it does not include the cost of depleting the environment. Not only does the cost of "meat" not include the loss of topsoil, the pollution of water, and other environmental effects (see below), but price supports of the dairy and beef "industry" mean that the government actively prevents the price of eating animals from being reflected in the commodity of "meat." My tax money subsidizes war, but it also subsidizes the eating of animals. For instance, the estimated costs of subsidizing the "meat" industry with water in California alone is $26 billion annually (Hur and Fields 1985a, 17). If water used by the "meat" industry were not subsidized by United States taxpayers, "hamburger" would cost $35 per pound and "beefsteak" would be $89. Tax monies perpetuate the cheapness of animals' bodies as a food source; consequently "meat" eaters are allowed to exist in a state of denial. They are not required to confront "meat" eating as a "pocketbook issue." Federal support of animal-based diet protects it from scrutiny from budget-conscious households. As much as we bemoan the war industry that is fed with our tax monies, we might also bemoan the support our tax monies give to the "meat" industry that wars upon animals and the environment.

INSTITUTIONAL VIOLENCE TARGETS "APPROPRIATE" VICTIMS.

I have referred to two different experiences I myself have had with the violence of "meat" eating. In one, I watched with fascination and dispassion as animals were slaughtered, bled, dunked into boiling water to rid them of their hair, skinned, disemboweled, and halved. In the other, I became upset by the death of my horse and connected that to the "hamburger" I was about to eat. How could I go home as a child each day from watching the bloody slaughter and eat flesh foods nonplussed, but as a young adult, greet the knowledge about eating animals with horror? Several answers come to mind; they all revolve around the notion of the appropriate victim. When cows and pigs were butchered, they had no names and no prior relationship to me. I had not affectionately combed their hair, bestowed upon them attention, recognized their individuality and personality. While their deaths were very vivid, indeed, the reason for our attendance at this ritual of slaughter, they remained absent referents. Images in our culture construct pigs and cows as appropriate victims—their sociability denied, given neither a past, present, nor future upon which we base our knowledge of them. I had little other understanding of them, except that as pigs and cows they were meant to be killed and eaten in our culture. As children, my friends and I recognized this and accepted it. I honestly cannot remember meeting with any qualms the pork chops or T-bones served at home the same night as the butchering we had watched. It was all a part of acceptable reality in our culture. Why else did cows and pigs exist?

However, horses are not generally meant to be killed and eaten in our culture. As a child, I begged that dog food made from horses be banned from our home.

Through my identification with Jimmy's death I came to see the meaning of institutional violence *for the victims rather than the consumers*. This painful experience allowed an ethic of inviolability to surface in my consciousness. There were no longer any appropriate victims.

Ideology makes the existence of "appropriate victims" appear to be natural and inevitable. Everything possible is done to keep us from seeing terminal animals as subjects of their own lives, and to keep us from seeing ourselves in any sort of relationship with a living, breathing, feeling being. Such animals are objectified in life and death. We ignore our radical biological similarity with these animals.

A logic of domination accompanies the making of appropriate victims. Differences have been deemed to carry meanings of superiority and inferiority. According to a logic of domination, that which is morally superior is morally justified in subordinating that which is not (Warren 1990, 128–133). The other animals are appropriate victims for "meat" eating simply because they are not humans. Once their inferiority is established through species differences, their subordination to humans' interests then follows. They become appropriate victims because they are not like us; they are not like us, in part because we dominate them.

INSTITUTIONAL VIOLENCE HAS IDENTIFIABLE DETRIMENTAL EFFECTS ON THE SOCIETY AS A WHOLE.

A remarkable aspect of institutional violence is that it is culturally protected and seen as beneficial, even though it is actually harmful in several ways besides the killings of billions of sentient beings. There are three areas of concern here: the consequences to the environment, to the health of eaters of animals, and to the workers who produce dead animals for consumption.

Consequences for the environment. Millions of acres are deforested to convert land to grazing and croplands to feed farm animals. Then overgrazing or intensive cultivation causes these lands to become desert. Eighty-five percent of topsoil erosion—the loss of the organic soil layer which provides plants with nutrients and moisture—is due to livestock raising. Because of conversion of land to feed animals, wildlife are losing their habitats, and are often crushed or wounded during the clearing operations.

Animal agriculture is the major industrial polluter in the United States. Feedlots and slaughterhouses are responsible for more of the country's water pollution than all other industries and households combined. A pound of animal flesh means that 100 pounds of livestock manure had to be disposed of, often in our waterways. Slaughterhouse waste—fat, carcass waste, fecal matter—is several hundred times more concentrated than raw waste, yet it is dumped into our rivers at the rate of more than two tons an hour. It is estimated that 125 tons of waste are produced every second by animals raised for human consumption; more than half of this waste is not recycled. "American livestock contribute five times more harmful organic waste to water pollution than do people, and twice that of industry" (Lappé 1982, 84). Agricultural crops—more than half of which are harvested to produce livestock feed—are the source of most of the pollutants such as pesticides, nutrients, leachates, and sediment that plague our water resources.

A by-product of livestock production is methane, a greenhouse gas that can trap twenty to thirty times more solar heat than carbon dioxide. Mainly because of their burps, "ruminant animals are the largest producers of methane, accounting for 12 to 15 percent of emissions, according to the EPA" (O'Neill 1990, 4).

The land and water needs of a vegetarian diet are substantially less than those of a "meat" based dietary: the same land that can be used to produce meat for 250 days would provide sustenance for 2,200 days if cultivated with soybeans. An animal-based diet requires about eight times more water than a plant-based diet. Over half the water used in this country is used to irrigate feed crops. "The fact is, a vegetarian diet is about the most ecologically efficient thing *anybody* can do."[3]

Consequences for "meat" eaters' health.   A study of the eating habits of 6,500 Chinese revealed that a flesh-eating and dairy-product consumption diet increases the risk of developing disease. Some if its findings include:

— While the Chinese consume 20 percent more calories than Americans, Americans are 25 percent fatter. The difference is attributed to the source for these calories. The Chinese eat only a third the amount of fat as we do, but twice the amount of starch, since the majority of their calories come from complex carbohydrates rather than from flesh foods.

— Overconsumption of protein, especially protein from animal flesh, is linked to chronic disease. Americans not only consume more protein than the Chinese (a third more) but 70 percent of that protein comes from flesh foods; only 7 percent of protein for Chinese is derived from dead animals. Those Chinese who increase their protein intake, especially animal protein intake, have the highest rates of "diseases of affluence": heart disease, cancer, and diabetes.

— Chinese cholesterol levels are much lower than ours, so that "their high cholesterol is our low," according to T. Colin Campbell (Brody 1990). Animal foods, including dairy products, are implicated in Americans' high cholesterol level. (A diet rich in fat also increases the risk of breast cancer, which strikes at least one out of every nine women.) Jane Brody notes a fivefold to tenfold difference in death rates between countries with high-fat diets and those with low-fat diets such as Japan (Brody 1981, 71)

— The Chinese diet contains three times more dietary fiber than the average American diet, because of the Chinese reliance on plant foods. Those with the highest fiber intake had the most iron-rich blood.

T. Colin Campbell, who oversaw the Chinese dietary study, concludes that "We're basically a vegetarian species and should be eating a wide variety of plant foods and minimizing our intake of animal foods" (Brody 1990).

Consequences for the workers who produce flesh. One of the basic things that must happen in the institutional violence of slaughtering is that the animal must be treated as an inert object, not as a living, feeling, breathing being. Similarly workers on the assembly line become treated as inert, unthinking objects whose creative, bodily, and emotional needs are ignored. They must view the living animal as the "meat" everyone outside the slaughterhouse accepts it as, while the animal is still alive.

Also, the "meat" packing industry has become increasingly centralized. A few large corporations that are strongly antiunion have driven down industry wages and benefits. Increased technology has permitted an industry-wide speedup, and resulted in some of the most dangerous jobs in America, jobs which, if they had a preference, most would choose not to hold. As Beverly Smith commented to Andrea Lewis: "It's not like they decided ... 'I'll go cut up chickens though I could go and be a college professor.' Those people don't have freedom of choice" (Lewis, 1990, 175–76). Smith was referring to "lung gunners" who must each hour scrape the insides of 5,000 chickens' cavities and pull out the recently slaughtered chicken's lungs. Ninety-five percent of these poultry workers are black women who face carpal tunnel syndrome and other disorders caused by repetitive motion and stress (Clift 1990; Lewis 1990, 175).

THE FINAL CONDITION OF INSTITUTIONAL VIOLENCE IS THAT CON-
SUMERS ARE MANIPULATED INTO PASSIVITY REGARDING THIS PRACTICE.
This manipulation occurs in several ways. As children we became convinced
that eating animals was good and proper. Any objections were quelled at the
dinner table. Since the 1950s the four basic food groups have contributed to our
passivity as beneficiaries of the institutional violence of "meat." Because of the
four basic food groups and their emphasis on flesh foods and dairy products,
many people continue to believe erroneously that they need to eat "meat" to
survive. Free recipes sent to newspapers around the country by the Dairy
Council, the Egg Council, and the Beef and Pork lobbies keep the idea of eating animals firmly in place, so firmly that many who perceive its deficiencies
despair of changing it.

It may seem to be a tautology to say that if we believe some other beings
are meant to be our "meat" (the appropriate victims) then we are meant to be
"meat" eaters. Conversely, if we are meant to be "meat" eaters then we also
believe that someone else is meant to die to be our "meat." These are inter-
locking givens, ontologies that become self-perpetuating and breed passivity.
Most of us think there is no problem, and those few who might initially detect
one are encouraged to dismiss it as unsolvable.

CHRISTIANITY AND THE INSTITUTIONALIZED VIOLENCE OF EATING ANIMALS

I have demonstrated the nature of institutional violence and how it is that
"meat" eating is a form of institutional violence. With this framework established, we can now turn to the Christian dimension to the institutional violence
of eating animals.

One reason that many Christians do not see animals as inviolable is
because they believe that only humans are in the image of God, and thus only
humans are inviolable. Animals become the appropriate victims because they are
not in God's image, but instead consumable entities: lambs of God, sacrificial
lambs, fatted calves. The same passage that establishes the relationship of humans
to God's image appears to bestow legitimacy on the exploitation of the other
animals. Genesis 1:26 reads: Then God said, "Let us make man in our image,
after our likeness; and let them have dominion over the fish of the sea, and over
the birds of the air, and over the cattle, and over all the earth, and over every
creeping thing that creeps upon the earth."

Genesis 1:26 is seen to be God's permission to dominate the other animals and make them instruments for human interests, thus de facto allowing "meat" eating. By interpreting "dominion" to mean God gave us permission to exploit animals for our tastes, several denial mechanisms are enacted. We are deflected from concern about animals by believing that we are absolved from the action that has cast animals as "meat." The comforting nature of this belief derives from the fact that the onus of the decision to eat animals is shifted from individual responsibility to divine intent. (Someone, but not me, is responsible for these animals' deaths. If I am not responsible, I do not need to examine what I am doing and its consequences.) In this viewpoint, God as the author of and authority over our lives has created us as "meat" eaters. In one act of authorization two ontological situations are created simultaneously: "meat" eater and "meat." As Bowie, the commentator in *The Interpreter's Bible*, remarks on this passage: "Fish and fowl and animals have been his [sic] food."

This interpretation of Genesis 1:26 requires associating dominion with exploitation. Some believe that the clue to this association is found in the choice of words in this passage. Von Rad opines that "[t]he expressions for the exercise of this dominion are remarkably strong: *rada*, 'tread,' 'trample' (e.g., the wine press); similarly *kabas*, 'stamp'" (60). But others see a less harsh meaning to the concept of dominion. James Barr suggests that *rada* was generally used about kings ruling over certain areas. "For instance in 1 Kings 5:4 the verb is used to express Solomon's dominion (expressly a peaceful dominion) over a wide area." He believes that *kabas*, "subdue," refers not to animals but to the tilling of the earth (Barr, 22). C. Westermann has suggested that the use of *rada*, "have dominion, govern," "can be compared with what is said in 1:16 about the sun and moon, which are to 'govern' the day and night" (Barr, 23).[4] According to this viewpoint, dominion carries no idea of exploitation, indeed, "man [sic] would lose his [sic] 'royal' position in the realm of living things if the animals were to him [sic] an object of use or of prey" (Barr, 23).

When dominion is equated with exploitation, people are conferring their own preconceptions concerning their relationship with animals upon the Bible, for an exploitative interpretation of Genesis 1:26 cannot be reconciled with the vegetarian passage quoted above found in Genesis 1:29. *The Interpreter's Bible* notes the difficulty of reconciling these two passages when it exegetes Genesis 1:29: "Man [sic] is thus to be a vegetarian. This is something of a contradiction to verse 26, according to which he was to *have dominion* over all living creatures" (Simpson, 486).[5] For others: "the human 'dominion' envisaged by Genesis 1 included no idea of using the animals for meat and no terrifying consequences for the animal world. Human exploitation of animal life is not regarded as an inevitable part of human existence, as something given and indeed encouraged by the ideal condition of the original creation (Barr, 21).[6]

Genesis 1:26 does not supersede the meaning of creation that extends to include Genesis 1:29. When severed from the meaning of creation and the direction to be vegetarian, the scriptures are used as a historically justificatory defense of actions. This is a denial mechanism at the theological level.

These defenses continue when considering God's explicit permission to consume animals in Genesis 9:3, "Every moving thing that lives shall be food for you; and as I give you the green plants, I give you everything." On a certain view of Genesis, one must argue that "meat" eating is a consequence of the fall. The end of vegetarianism is "a necessary evil" (Phillips, 48), and the introduction of flesh eating has a "negative connotation" (Soler, 24; see also Kook). In his discussion of the Jewish dietary laws, Samuel H. Dresner argues that "the eating of meat [permitted in Genesis 9] is itself a sort of compromise" (21), "*a divine concession to human weakness and human need*" (26). Adam, the perfect man, "is clearly meant to be a vegetarian" (22). In pondering the fact that Isaiah's vision of the future perfect society postulates vegetarianism as well, Dresner observes: "At the 'beginning' and at the 'end' man [sic] is, thus, in his [sic] ideal state, herbivorous. His [sic] life is not maintained at the expense of the life of the beast. In 'history' which takes place here and now, and in which man [sic], with all his [sic] frailties and relativities, lives and works out his [sic] destiny, he[sic] may be carnivorous." (24)

What is interposed between Genesis 1:29 and Isaiah is human history. In this sense, history is the concrete, social context in which we move. Moreover, history becomes our destiny.

We come to believe that because an action of the past was condoned by the ethical norms of the time, it may continue unchanged and unchallenged into our present time, history becomes another authority manipulating and extending our passivity. It allows us to objectify the praxis of vegetarianism: it is an ideal, but not realizable. It is out of time, not in time. When Genesis 9 is used to interpret backward to Genesis 1 and forward to our own practice of "meat" eating, history is read into creation, and praxis is superseded by an excused fallibility. History will then immobilize the call to praxis—to stop the suffering, end institutional violence, and side with the oppressed animals. If vegetarianism is out of time, in the Garden of Eden, then we need not concern ourselves with it.

Objectifying the praxis of vegetarianism makes it ahistorical, outside of history and without a history. This may explain why vegetarianism throughout the ages has been called a fad despite its recurrence. "Meat" eating has not constituted a large part of the diets of humankind and, I believe, each individual at some point experiences some discomfort with the eating of animals. In the light of what I have called "the sexual politics of meat"—i.e., women, second-class citizens, are more likely to eat what are considered to be second-class foods in a patriarchal culture, vegetables, fruits, and grains rather than "meat"—the question becomes who exactly has been eating the "meat" after Genesis 9? Consider, for instance, this terse comment on Leviticus 6 by Elizabeth Cady Stanton, a leading nineteenth-century feminist: "The meat so delicately cooked by the priests, with wood and coals in the altar, in clean linen, no woman was permitted to taste, only the males among the children of Aaron" (Stanton, 91).

RESISTING INSTITUTIONALIZED VIOLENCE

We are estranged from animals through institutionalized violence and have accepted inauthenticity in the name of divine authority. We have also been estranged from ways to think about our estrangement. Religious concepts of alienation, brokenness, separation ought to include our treatment of animals. Eating animals is an existential expression of our estrangement and alienation from the created order.

Elisabeth Schüssler Fiorenza reminds us that "The basic insight of all liberation theologies, including feminist theology, is the recognition that all theology, willingly or not, is by definition always engaged for or against the oppressed" (6). To side with history and posit vegetarianism as unattainable is to side against the oppressed animals; to side with the praxis of vegetarianism is to side with the oppressed and against institutional violence. Insofar as Christians are called to live in the reign of God initiated by Jesus, they cannot legitimately take the "practical" fallen history of Genesis 9 as authority.

It is here, in the conflict between history and eschatology, that I would place a Christology of vegetarianism. This Christology is not concerned with whether Jesus was or was not a vegetarian just as feminist theology rejects the relevance of the maleness of the twelve disciples. This is not a quest for historical duplication but for the acquisition of an ability to discern justice-making according to the Christological revelation. With this perspective we should come to see that a piece of "meat" turns the miracles of the loaves and fishes on its head. Where Jesus multiplied food to feed the hungry, our current food-producing system reduces food sources and damages the environment at the same time, producing plant food to feed terminal animals.

A Christology of vegetarianism would argue that just as Jesus challenged historical definitions such as Samaritan, or undercut identities such as the wealthy man, so we are equipped to challenge the historical and individual identity of a food habit that fosters environmental and ethical injustice. We are not bound by our histories. We have been freed to claim an identity based on current understanding of animal consciousness, ecological spoilage, and health issues. A Christology of vegetarianism would affirm that no more crucifixions are necessary, and insist that animals, who are still being crucified, must be freed from the cross. The suffering of animals, our sacrificial lambs, does not bring about our redemption but furthers our suffering, suffering from preventable diseases related to eating animals, suffering from environmental problems, suffering from the inauthenticity that institutionalized violence promotes. In the following quotation feminist ethicist Beverly Harrison (1985) contributes important insights into this process of Christians resisting institutional violence, which can be readily connected to the eating of animals. (I add these connections in brackets.)

> Each of us must learn to extend a critical analysis of the contradictions affecting our lives in an ever-widening circle, until it inclusively incorporates those whose situations differ from our own [such as animals.] This involves naming structures that create the social privilege we possess [to eat animals and make them appropriate victims] as well as understanding how we have been victims [manipulated into passivity so that we believe that need to eat dead animals] . . . Critical consciousness and, therefore, genuine social and spiritual transcendence, do not and cannot emerge apart from our refusing complicity in destructive social forces and resisting those structures that perpetuate life-denying conditions [including eating animals]. (235–36)

Perhaps our greatest challenge is to raise the consciousness of those around us to see the institutional violence of eating animals as an ethical issue. But how does something become an ethical issue? Sarah Bentley has described the process by which wife beating has become an ethical concern.[7] She does so by drawing on Gerald Fourez's *Liberation Ethics* which demonstrates that " 'concrete historical struggles' " are the basis for the development of "the discipline called 'ethics.' " For something to become an ethical issue we need " 'a new awareness of some oppression or conflict.' " This is critical consciousness.

I would suggest that an example of this critical consciousness is the animal liberation movement and its identification of the eating of animals as inhumane and exploitative. As Bentley explains, after a time of agitation by a group living with the critical consciousness of this oppression, others besides the group with the critical consciousness begin to question the oppression as well. The social consciousness of a community or a culture is transformed by this agitation. "Ethical themes, therefore, are *historically specific*, arising from 'the particular questions that certain groups are asking themselves.' "

Christians responding to the insights of the animal liberation movement must ask questions about the institutional violence that permits them the personal satisfaction of eating flesh. "In effect, the [particular] questions represent 'problems *raised by practices* that have to be faced.'" Farming and slaughtering practices such as caging, debeaking, liquid diets for calves, twenty-four-hour starvation before death, transporting and killing animals are all troublesome practices. We must stop denying them. But of course, denial is necessary when concrete practices are challenged. Indeed, ethical statements "always evolve 'as particular ways of questioning in which people, individually or in groups, *stake their lives* as they decide what they want to do and what their solidarity is.' Thus, if *no one questions*, if *no practical engagement* takes place, no problem exists."

This can be linked with the success of false naming and other denial mechanisms we have mentioned. They cannot be overcome at a merely theoretical level. Unless we acquaint ourselves with the *practice* of farming and slaughtering animals, we will not encounter the *problems* raised by these practices, such as the abuse of animals, the environment, our health, and workers in the "meat" industry. If the problem is invisible, in a sense mirroring the physical invisibility of intensively farmed animals, then there will be ethical invisibility.

A Christian ethics adequate to challenging the institutional violence of eating animals and modeled on this understanding of the evolution of an ethical stance involves three connected parts: certain practices raise problems; practical engagement and solidarity ensues when these problematic practices are perceived; an ethical position arises from this ongoing solidarity that forges critical community consciousness. As we become personally aware of the contradictions between Christianity and the practice of eating animals, we find that we must enter into a struggle regarding our own and this culture's practice.

To overcome our failure to acknowledge another's inviolability we need to find alternative ways of relating to animals rather than eating them. Beverly Harrison proposes that "We know and value the world, *if* we know and value it, through our ability to touch, to hear, to see" (13). We have not known and valued the domestic animals that are eaten because we have not touched, heard, or seen them. To most of us, animals are disembodied entities. Disembodied animals have little potential of being touched, heard, or seen, except as "meat."

Demonstrating Harrison's sensual understanding of how we know the world, Alice Walker describes what happens when she touches, hears, and sees an animal. With Blue the horse she sees the depth of feeling in his eyes and recalls something she feels adults fail to remember: "human animals and non-human animals can communicate quite well" (Walker 1988, 5). Shortly after having that insight, Walker experiences the injustice of a steak: "I am eating misery" she thinks. Walker touches, hears, sees, and describes interactions with very specific animals, and she is changed by this, called to authenticity.

We all have an option to dispense with the consumption of misery: We can feed instead on the grace of vegetables. Virginia de Araujo describes such a perspective, that of a friend, who takes the barrenness of a cupboard, filled only with "celery threads, chard stems, avocado skins" and creates a feast

> & says, On this grace I feed, I wilt
> in spirit if I eat flesh, let the hogs,
> the rabbits live, the cows browse,
> the eggs hatch out chicks & peck seeds.

The choice is institutionalized violence or feeding on grace. One cannot feed on grace and eat animals. Our goal of living in right relationships and ending injustice is to have grace *in* our meals as well as *at* our meals. Socially responsible persons, justice-oriented persons, must recognize that we are violating others in eating animals, and in the process wilting the spirit. There are no appropriate victims. Let the hogs, rabbits, cows, chicks live. In place of misery, let there be grace.

NOTES

1. I use the term God/ess after Rosemary Radford Ruether in *Sexism and Godtalk: Toward a Feminist Theology*. Ruether explains: "when discussing fuller divinity to which this theology points, I use the term God/ess, a written symbol intended to combine both the masculine and feminine forms of the word for the divine while preserving the Judeo-Christian affirmation that divinity is one ... [I]t serves here as an analytic sign to point toward that yet unnameable understanding of the divine that would transcend patriarchal limitations and signal redemptive experience for women as well as men" (Ruether, 46).

2. The structure of the absent referent is fulfilled in intensive or factory farming, but did not originate with it. Indeed, in *The Sexual Politics of Meat* (Adams, 1990), I gave little attention to factory farming per se because I see the problem as the objectification of animals, not any single practice of producing flesh foods. On the problem of the hunt as the way of obtaining flesh foods, see Adams 1991.

3. Paul Orbis, 4. This information was gathered from material including Fund for Animals, 1990; Robbins, 1989; Akers, 1983; Hur and Fields, 1984; 1985a, 1985b; Hur, 1985; Krizmanic, 1990a, 1990b; Lappé, 1982; O'Neill, 1990; Pimental, 1975, 1976.

4. James Barr adds parenthetically, "a different Hebrew word indeed, but there is no reason to suppose that this makes much difference" (Barr, 23).

5. Cuthbert Simpson's explanation is that verse 29 may have been an addition to P's original narrative, containing the classical conceptualization of the Golden Age—which was seen as vegetarian and peaceful between humans and animals—and so it is more linked to the visions of Isaiah 11:6–8, 65:25; Hosea 2:18. Thus it posits potentiality rather than reality.

6. Jean Soler agrees with Barr's conclusion, stating "meat eating is implicitly but unequivocally excluded" and that the reason for this has to do with the way that God and humans are defined in Genesis 1:26 by their relationship to each other (Soler, 24). See also Cohen.

7. The quotations which follow about the development of an ethical issue are from Sarah Bentley, pp. 16–17. Those quotations with both single and double quotation marks are Bentley's references to Gerard Fourez's *Liberation Ethics* (Philadelphia: Temple University Press, 1982), 108–109. Italicized words within the quotation marks contained this emphasis in the original source.

REFERENCES

Adams, Carol. 1990. *The Sexual Politics of Meat: A Feminist-Vegetarian Critical Theory*. New York: Continuum.

———. 1991. "Ecofeminism and the Eating of Animals." *Hypatia* 6 (1).

Akers, Keith. 1983. *A Vegetarian Sourcebook: The Nutrition, Ecology, and Ethics of a Natural Foods Diet*. New York: G.P. Putnam's Sons.

Barr, James. 1972. "Man and Nature—The Ecological Controversy and the Old Testament." *Bulletin of the John Rylands University Library of Manchester*: 9–32.

Bentley, Sarah R. 1989. *For Better or Worse: The Challenge of the Battered Women's Movement to Christian Social Ethics*. Union Theological Seminary doctoral diss.

Brody, Jane. 1981. *Jane Brody's Nutrition Book*. New York: W. W. Norton & Co.

———. 1990. "Huge Study Indicts Fat and Meat." *New York Times*, 8 May.

Clift, Elayne. 1990. "Advocate Battles for Safety in Mines and Poultry Plants." *New Directions for Women* (May/June): 3.

Daly, Lois. 1990. "Ecofeminism, Reverence for Life, and Feminist Theological Ethics." In Birch, et at. *Liberating Life: Contemporary Approaches to Ecological Theology*. Maryknoll, NY: Orbis Books, 1990.

Fiorenza, Elisabeth Schüssler. 1984. *In Memory of Her: A Feminist Theological Reconstruction of Christian Origins*. New York: Crossroad.

Fund for Animals. 1990. "Animal Agriculture Fact Sheet #2. Factory Farming: Misery on the Menu."

Harrison, Beverly. 1985. *Making the Connections: Essays in Feminist Social Ethics*. Carol S. Robb, ed. Boston: Beacon Press.

Hur, Robin. 1985. "Six Inches from Starvation: How and Why America's Topsoil Is Disappearing." *Vegetarian Times* (March): 45–47.

Hur, Robin, and David Fields. 1984. "Are High-fat Diets Killing Our Forests?" *Vegetarian Times* (February): 22–24.

———. 1985a. "America's Appetite for Meat is Ruining Our Water." *Vegetarian Times* (January): 16–18.

———. 1985b. "How Meat Robs America of its Energy." *Vegetarian Times* (April): 24–27.

Kellog, Kathy and Bob. 1985. *Raising Pigs Successfully*. Charlotte, Vt: Williamson Publishing.

Kook, Abraham Isaac. 1990. "Fragments of Light: A View as to the Reasons for the Commandments." In *Abraham Isaac Kook: The Lights of Penitence, The Moral Principles, Lights of Holiness, Essays, Letters, and Poems*. Trans. Ben Zion Bokser. New York: Paulist Press.

Krizmanic, Judy. 1990a. "Is a Burger Worth It?" *Vegetarian Times* (April): 20–21.

———. 1990b. "Why Cutting Out Meat Can Cool Down the Earth." *Vegetarian Times* (April): 18–19.

Lappé, Francis Moore. 1982. *Diet for a Small Planet*. New York: Ballantine.

Lewis, Andrea. 1990. "Looking at the Total Picture: A Conversation with Health Activist Beverly Smith." In Evelyn C. White, ed. *The Black Women's Health Book: Speaking for Ourselves*. Seattle: The Seal Press, 172–181.

Mason, Jim, and Peter Singer. 1980. *Animal Factories*. New York, Crown.

O'Neill, Molly. 1990. "The Cow's Role in Life is Called into Question by a Crowded Planet." *New York Times*, 6 May, Section 4: 1, 4.

Phillips, Anthony. 1983. *Lower than the Angels: Questions Raised by Genesis 1–11*. The Bible Reading Fellowship.

Pimental, David. 1975. "Energy and Land Constraints in Food Protein Production." *Science* 190 (November 21): 754–761.

———. 1976. "Land Degradation: Effects on Food and Energy Resources." *Science* 194 (October 8): 149–55.

Robbins, John. 1989. *Diet for a New America*. New York: Stillpoint Press.

Ruether, Rosemary Radford. 1975. *New Woman, New Earth*. New York: Seabury Press.

Simpson, Cuthbert, and Walter Russell Bowie. 1952. *The Interpreter's Bible (Genesis)*. New York and Asheville: Abingdon Press.

Stanton, Elizabeth Cady. (1989), 1974. *The Woman's Bible: Part I*. New York: European Publishng Co.; Seattle: Coalition Task Force on Women and Religion.

Walker, Alice. 1988. "Am I Blue." In *Living by the Word: Selected Writings: 1973–1987*. San Diego: Harcourt Brace Jovanovich.

Warren, Karen J. 1990. "The Power and the Promise of Ecological Feminism." *Environmental Ethics* 12 (Summer): 125–146.

THE ISLAMIC
TRADITION

> *God*
> *there is no god but He, the*
> *Living, the Everlasting.*
> *Slumber seizes Him not, neither sleep;*
> *to Him belongs*
> *all that is in the heavens and the earth.*
> —*Qur'ān* 2:256

Originating in the divine revelation to Muḥammad in early seventh-century Arabia, the *Qur'ān* speaks of a single God who is creator and sustainer of the universe. To God is said to belong all that exists on earth and in heaven. No creature moves but God moves it; no star shines but God illumines it. The shoots of plants, thick-clustered dates, olives, pomegranates, the gardens of vines: all these are signs for those who believe. "And earth—He set it down for all beings, therein fruits, and palm-trees with sheaths, and grain in the blade, and fragrant herbs." In the Islamic vision of the universe, order and meaning exist in the natural arrangement of nature; nature has been "set down" for all beings, not as wilderness or brute enemy, but as provision for life. Everywhere signs of God's majesty and providence suffuse creation. Yet it is to God above all, not his creation, that one is to submit.

Islamic theology and jurisprudence traditionally have focused on religious questions regarding God's nature, God's relationship to his creation, human destiny, and the laws that govern community life. Questions regarding nature and the relationship of humans to other forms of life—especially the responsibilities humans have to animals and to the natural world—for the most part are indirectly treated.

Still, there is no doubt that in the *Qur'ān* and the writings inspired by it, God is conceived as the God of *all* living things. God's relationship is vividly understood as encompassing the whole creation, not just human beings. In the unity of creation—of sun and moon, stars and trees, goats, sheep, and humans—created things share their creaturehood and possess a commonality one might not discern from the scarcity of Islamic writings on nature and animal life. Few declarations of the kinship of all life exist to express this commonality; noninjury to life and compassion for all living things are rarely invoked. Yet a sense of the generous beauty and abundance of the earth pervades Islamic texts—its rivers and fruits, its pearl and coral, the clay from which God fashioned human form. However we are to understand the spirit of the *Qur'ānic* verses, the seeds of empathy for animal suffering and a sense of the kindredness of all life exist in the pervasive recognition of the unity of creation and the mercy of God. All things belong to God, and should be treated accordingly.

Sacred places in which humans are forbidden to slay animals except in self-defense play a preeminent role in Muslim culture. The holy areas around Mecca and Medina are often referred to as *ḥaramān*, the "two sacred sites." Jerusalem is sometimes referred to as a third one. The existence of sacred sites where slaughter is forbidden suggests a spiritual aversion to the violence inherent in killing animals, even when its occasional necessity is recognized.

For Muslims, meat that is considered acceptable to eat is called *ḥalāl*. Its propriety as food derives from its being the flesh of "clean" animals that have been properly slaughtered, and is thus reminiscent of the *kashrut*-purified meat in the Judaic tradition. Scavenger animals, for example, are forbidden as food. During acts of ritual slaughter, a Muslim must consecrate the act of killing by pronouncing the words *Bismi-Llāh, Allāhu Akbar*, and cutting the throat of the animal with mercifully quick strokes. When animals are hunted, their meat is *ḥalāl* if the words of consecration are spoken when the animal is killed. Fish are *ḥalāl* if caught when alive, but dead fish are not.

'Īd al-Aḍḥā, the most important feast in the Islamic calendar, involves communal prayer and animal sacrifice. Commemorating Abraham's sacrifice of the ram, the feast recalls the divine dispensation to Abraham which relieved him of the burden of sacrificing his son Ismael. When Abraham had demonstrated his obedience to God, the Angel Gabriel brought a ram at the final moment as a surrogate for Abraham's son. Abraham's obedience to God, expressed in his willingness to sacrifice what was most dear to him, is embodied in the gift of the ram,

a sacrificial creature whose life absorbs the suffering that was to be Ismael's. The deep mysteries of animal sacrifice, wherever practiced, indebt humans to those creatures whose suffering transfigures their own. That ram could be surrogate for child bespeaks Islam's deep message of the commonality of creaturehood.

Islam's mystical Sufi tradition, which originated in the seventh century, is particularly sensitive to the spiritual dangers of animal slaughter. Sufism teaches that union with God is achievable through ascetic discipline motivated by love, and many individual Sufis have extended that love to animals. Legend records that an early female Sufi saint, Zaynab, found herself in trouble with the authorities for refusing to eat meat. Another story is told of the eighth-century Sufi Rābi'a al-'Adawiyya. According to the tale, Rābi'a went to the mountains, where deer, gazelle, mountain goats and wild asses joyfully gathered around her. Suddenly a man appeared, Ḥasan al-Basri, and the wild creatures fled. Confused, Ḥasan asked Rābi'a why the animals ran in terror when he came. Rābi'a said to him, "What have you eaten today?" "Onions in fat," he replied. She answered, "You eat their fat, how should they not flee from you?"[1]

Two Sufi perspectives on religious vegetarianism are included here. The first comes from the thirteenth-century mystic and poet Rūmī. Rūmī was fascinated by the dance of all creation out of nonbeing and jubilant at a world inflamed with divine love. In a chilling parable, he warns of the retribution that befalls humans who rupture that love by savagely slaughtering animals for food.

Similarly, the twentieth-century Sufi master M. R. Bawa Muhaiyaddeen seeks to awaken us to the spiritual imperative of imitating God's compassionate love for creation. In his discussion of *qurbān*, the Islamic parallel to *kashrut*, Bawa Muhaiyaddeen reminds us that "every life is truly the property of God," and that if one must eat meat, the slaughter of food animals should be performed compassionately and responsibly. It's not enough, says the Bawa, merely to follow conventional canons of *qurbān*. In addition, love requires that the butcher "must look into the eyes of the animal [and] he must continue to look into [its] eyes until its soul departs." In this way, the Bawa seeks to honor the purification implied in qurbānic slaughter as well as to awaken the heart of the one who kills. That such purification is believed necessary speaks to the deep ambivalence with which the taking of life is regarded in the Islamic tradition. This ambivalence is born from the intuition that animal life belongs to God no less than human life, a point beautifully conveyed in the second selection from Bawa Muhaiyaddeen. The Bawa's tale about the hunter and the orphaned fawn reminds us, as does Rūmī's parable, of the sacredness of all creation.

Such sacredness is also the theme of the selection from the Sunni Muslim Al-Ḥāfiẓ B.A. Masri ("Ḥāfiẓ" is an honorific title given to one who has memorized the entire *Qur'ān* by heart). Masri examines the place accorded animals in both the *Qur'ān* and Islamic tradition. Passionately decrying the contempt with which humans regard animals, he defends an alternative spiritual position, rooted in Qur'ānic study, that emphasizes the dignity and sacredness of animal life. Animals glorify God, symbolize God's love for creation, and know their own prayer and psalm.

N O T E

1. Margaret Smith writes about Zaynab and Rābi'a al-'Adawiyya in, respectively, *The Way of the Mystics* (New York: Oxford University Press, 1978), 154–162, and *Rābi'a the Mystic and Her Fellow-Saints in Islam* (Cambridge: Cambridge University Press, 1984), 34–35.

The Men Who Ate the Elephant

RŪMĪ

Jalāl al-Dīn Rūmī, author of Persian odes and lyrics, saint, great teacher, and founder of the famous Sufi Order of Whirling Dervishes, was born in 1207 in modern day Afghanistan and died in Asiatic Turkey in 1273. In ecstatic torrents of poetry that flowed from Rūmī after his 1244 meeting with the wandering dervish Shams al-Dīn, the moving power of love—its mystery, the encounter between lover and beloved—is evoked through images of transformation and rebirth. The lowliest manifestations of life are worthy of poetic verse; everything is symbolic of the divine unity that exists behind the distracting beauty and multiplicity of the world. Out of love for the source of all things, the mystic seeks the Beloved, the divine essence hidden and elusive in all that is seen, heard, and felt.

In this tale, Rūmī reminds us that any violation of the love that permeates the universe is swiftly retributed. In the process, he speaks eloquently against the slaughter of animals for food.

Have you heard the tale of how a certain sage of India once espied a party of friends? Naked and destitute, without provender, ahungered, they were arriving from a far journey. His wisdom's love surged within him and he greeted them kindly, blossoming like a rose-bush.

"I know," he said, "what anguish has gathered upon you, hungry and empty, on this pilgrimage of pain. But by Allah, I adjure you, illustrious folk, let not your food be the elephant's young! The elephant is in the direction where you are now going; give heed, and do not rend the elephant's child! Young elephants there are upon your way; to hunt them down would delight your hearts mightily. Very weak they are, and tender and very fat, but their mother lies in wait, searching for them; she would wander a hundred leagues seeking her offspring with many a moan and many a sigh. Fire and smoke issue from her trunk: beware that you harm not her fondly cherished little ones! The elephant takes a sniff at every mouth and twists her snout round the belly of every man, seeking where she may find the roast flesh of her offspring, that she may display her vengeance and her might.

"Listen to my advice," the good counselor went on, "that your hearts and souls may not be sorely tried. Satisfy yourselves with grasses and leaves; go not in chase of the young elephants. Now I have discharged the debt of good counsel; what should the fruit of good counsel be but felicity? I came in order to deliver the Message, that I may rescue you out of repentance. Take heed, and let not greed waylay you, let not greed for the leaf tear you up from the roots!"

So saying, he wished them farewell and departed.

As they went on their way, their famine and hunger waxed mighty. Suddenly they espied toward the highroad a fat young elephant, just newly born. Like ravening wolves they fell upon it, ate it clean up, and washed their hands.

One of the travelers however did not eat; he counseled his fellows, for he recalled what the dervish had said. The sage's words prohibited him from eating the roast flesh: old sense frequently bestows on you new fortune.

Then they all dropped to the ground and fell fast asleep; but the still hungry one watched like a shepherd amidst the flock. Presently he saw a terrible elephant approaching. First of all she came running toward him as he kept guard, and thrice sniffed his mouth, but no unwholesome odor came from it. Several times she circled him, and then departed; that huge queen-elephant harmed him not at all. Next she smelt the lips of every man that lay sleeping; the smell of her young one's flesh came to her from them each as they slumbered, for each had eaten of the roast-flesh of her offspring. The mother-elephant swiftly rent and slew them one by one, tossed each in the air at random so that he dashed upon the ground and split asunder.

Qurbān and

The Hunter Learns

Compassion from the Fawn

HIS HOLINESS M. R. BAWA MUHAIYADDEEN

Little is known of the early life of Sufi mystic Muḥammad Raheem Bawa Muhaiyaddeen of Sri Lanka. The first records date to the early 1900s, when traveling religious pilgrims came to know him and were inspired by the depth of his spiritual vision. He subsequently visited the United States, where he inspired the founding of the Bawa Muhaiyaddeen Fellowship in Philadelphia, a community devoted to the study and dissemination of his teachings. The Bawa died in 1986.

In the first selection here, Bawa Muhaiyaddeen interprets the practice of qurbān *as a ritual method for the slaughter of animals intended both to reduce killing and, more important, as a spiritual reminder that life belongs to God. The Bawa's treatment of* qurbān *clearly suggests that it parallels the "ambiguous permission" to kill animals Andrew Linzey discusses in his defense of Christian vegetarianism*

The second selection is a parable that teaches us how to become "true" human beings. An orphaned fawn reminds the hunter who has slain its mother that God has created both of them from the same elements. "Even though our skin and color are different," the fawn says, "our flesh is the same." Spiritually enlightened, the hunter learns compassion and the truth that all living things are God's sacred property.

175

QURBĀN

If a person is to take food for himself, he must remember that every life is the sole property of God. And if he would desire a life that is truly the property of God, he must first hand over all responsibility to God in *tawakkal-Allāh* (absolute trust and surrender to Allah). In that state, he must praise the glory of God before slaughtering the animal. This is one meaning of *qurbān*.

Allah has laid down certain laws for this. "You desired this animal, this flesh, but you must realize that this is also a life like you. You have not realized this, and therefore, I am laying down certain conditions or laws from which I hope you will realize this." Allah passed these commandments down to Prophet Muḥammad (*Salaam*). In those times, about 1,399 years ago, people did not realize this state of equality of life. Each individual would take a life according to his own wishes. They would wring or cut the animals' necks and slaughter them any way they liked, each in their own houses or compounds. Whenever they had celebrations or festivals, they would sacrifice millions and millions of animals in order to enjoy their festivities. They would even steal animals from others, to slaughter and eat.

So in the time of Prophet Muḥammad (*Sal.*), many people brought this complaint to him. The Prophet (*Sal.*) asked, "O God, what does this mean?" Then Allah sent down these laws or commandments which are called the *qurbān*. According to the commands of Allah, the people must not slaughter in this loose manner any longer. They must not take food that is *ḥarām* (forbidden), and they must take only the food that is *ḥalāl* (permissible). *Ḥarām* is mingled within everything you eat. There are evil things mingled into the body, and you must make them *ḥalāl* according to the words of Allah.

In order to do this, God said that you must recite the *Subhan Allāhi Kalimah* [ejaculatory prayer signifying "Holiness be to God!"] three times before you slaughter the animal. While you recite the *Kalimah*, you must complete the severing in three strokes of the knife, one for each recitation. The knife is to be swept around three times, and it must not touch the bone. It must be extremely sharp, and the length is prescribed according to each animal—so much for a fowl, so much for a goat, so much for a cow, so much for a camel. Also, the animal must not regurgitate any food, and it must not make any noise; otherwise, it becomes *ḥarām*.

The person who holds the animal and the person who cuts it must always observe the five times prayer. Therefore, it must be the *Imām* and the *mu'azzin* who perform the *qurbān*, because very often they are the only ones who regularly observe the five times prayer. This also means that the *qurbān* must take place near a mosque where two such people can always be found.

Before beginning the slaughter, they must first perform their ablutions, and then they must recite the *Kalimah* three times and feed water to the animal which is to be sacrificed. The neck of the animal must be turned in the direction of the *Quiblah* [the Ka'bah, in Mecca, which devout Muslims face in prayer], so that the eyes of the sacrificial animal look into the eyes of the person who is doing the sacrifice. The person must look into the eyes of the animal and then, saying the *Kalimah*, he must cut the neck. And he must continue to look into the eyes of the animal until its soul departs, repeating the *Zikr* [invocation and remembrance of God referred to in the *Qur'ān* as an act of worship] all the while. Then after the soul has departed, he must say the *Kalimah* once again and wash the knife. Only then can he move on to the next animal. He has to look into the animal's eyes, he has to watch the tears of the animal, and he has to watch the animal's eyes until it dies—hopefully, his heart will change.

Allah told Muḥammad (*Sal.*), "With the *qurbān* the killing will be greatly reduced, for where they used to kill 1,000 or 2,000 in one day, they will now be able to slaughter only ten or fifteen animals. If they started after the morning prayers, it would be ten o'clock by the time they are ready to begin, and they could slaughter only until eleven o'clock when they must prepare for the next prayer. In addition, it takes about fifteen or twenty minutes for each animal, because he has to wait until the soul has departed." This is how Allah instructed the Prophet (*Sal.*).

Then the people complained, "How can we do this? We can cut only so few! Our enjoyments and our festivals are being curtailed."

But Allah said, "Each one of you does not need to sacrifice one animal; you do not need to sacrifice one animal for each family. In place of forty fowls, kill one goat. In place of forty goats, kill ten cows, and in place of forty cows, kill ten camels. Sacrifice ten camels and then share the meat among the different families." So in place of four hundred animals only forty might be killed. The killing was reduced by that much. Thus, Allah passed down the commands to the Prophet (*Sal.*) to reduce the taking of lives. These are the commandments or laws according to the word of Allah, and this was the explanation in the *Qur'ān*.

If you understand the *qurbān* from within with wisdom, its purpose is to reduce this killing. But if you look at it from outside, it is meant to supply desire with food, to supply the craving of the base desires (*nafs ammārah*). Only Muslims and Jews (the followers of Moses) still continue to do the *qurbān* in this manner. Only these two people follow the law as it was handed down.

Man must understand through his wisdom, realize what is right, and if we can develop sufficient wisdom to avoid causing hurt and harm to other lives, then we will understand the meaning of this *qurbān*.

THE HUNTER LEARNS COMPASSION
FROM THE FAWN

My love to you, my grandchildren, my sons and daughters, my brothers and sisters. Have you ever seen a baby deer? Let me tell you a story about a fawn and its mother. Please listen carefully. This story will show you the difference between the awareness of a man and the awareness of animals.

Once there was a man who liked to go hunting. He would go into the forest carrying a gun or a bow and arrow, and he would shoot deer, elk, and other animals. Like most hunters he enjoyed eating all the animals he killed, but he found deer meat especially tasty.

Now, this man had been hunting, killing, and eating like this for most of his life. Then one day he came upon a deer giving milk to her fawn. This made him happy because he was tired, and he knew that the deer could not run away while her baby was nursing. So he shot her. But before dying, the deer cried, "O man, you have shot me, so go ahead and eat me, but do not harm my child! Let it live and go free!"

"I understand what you are asking," the hunter replied, "but I plan to take your child home, raise it, and make it nice and fat. Then one day it too will become meat for me to eat."

The little fawn heard this and said, "O man, are such thoughts acceptable to God?"

The hunter laughed. "God created animals for men to kill and eat."

"O man, you are right. God did create some beings so that others could eat them. But what about you? If there is a law like that for us, then perhaps there is also such a law for you. Think about it. There is only one person ready to eat me, but there are so many eagerly waiting to eat you. Don't you know that? Someday in the very presence of God Himself, grubs, worms, the tiny insects of hell, and even the earth itself will be quite happy to devour you. You who are a human being must think about this. When we deer are killed, we are eaten right away, but when you die you will be consumed in hell ever so slowly, over a long period of time. You will be subjected to hell in so many rebirths.

"O man, God created me and He created you. You are a man. God created you from earth, fire, water, air, and ether. I am an animal, but God created me from these same elements. You walk on two legs, I walk on four. Even though our skin and color are different, our flesh is the same. Think about the many ways in which we are alike.

"If someone had killed your mother while you were nursing, how would you feel? Most men would feel sorry if they killed a deer with her fawn. They would cry, 'Oh, I didn't know!' But you don't seem to have any compassion. You are a murderer. You have killed so many lives, but you never stop to think how sad you would be if someone killed your mother. Instead you are happy to kill not only my mother, but you also want to kill me and eat me. Since you are a human being, you should think about this. Even the cruelest and most demonic of beasts would stop to think about what I have said.

"Can't you understand the sadness of a child whose mother has just been killed? What you said to my mother and to me is terrible and has caused me great pain. O man, you have neither God's compassion nor human compassion. You do not even have a human conscience. All your life you have been drinking the blood and eating the flesh of animals without realizing what you have been doing. You love flesh and enjoy murder. If you had a conscience or any sense of justice, if you were born as a true human being, you would think about this. God is looking at me and at you. Tomorrow His justice and His truth will inquire into this. You must realize this.

"Even though you are a man, your thoughts are much worse than those of four-legged animals. Do not think you are a human being. We certainly don't think so. You have the face of a man, but to us you are worse than a demon or the most dangerous beast in the jungle. When we look at you, we are afraid. But when we see a true human being, we have no fear. We might even walk up to him, because we are like small children who embrace everyone as readily as they embrace their own mother.

"O man, I am only a baby. If I lie down by mistake on a poisonous snake, it will not hurt me. Or if I accidentally step on a snake, it still won't hurt me, because it realizes that I am young. Even insects know I am small and will not sting me.

"So how can you do this, O man? You who have been born as a human being must consider your actions. It is terrible to keep me as a pet only to eat me later. Every day when you fed me, I would be thinking, 'I might be eaten tomorrow.' This would torture me constantly. Day by day, my weight, my happiness, and my life would decrease. In the end all that would be left of me would be skin and bones. I would be griefstricken and emaciated. I would be no good to you at all. I would be too sad to live, so just kill me and eat me right now.

"It is better to eat me at the same time you eat my mother. If you kill me know, before I experience that sorrow, at least you can enjoy the innocent, happy flesh that has drunk its mother's milk. Later I will have no flesh. Do not make me suffer any longer. Kill me now, so that I will suffer for only one day. I am too sad to talk about it anymore."

"Little fawn, everything you have said is true," the hunter admitted. Then he gently picked up the body of the mother and led the baby deer home.

All who heard the story cried. "So often we have eaten deer meat, but now that you have told us this, we see the *karma* that has come to us through the food we enjoyed. Our bodies are in a state of turmoil. We realize now that we had no compassion or wisdom." And they all decided to stop eating such food.

"Let the baby deer go," one man said.

"No, give me the deer," said another. "I will raise it until it grows up and then I will set it free."

But the hunter decided to raise the fawn by himself. And over the years that deer showed him more love than his own children did. "This gentle being is capable of more love and gratitude than a human being," the man thought. "It kisses and licks me and makes contented sounds when I feed it. And it even sleeps at my feet."

So the years passed until the deer was fully grown. Then one day the man took it into the forest and set it free.

My children, each of us must be aware of everything we do. All young animals have love and compassion. And if we remember that every creation was young once, we will never kill another life. We will not harm or attack any living creature.

My children and grandchildren, think about this. If we think and act with wisdom, it will be very good for our lives. My love to you.

They Are Communities Like You

AL-ḤĀFIẒ B. A. MASRI

Al-Ḥāfiẓ B. A. Masri was born in 1914 in India. For several years he lived in British East Africa, where his interest in animal welfare and his international work on behalf of animals began. He was appointed the first Sunni Imām of the Shah Jehan Mosque in Woking, Surrey, England in 1964. Until his death in 1993, he spent his later years writing about animal welfare from the perspective of the Islamic tradition.

In the selection offered here, Masri examines the lamentable treatment of animals and proposes a way of looking at animals and humans as tenants of a common world. Inspired by the Qur'ānic notion of God as creator and sustainer of all that is, Masri sees animals as the embodiment of God's love, each with its own way of reflecting the unity of creation.

Through a careful analysis of Islamic law and Ḥadīth, or commentary based on the sayings and deeds of the Prophet, Masri confronts difficult questions about the customary treatment of animals in the Islamic world, particularly when it comes to animal sacrifice. Although a vegetarian himself, who elsewhere insists "If only the average simple and God-fearing Muslim consumer of . . . food animals knew of the gruesome details of [factory farming], they would become vegetarians rather than eat such sacrilegious meat,"[1] Masri recognizes that his position runs counter to mainstream Islam, so he struggles to at least convince his fellow religionists to ameliorate obviously wasteful or unnecessary taking of animal life. But his discussion of Islam's horror of cruelty to animals leaves no doubt about his conviction that vegetarianism is compatible with Qur'ānic and Ḥadīthic teachings.

ANIMAL PSYCHES AND COMMUNITIES

The *Qur'ān* and *Ḥadīth* instruct us that all species of animals are "communities" like the human community. In other words, they are communities in their own right and not merely in relation to humankind or its values. The exact words of the *Qur'ān* are

> There is not an animal on earth
> Nor a bird that flies on its wings,
> But they are communities like you.
> (ch. 6 v. 38)

According to the learned commentators of the *Qur'ān*, the word *communities* is used here in the sense of genera and animals and birds for all kinds of vertebrates, quadrupeds, mammals, birdlike mammals such as bats, crustaceans, reptiles, worms, and insects. They all live a life, individual and social, like the members of the human society.

To define what it means by the "communities of animals," the *Qur'ān* says:

> Allah has created every animal from water:
> Of them there are some that creep on their bellies:
> Some that walk on two legs:
> And some that walk on four.
> (ch. 24 .v 45)

The first category includes all kinds of worms, reptiles, centipedes, insects, and all such creatures. The second category includes birds and human beings; and the third category covers all kinds of mammals. The significant point to note is that, physically, humans have been put in the same bracket as all other creatures.

The following *Ḥadīth* leaves no ambiguity about the sense in which the *Qur'ān* uses the word *communities*:

> Abu Huraira reported the Prophet Muhammad as
> telling of an incident that happened to a prophet in
> the past. This prophet was stung by an ant and, in
> anger, he ordered the whole of the nest of ants to be
> burned. At this God reprimanded this prophet in these
> words: 'Because one ant stung you, you have burned
> a whole community which glorified Me.'[2]

One of the reasons why the human and all other species have been classified together throughout the *Qur'ān* is that even animals possess a psyche. Although their psychic force is of a lower level than that of human beings, there is ample evidence in the *Qur'ān* to suggest that animals' consciousness is of a higher degree than mere instinct and intuition.

We are told in the *Qur'ān* that animals have a cognizance of their Creator, and hence they pay their obeisance to him by adoration and worship. Out of the many verses of the *Qur'ān* on this proposition, a few must suffice here:

> Seest thou not that it is Allah Whose praises are celebrated
> By all beings in the heavens and on earth,
> And by the birds with extended wings?
> Each one knows its own [mode of] prayer and psalm.
> And Allah is aware of what they do.
>
> (ch. 24 v. 41)

The statement that "Each one knows its own prayer and psalm" is worth noting. The execution of a voluntary act, performed knowingly and intentionally, requires a faculty higher than those of instinct and intuition.

In the event that some may doubt that animals could have such a faculty, the following verse points out that it is human ignorance, not animals, that prevent us from understanding their celebration of God.

> The seven heavens and the earth and all things therein,
>   declare His glory,
> There is not a thing but celebrates His praise;
> And yet ye mankind! ye understand not
> How do they declare His glory.
>
> (ch. 17 v. 44)

The following verse tells us how all the elements of nature and all the animal kingdom function in harmony with God's laws; only some humans disobey and so bring affliction on themselves. The *Qur'ān* dwells on this subject repeatedly to emphasize the point that humans should bring themselves into harmony with nature, as the rest of creation does:

> Seest thou not that unto Allah payeth adoration
> All things that are in the heavens and on earth;
> The sun, the moon, the stars, the hills, the trees, the animals;
> And a large number among mankind?
> But there are many [humans] who do not,
> And deserve chastisement.
>
> (ch. 22 v. 18)

It is understood that the inanimate elements of nature perform the act of worshipping God without verbal communication by functioning in conformity with the divine ordinances known as the laws of nature.

In the case of animals, however, the *Qur'ān* teaches that God actually communicates with them, as the following verse shows:

> And your Lord revealed to the bee, saying:
> Make hives in the mountains,
> And in the trees,
> And in [human] habitations.
>
> (ch. 16 v. 68)

It is anybody's guess what form God's communication with animals takes. We know only that the *Qur'ān* uses the same Arabic word *Waḥy* for God's revelations to all his prophets, including Prophet Muḥammad, as well as to the bee. It is obvious that the connotation of God's revelations to his messengers would be different from that of his revelations to animals. But this is too complex a theological subject that cannot be dealt with here. Nevertheless, it proves the basic fact that animals have enough psychic endowment to understand and follow God's messages—a faculty higher than instinct and intuition.

Animals are not inferior to us because they have a different vocal apparatus; nor does the fact that they cannot make articulate speech, like we can, mean that they are "contemptible dumb animals." Science has proved now that they communicate not only with each other but also with humans, at least enough to express their social interests and biological needs. Those of us who enjoy the privilege of a loving and caring relationship with our pets will bear witness to the fact. . .

ANIMALS' FAIR SHARE IN FOOD

In the Islamic view, animals are tenants in common with humans. Let us see now why some humans do not act according to the terms of this partnership.

Man has always been in competition with animals for food, and the problem has been aggravated in the modern world, especially because of human overpopulation.

The *Qur'ān* tried to allay this fear of man by reassuring him that God is not only the creator but also the nourisher of all that he creates. For human beings, however, the *Qur'ān* lays down the condition that they will have to work for their sustenance and that their emolument will be proportionate to their labor. The following verse serves as the maxim for this principle:

> And that man shall have nothing
> But what he strives for.
>
> (ch. 53 v. 39)

In the next verse, this stipulation is repeated in the words "those who seek," with the additional proviso that God provides according to the needs of the people:

> And [God] bestowed blessings on the earth,
> And measured therein sustenance in due proportion...,
> In accordance [with the needs of] those who seek.
>
> (ch. 41 v. 10)

The conditions laid down in these two verses for human beings to work for the necessities of life seem to be conveniently ignored by some people. Some of us tend to rely solely on God's beneficence and to just lie down on our backs with our mouths open and wait for the manna from heaven to fall. Others have invented dubious ways and means to get more than their share by as little work as possible. Some of those who do work muscle in and poach on others' preserves.

As for animals, the *Qur'ān* repeatedly emphasizes the fact that food and other resources of nature are there to be shared equitably with other creatures. Below are just a few of many such verses:

> Then let man look at his food:
> How we pour water in showers,
> Then turn up the earth into furrow-slices,
> And cause cereals to grow therein—
> And grapes and green fodder,
> And olive-trees and palm-trees,
> And luxuriant orchards,
> And fruits and grasses.

Let us stop at this point of the quotation and ask ourselves the question: For what and for whom has this sumptuous meal been laid out? The last line of the verse tells us that all these bounties of nature are as "provision for you as well as for your cattle." (ch. 80 vv. 24–32).

Again, in the following verse, the bounties of nature are enumerated, with the accent on animals' share in all of them:

> And He [God] it is Who sends the winds
> As glad tidings heralding His mercy;
> And We send down pure water from the clouds,
> That We may give life thereby,
> By watering the parched earth,
> And slake the thirst of those We have created—
> Both the animals and the human beings
> In multitude.
>
> (ch. 25 vv. 48, 49)

And what is the reason for creating everything, viz., the cosmos as an ordered whole, the dark nights and the bright days, the earth with its immense expanse, shooting forth its moisture and its pastures, and the stable mountains—all this has been created for whom and why? The Qur'ānic answer, again, is "as a provision for you and your cattle." (ch. 28 v. 33.)

> And do they not see?
> That We meander water to a barren land,
> And sprout forth from its crops—
> Whereof their cattle as well as they themselves eat;
> Will they take no notice of it?
>
> (ch. 32 v. 27)

One could obtain the impression from these verses that they refer only to livestock in whose welfare we have a vested interest. But the message of the Qur'ān, in this context, comprehends the entire animal kingdom, as is made clear in the following verses:

> There is no moving creature on earth,
> But Allah provides for its sustenance.
>
> (ch. 11 v. 6)

In the words of Moses, as recorded in the Qur'ān:

> Surely the earth belongs to Allah;
> He bequeaths it to whosoever He pleases
> Of His servants.
>
> (ch. 7 v. 128)

> And the earth!
> He has assigned to all living creatures.
>
> (ch. 55 v. 10)

The Qur'ān has recounted the history of some past nations to show how they fell into error and perished. We come across a pertinent incident that is relevant to our discussion here. The tribe of Thamud were the descendants of Noah. Their name is also mentioned in the Ptolemaic records of Alexander's astronomer of the second century. The people of Thamud demanded that the Prophet Salih show them some sign to prove that he was a prophet of God. At that time the tribe was experiencing a dearth of food and water and was, therefore, neglecting its livestock. It was revealed to the Prophet Salih to single out a she-camel as a symbol and ask his people to give her her fair share of water and fodder. The people of Thamud promised to do that, but later killed the camel. As a retribution, the tribe was annihilated (ch. 11 v. 26; ch. 26 vv. 155, 156; ch. 54, vv. 27–31).

This historic incident sets forth the essence of the *Qur'ān's* teaching on "animal rights." Cruelty to animals is so offensive to God that it is declared as a serious sin... Cruelty to animals does not end there. It generates sadistic characteristics leading to acts of cruelty against fellow human beings...

ISLAMIC LAWS

Islam's concern for animals goes beyond the prevention of cruelty to them which, logically, is a negative proposition. On the positive side, Islam enjoins us to take responsibility for the welfare of all creatures. In the spirit of the positive philosophy of life, we are to be their active protectors. Even in the case of cruelty, prevention of physical cruelty to animals is not enough; mental cruelty is equally condemned. In the following *Ḥadīth*, a bird's emotional distress, for example, is called an injury:

> We were on a journey with the apostle of God, who left us for a short space. We saw a *hummara* [a bird] with its two young, and took the young birds. The *hummara* hovered with fluttering wings, and the prophet returned, saying, 'Who has injured this bird by taking its young? Return them to her.'[2]

Islam, like most other religions, has laid down a code of law governing the use of animals for the necessities of our life. [It] comprises specific instructions regarding the treatment of domestic animals, beasts of burden, pets, and other such animals who have become a part of human society.

The spirit and letter of these laws strongly deprecate all direct or indirect acts of cruelty to animals, such as:

— Subjecting animals to pain, both physical and, as we have just seen, mental, or killing them for sport, such as in blood sports and fishing, except for food.

— Killing them for luxuries (for their fur or tusks, for example) or of other inessential by-products, such as cosmetics.

— Depriving free-born animals and birds of their natural life by enclosing them in zoos, cages, and aquariums, except when this is necessary for their safety and preservation.

— Breeding animals and birds in confined and unhygienic conditions, and increasingly common practice in modern farming.

— Using snares, leghold traps, and other contraptions that maim and cause lingering death...

TRADITIONAL SLAUGHTER

The Islamic traditional method of slaughter, like that of Judaism, dispenses with preslaughter stunning. Western animal welfare workers are at a loss to understand why, in spite of all the Islamic concern we have seen in the foregoing pages for animal well-being, the Muslims are adamant in rejecting the use of preslaughter stunners. Even the apparently convincing sayings of Prophet Muḥammad, as quoted below, are not helpful in resolving the issue:

> Shaddad bin Aus reported God's Messenger as saying: 'God Who is Blessed and Exalted has declared that everything should be done in a good way; so when you kill, use a good method, and when you cut an animal's throat, you should use a good method; for each of you should sharpen his knife and give the animal as little pain as possible.'[3]

Even a cursory discussion of this subject is beyond the scope of this paper, especially if the perennial controversy between the vegetarian and the nonvegetarian disciplines is included. In the absence of any central religious authority within the Islamic community of nations, such as the caliphate, each country's accredited jurists (*muftīs*) decide whether or not a particular thought or action conforms to the ecclesiastical tenets of the Islamic law (*Sharī'a*)... Less than half a century ago, no one had even heard of the stunners and no *muftī* had ever thought of slaughtering animals by stunning them prior to the use of a sharp knife. Today, mainly because of intercontinental emigration and the interlacing of cultures, such problems have become conspicuous and must be addressed.

The only way to solve the controversial problem of the use of stunners is to go to each of the major Islamic countries and demonstrate to the accredited *muftīs* that the use of stunners meets the laws of the Islamic *Sharī'a* ... [A] jointly issued decree or *fatwā* will go a very long way in convincing the Muslim population once and for all...

Animal sacrifice is another issue that is not easy for Westerners to understand or condone... Islam also carried on with this practice, but with a difference. It channeled the whole concept of animal sacrifice into an institution of charity. Instead of burning the meat of the sacrificed animal at the altar or letting it rot, Islam ordered it to be distributed either wholly or partly among the poor. Since then Muslims from all over the world sacrifice animals and distribute the meat among the poor in their neighborhoods. Especially during the Festival of Sacrifice (*ʿĪd al-Adha*), which the Muslims celebrate annually in commemoration of Prophet Abraham's willingness to sacrifice his son, every Muslim who can afford it is required to offer this animal sacrifice and distribute the meat among the poor, keeping a portion for his own consumption...

Another relevant point to understand in this respect is that the age-old concepts of atonement for sins or peace offerings to God by way of animal sacrifices were discredited by Islam. According to verse 37, chapter 22:

> It is not their meat, nor their blood,
> That reaches Allah;
> It is your piety that reaches Him.

CRUELTY

Many practices in the West, because they involve cruelty to animals, are not only against the spirit of Islam but also against the teachings of all religions. Factory farming is an example. Perhaps the most distressing aspect of this development is that the so-called undeveloped and developing countries of the world have begun to emulate their Western models. Better and quicker profits, plus the feeling that "civilized" Western society has given its tacit approval to the intensive rearing of farm animals, are eroding the gentler and more humane methods once the rule in these countries. The same is true in the case of other cruel practices now current in the West. Cruelty to animals seems to export well.

Islam has a number of things to say about the general treatment of animals. Imām 'Alī has laid down the following maxim in simple words: "Be kind to pack animals; do not hurt them; and do not load them more than their ability to bear."[4]

The late Mawlānā Mawdūdī was an internationally honored Muslim theologian of this century and the founder of a movement called *Jamā'at-i-Islāmī*. His views are very pertinent to our subject:

> God has honored man with authority over His countless creatures... This superior position... does not mean that God has given him unbridled liberty.

> Islam says that all the creation has certain rights upon man. They are: he should not waste them on pointless ventures nor should he unnecessarily hurt or harm them.

> We have been forbidden to kill them merely for fun or sport.

> Killing an animal by causing continuous pain and injury is considered abominable in Islam.

> . . .It does not allow their killing (even of dangerous and venomous animals) by resort to prolonged painful methods.

> To catch birds and imprison them in cages without any special purpose is considered abominable.[5]

Mawlānā Mawdūdī's advice about beasts of burden is the same as that of Imām 'Ali, quoted above.

In spite of modern mechanization, animals are still very much in use in farming and transport, especially in the rural areas of the East. Their use, and sometimes their misuse, often entails great labor and hardship for them.

Islam's directives in this respect are very specific, as the few Ḥadīth we will cite show: "The Prophet once passed by a camel whose belly clave to its back. 'Fear God,' said he, 'in these dumb animals, and ride when they are fit to be ridden, and let them go free when it is meet they should rest.'"[6]

The following Ḥadīth lays down the principle that animals should be used only for the purpose for which they are meant and only for the necessities of life: "Abu Huraira reports that the Prophet said: 'Do not use the backs of your beasts as pulpits, for God has made them subject to you in order that they may bring you to a town you could not otherwise reach without fatigue of body.'"[7]

Daily prayer is one of the five pillars of the Islamic faith. The following Ḥadīth shows that even this very important obligation used to be deferred by the Prophet and his companions in favor of the comfort of animals: "Anas says: 'When we stopped at a halt, we did not say our prayers until we had unburdened the camels.'"[8]

CONCLUSION

. . . After all is said and done, one wonders why, in our so-called civilized society today, man's cruelty to animals is on the increase. Why is it that human attitudes toward animals are hard to change? The organized religious institutions could have played an important role in educating the people. Almost 90 percent of the world's population owes allegiance to one of the major religions. Each of these religions has the benefit of platforms whereupon captive audiences could be influenced and educated. But one never hears from their pulpits any sermons preaching the word of God about animals. The dictum "Love thy neighbor" embraces all neighbors, including animals. . .

Most of the sermons from our religious pulpits are admonitions against sin. If someone were inclined to choose a subject pertaining to animal welfare, there is enough material in every scripture to choose from. For example, there are two sayings of Prophet Muḥammad that would make very appropriate themes for such sermons. In the following *Ḥadīth*, the Prophet placed the unauthorized killing of animals as second on the list of the seven deadly sins: "Avoid ye the seven deadly things: Polytheism; the killing of breathing beings which God has forbidden except by right."[9]

In the following *Ḥadīth*, it has been placed as third in the list of four sins: "The grievous things are: Polytheism; disobedience to parents; the killing of breathing beings."[10]

... To end this paper, there could not be a better conclusion than the following aphoristic *Ḥadīth* of the Holy Prophet Muḥammad: "Whoever is kind to the creatures of God, is kind to himself."[11]

NOTES

1. Al-Ḥafiẓ B.A. Masri, *Animals in Islam* (Petersfield: The Athena Trust, 1987), 23.

2. Bukhāri and Muslim.

3. Muslim. Alfred Guillaume, *The Traditions of Islam* (Beirut, Lebanon: Khayats Oriental Reprinters, 1966), 106.

4. Narrated by Shaddad bin Aus. Muslim, vol. 2, ch. 11, section on "Slaying," 10:739, verse 151. Also *Mishkat al-Masabih*, 872. English translation by James Robson, in four volumes (Lahore, Pakistan: Sh. Muḥammad Ashraf, 1963).

5. *Maxims of 'Ali*, translated by A. Halal from the famous book *Nahj-ul-Balagha*, Elmi (Lahore, Pakistan: Sh. Muḥammad Ashraf, 1963, 436.

6. Sayyid Abu al-A'lā Mawdūdī, *Towards Understanding Islam*, English translation by Dr. Khurshīd Ahmad (Lahore, Pakistan: Islamic Publications, Ltd., 1967), 174–176.

7. Narrated by Abū Hurayra. Guillaume, *Traditions*, 106, 107.

8. Ibid.

9. Ibid.

10. Narrated by Abū Hurayra. Bukhāri and Muslim.

11. Narrated by Abdallah bin 'Amru. Bukhāri and Muslim.

12. Muḥammad Amīn, *Wisdom of Prophet Muḥammad* (Lahore, Pakistan: Sh. Muḥammad Ashraf, 1965), 200.

For Further Reading

In the bibliographical essay for *Ethical Vegetarianism from Pythagoras to Peter Singer*, we noted that although moral defenses of vegetarianism are numerous and ancient, they are also widely scattered and difficult to find. This is even more true in the case of religious defenses of vegetarianism. In this essay we can hope to do no more than plant a few signposts for the reader who wishes to explore more fully the rich tradition of religious vegetarianism. Fortunately, most of the works listed here (as well as many of the anthologized selections in this volume) contain extensive bibliographies helpful in steering the reader in ever wider directions.

A good starting point is Judith C. Dyer's *Vegetarianism: An Annotated Bibliography* (Meutchen, N.J.: Scarecrow Press, 1982). Dyer's bibliography is the best one available, but its usefulness is limited for three reasons: first, it badly needs updating; second, it focuses primarily on twentieth-century titles; and third, its listing of source materials on religious vegetarianism is somewhat limited—information on ethical vegetarianism preponderates. Two other bibliographical references are also helpful. One is Charles R. Magel's *Keyguide to Information Resources in Animal Rights* (Jefferson, N.C.: McFarland, 1989). The other, also compiled by Magel, is the appendix on twentieth-century works on vegetarianism and animal rights in a recent reprint of Henry Salt's 1892 classic *Animal Rights: Considered in Relation to Social Progress* (Clarks Summit, Pa.: Society for Animal Rights, 1980). Worth consulting in the same volume is Salt's own bibliography of pertinent works, which extends from the early eighteenth to the early nineteenth centuries. In both bibliographies listings on ethical vegetarianism again preponderate, although each does have a scattering of source materials on religious vegetarianism. Most of these, however, are in the Christian tradition.

Two books that focus on religious vegetarianism from a multifaith perspective are indispensable: Rynn Berry's *Food for the Gods: Vegetarianism and the World's Religions* (New York: Pythagorean Publishers, 1998) and Steven Rosen's *Diet for Transcendence: Vegetarianism and the World Religions* (Badger, Calif.: Torchlight, 1997). Berry's book consists of essays about vegetarianism in different faith traditions and interviews with representatives from each of those traditions. Rosen's book, previously published as *Food for the Spirit* (New York: Bala Books, 1987) offers a shorter but nonetheless invaluable overview.

Although not devoted to religious vegetarianism, several books contain discussions of it. The classic is Howard Williams's *The Ethics of Diet: A Catena of Authorities Deprecatory of the Habit of Flesheating* (London: Richard J. James and Manchester: Albert Broadbest, 1883). Despite its somewhat cumbersome title, Williams presents the reader with concise and elegant essays on vegetarians from Hesiod through the nineteenth century. About half the figures he discusses are from a religious vegetarian tradition. Rynn Berry's *Famous Vegetarians and their Favorite Recipes: Love and Lore from Buddha to Beatles* (Los Angeles, Calif.: Panjandrum Books, 1989), is a twentieth-century parallel to Williams. Religious vegetarians discussed include Pythagoras, the Buddha and Jesus. Mark Mathew Braunstein's *Radical Vegetarianism* (Los Angeles, Calif.: Panjandrum Books, 1988), Dudley Giehl's *Vegetarianism: A Way of Life* (New York: Harper & Row, 1979) and Gary Null's *The Vegetarian Handbook* (New York: St. Martin's Press, 1987) each contain brief discussions of religious vegetarianism. Insightful historical accounts of certain aspects of religious vegetarianism may be found in Jon Gregerson's *Vegetarianism: A History* (Freemont, Calif.: Jain Publishing, 1994) and Colin Spencer's *The Heretic's Feast: A History of Vegetarianism* (Hanover, N.H.: University Press of New England, 1995). Gregerson discusses religious vegetarianism from the perspective of a number of religious traditions, while Spencer limits himself mainly to the Orphic-Pythagorean and Christian traditions.

Daniel A. Dombrowski's *The Philosophy of Vegetarianism* (Amherst, Mass.: University of Massachusetts Press, 1984) is unquestionably the single best discussion of vegetarianism in the Orphic-Pythagorean tradition. Peter Gorman briefly discusses vegetarianism in his *Pythagoras: A Life* (London: Routledge and Kegan Paul, 1978). J. Donald Hughes examines the underpinnings of Pythagorean vegetarianism in "The Environmental Ethics of the Pythagoreans," and Hwa Yol Jung focuses on Orphism in his fine essay "The Orphic Voice and Ecology," *Environmental Ethics* 3 (1980): 195–213 and 329–340, respectively. P. Vidal-Naquet explores the golden age legend in "Plato's Myth of the Statesman, the Ambiguities of the Golden Age and of History," *Journal of Hellenic Studies* 98 (1978): 132–141. Discussions of Orphic-Pythagorean vegetarianism may also be found in Williams's *Ethics of Diet*, Gregerson's *Vegetarianism: A History*, and Spencer's *Heretic's Feast*.

Interesting discussions of religious vegetarianism in the Indian tradition include J. M. Jussawalla's *Living the Vegetarian Way* (Bombay: Lalvani Publishing, 1971); the essays collected by R. S. Khare in *The Eternal Food: Gastronomic Ideas and Experiences of Hindus and Buddhists* (Albany, N.Y.: State University of New York Press, 1992); Swaran Singh Sanehi's *Vegetarianism in Sikhism* (Madras: The

Vegetarian Way, 1977); and Julie Sahni's *Classic Indian Vegetarian and Grain Cooking* (New York: William Morrow, 1985). The concept of *ahiṃsā*, so crucial to both Indian and Buddhist vegetarianism, is explored in Christopher Chapple's *Nonviolence to Animals, Earth, and Self in Asian Traditions* (Albany, N.Y.: State University of New York Press, 1993), as well as his "Noninjury to Animals: Jain and Buddhist Perspectives," in *Animal Sacrifices: Religious Perspectives on the Use of Animals in Science*, ed. Tom Regan (Philadelphia, Pa.: Temple University Press, 1986), Unto Tahtinen's *Ahiṃsā: Nonviolence in Indian Tradition* (London: Rider & Co., 1976) and Koshelya Walli's *The Conception of Ahiṃsā in Indian Thought* (Varanasi: Battacharya, 1974). A convenient compendium of "voices of *ahiṃsa*" is provided by Nathaniel Altman in his *Ahiṃsā: Divine Compassion*. Stephen Rosen insightfully discusses Indian religious vegetarianism in his *Diet for Transcendence*, and Berry interviews Rosen (who, as a Hare Krishnaite, is also called Satyaraj Das) in his *Food for the Gods*. An overview of Indian religious vegetarianism may also be found in Gregerson's *Vegetarianism: A History*, and a shorter discussion is in Spencer's *Heretic's Feast*.

The studies of *ahiṃsā* cited in the preceding paragraph are also useful, as is Daisetz T. Suzuki's *The Chain of Compassion* (Cambridge, Mass.: Cambridge Buddhist Association, 1966), in further exploration of Buddhist defenses of vegetarianism. Another good discussion of Buddhist vegetarianism, particularly in the Chinese context, is in Gregerson's *Vegetarianism: A History*. Steven Rosen's *Diet for Transcendence* devotes a chapter to Buddhist vegetarianism, as does Berry's *Food for the Gods*. Berry's book also includes a fascinating interview with Roshi Kapleau.

A great number of interesting and valuable treatments of Jewish vegetarianism have appeared in recent years. One of the most prolific authors in this tradition is Roberta Kalechofsky. In addition to her *Vegetarian Judaism: A Guide for Everyone*, a selection from which is reprinted in this volume, her works also include two important anthologies: *Judaism and Animal Rights* (Marblehead, Mass.: Micah Publications, 1992) and *Rabbis and Vegetarianism: An Evolving Tradition* (Marblehead, Mass.: Micah Publications, 1995). Both collections contain exceptionally fine discussions of vegetarianism from a Jewish perspective. Also worth consulting are Samuel H. Dresner's *The Jewish Dietary Laws* (New York: The Rabbinical Assembly of America, 1982) and Richard H. Schwartz's *Judaism and Vegetarianism*, 2nd ed. (Marblehead, Mass.: Micah Publications, 1988). Rosen devotes a chapter to Jewish vegetarianism in his *Diet for Transcendence*, as does Berry in his *Food for the Gods*. Gregerson includes a very brief discussion in his *Vegetarianism: A History*.

No individual has done more to elucidate and defend vegetarianism from a Christian perspective than Andrew Linzey. In addition to his *Animal Theology*, excerpted in this volume, his many fine works include *Animal Rights: A*

Christian Assessment of Man's Treatment of Animals (London: SCM Press, 1976), *Christianity and the Rights of Animals* (New York: Crossroad, 1987), *After Noah: Animals and the Liberation of Theology*, co-authored with Dan Cohn-Sherbok (London: Cassell, 1997), and *Animals on the Agenda: Questions about Animals for Theology and Ethics*, co-edited with Dorothy Yamamoto (London: SCM Press, 1998). Along with Tom Regan (another of this anthology's contributors), Linzey also edited *Animals and Christianity: A Book of Readings* (New York: Crossroad, 1988). Although not an explicit defence of Christian vegetarianism, Carol J. Adams's (also one of the contributors to this volume) excellent *The Sexual Politics of Meat: A Feminist-Vegetarian Critical Theory* (New York: Continuum, 1990), deserves mention. Its brilliant analysis of "absent-referencing" is one of the foundations for her defences of religious vegetarianism. Also worth consulting are Gary Comstock's "Pigs and Piety: A Theocentric Perspective on Food Animals," *Between the Species: A Journal of Ethics* 8 (1992): 121–35), Charles P. Vaclavik's *The Vegetarianism of Jesus Christ: The Pacifism, Communalism, and Vegetarianism of Primitive Christianity* (Platteville, Wisc.: Kaweah Publishing Company, 1986), and Richard Alan Young's *Is God a Vegetarian? Christianity, Vegetarianism, and Animal Rights* (Chicago, Ill.: Open Court, 1999). Gregerson briefly discusses Christian vegetarianism in his *Vegetarianism: A History*, Spencer offers a detailed and frequently insightful analysis in *Heretic's Feast*, and Rosen's *Diet for Transcendence* devotes two chapters to it. Rynn Berry's *Food for the Gods* deals with Christian vegetarianism in no fewer than three chapters. Particularly valuable is his interview with Andrew Linzey.

Discussions of vegetarianism from a Muslim perspective are sparse. But well worth consulting is Al-Ḥāfiẓ B. A. Masri's *Animals in Islam* (Petersfield: The Athena Trust, 1987). Rosen's *Diet for Transcendence* and Berry's *Food for the Gods* include chapters on vegetarianism in the Islamic tradition. Both of them understandably focus on Sufism, the Muslim tradition most sympathetic with a meatless diet.

Two final resources: First, the British vegetarian and animal rights activist Jon Wynne-Tyson's *The Extended Circle: A Commonplace Book of Animal Rights* (New York: Paragon House, 1989) is a joyful and comprehensive collection of texts, religious as well as ethical, which defend compassion for all living beings. Second, Internet users may access information about dozens of vegetarian organizations, ranging geographically from the United States to Botswana, by following the links listed on the homepage of the International Vegetarian Union: http://www.ivu.org. Most of these offer additional access to thousands of links that discuss, among other topics, religious vegetarianism. Some sites are superficial, others are downright crackpotted. But most are interesting, informative, and sometimes substantive.

Sources

THE ORPHIC-PYTHAGOREAN TRADITION

Hesiod, *Works and Days*, trans. Richard Lattimore, in *Hesiod* (Ann Arbor, Mich.: University of Michigan Press, 1962), lines 109–201, pp. 31, 33, 35, 37, 39, 41.

Porphyry, *On Abstinence from Animal Food*, trans. Thomas Taylor (London: Centaur Press, Ltd, 1965), Bk. IV, pp. 145–48.

Ovid, *Metamorphosis*, trans. Frank Justus Miller (London: Wm Heinemann, 1916), Bk. 15, lines 61–175, 546–478, pp. 369, 371, 373, 377, 397, 399.

Empedocles, selections from *The Presocratic Philosophers: A Critical History with a Selection of Texts*, ed. G. S. Kirk, J. S. Raven, M. Schofield. 2nd ed. (Cambridge: Cambridge University Press, 1983), p. 314, line 16; p. 315, lines 1–12; p. 316, lines 8–18; p. 317, lines 4–9 and 32–36; p. 318, lines 16–26; p. 319, lines 22–36.

Philostratus, *The Life of Apollonius of Tyana*, trans. F. C. Conybeare. Vol. 2 (London: Wm Heinemann, 1922), Book VI, pp. 37, 39, 41, 43.

THE INDIAN TRADITION

The Laws of Manu, trans. G. Buehler (Oxford: Clarendon Press, 1986), p. 176, lines 3–29.

Ākārāṅga Sūtra, in *Jaina Sūtras*, trans. Hermann Jacobi, in *Sacred Books of the East*. Vol. 22 (Oxford: Clarendon Press, 1884), Bk. 1, Lecture 1, Lesson 6, pp. 10–13; Bk. 1, Lecture 7, Lesson 1, pp. 62–64; Bk. 2, Lecture 15, Lesson 1, 202–203.

Kabīr, from *A Translation of Kabīr's Complete Bījak*, trans. Prem Chand (Calcutta: Baptist Mission Press, 1911), pp. 43–44, 64–65, 232, 233.

Swami Vivekānanda, *Jnāna-Yoga*, in *The Yogas and Other Works* (New York: Ramakrishna-Vivekānanda Center, 1984), mid-page 341, p. 343, lines 1–7.

Mohandas Gandhi, *The Collected Works of Mahatma Gandhi* (Delhi: Ministry of Information and Broadcasting, 1958), Vol. 1, pp. 289–90, 291–92; Vol. 35, pp. 380–81.

A. C. Bhaktivedanta Swami Prabhupāda, "'Thou Shalt Not Kill' or 'Thou Shalt Not Murder'?" in *The Science of Self Realization* (New York: Bhaktivedanta Book Trust, 1981), pp. 137–141.

THE BUDDHIST TRADITION

Śūraṅgama Sūtra, trans. Lu K'uan Yu (London: Rider & Co., 1966), pp. 153–54.

Laṅkāvatāra Sūtra, trans. Daisetz Testaro Suzuki (London: Routledge & Kegan Paul, 1932), chapter 9, pp. 211–22.

Aśoka's *Edicts*, from *Sources of Indian Tradition. Vol. 1: From the Beginning to 1800*, ed. Ainslie T. Embree (New York: Columbia University Press, 1988), p. 143, lines 17–26, 28–31; p. 144, lines 2–7, 14–20, 22–24, 29–30; p. 145, lines 1–6; p. 148, lines 12–34; p. 149, lines 1–5.

Sir Edwin Arnold, *The Light of Asia* (Philadelphia: Henry Allemus, 1879), pp. 130–34.

Chu-hung, *Selections*, from Chun-fang Yu, *The Renewal of Buddhism in China: Chu-hung and the Late Ming Synthesis* (New York: Columbia University Press, 1981), p. 78, lines 22–27; p. 80, lines 5–10, 19–39; midpage 85 to midpage 86.

Philip Kapleau, *To Cherish All Life: A Buddhist Case for Becoming Vegetarian*. 2nd ed. (Rochester, N.Y.: The Rochester Zen Center, 1986), pp. 19–20.

The Dalai Lama, "Animals and Suffering," in *Worlds in Harmony: Dialogues on Compassionate Action* (Berkeley, Calif.: Parallax Press, 1992), midpage 19 to midpage 21; bottom of page 133 to 39.

THE JUDAIC TRADITION

Roberta Kalechofsky, *Vegetarian Judaism: A Guide for Everyone* (Marblehead, Mass.: Micah Publications, 1998), pp. 14, 15, 19–22, 23, 24, 25–26, 30.

Rabbi Everett E. Gendler, "The Life of His Beast," in Philip L. Pick, ed., *Tree of Life: An Anthology of Articles Appearing in The Jewish Vegetarianism, 1966–1974* (South Brunswick & New York: A. S. Barnes & Co.), pp. 40–47.

Rabbi Joseph Rosenfeld, "The Religious Justification for Vegetarianism," in Ibid., pp. 96–102.

Rabbi Abraham Isaac Kook, selections from "Fragments of Light: A View as to the Reasons for the Commandments," in *Abraham Isaac Kook*, ed and trans. Ben Zion Bokser (Mahweh, N.J.: Paulist Press, 1978), pp. 317–21.

The Christian Tradition

Andrew Linzey, "Vegetarianism as Biblical Ideal," from *Animal Theology* (Urbana and Chicago: University of Illinois Press, 1995), Chapter 8, pp. 125–37.

Tom Regan, selection from "Christianity and Animal Rights: The Challenge and Promise," in *Liberating Life: Contemporary Approaches to Ecological Theology*, ed. Charles Birch et. al. (Maryknoll, N.Y.: Orbis Books, 1991), pp. 81–83.

Francis X. Clooney, "Vegetarianism and Religion," *America* 140 (24 February 1979), pp. 133–34.

Carol J. Adams, "Feeding on Grace: Institutional Violence, Christianity, and Vegetarianism," in *Good News for Animals? Christian Approaches to Animal Well-Being*, ed. Charles Pinches & Jay B. McDaniel (Maryknoll, N.Y.: Orbis Books, 1993), pp. 142–59.

The Islamic Tradition

Rūmī, "The Men Who Ate the Elephant, on the Penalty of Greed," in *Tales of the Masnavi*, trans. Arthur J. Arberry (Richard, Eng.: Curzon Press, 1993), pp. 184–85.

M. R. Bawa Muhaiyaddeen, "Explanation of Qurbān," in *al-Asma'ul-Husna, The 99 Beautiful Names of Allah* (Philadelphia: Fellowship Press, 1993), pp. 180–84; and "The Hunter Learns Compassion from the Fawn," in *Come to the Secret Garden: Sufi Tales of Wisdom* (Philadelphia: Fellowship Press, 1985), pp. 25–28.

Al-Ḥafiẓ B.A. Masri, selections from "Animal Experimentation: The Muslim Viewpoint," in *Animal Sacrifices: Religious Perspectives on the Use of Animals in Science*, ed. Tom Regan (Philadephia: Temple University Press, 1986), pp. 172–75, 181–90, 194–95.

Index